enVision Mathematics

Common Core

P9-CRZ-568

Volume 2 Topics 8-15

Authors

Randall I. Charles
Professor Emeritus
Department of Mathematics
San Jose State University
San Jose, California

Jennifer Bay-Williams
Professor of Mathematics Education
College of Education and Human
Development
University of Louisville
Louisville, Kentucky

Robert Q. Berry, III
Professor of Mathematics Education
Department of Curriculum,
Instruction and Special Education
University of Virginia
Charlottesville, Virginia

Janet H. Caldwell
Professor Emerita
Department of Mathematics
Rowan University
Glassboro, New Jersey

Zachary Champagne
Assistant in Research
Florida Center for Research in Science,
Technology, Engineering, and
Mathematics (FCR-STEM)
Jacksonville, Florida

Juanita Copley
Professor Emerita, College of Education
University of Houston
Houston, Texas

Warren Crown
Professor Emeritus of Mathematics
Education
Graduate School of Education
Rutgers University
New Brunswick, New Jersey

Francis (Skip) Fennell
Professor Emeritus of
Education and Graduate and
Professional Studies
McDaniel College
Westminster, Maryland

Karen Karp
Professor of
Mathematics Education
School of Education
Johns Hopkins University
Baltimore, Maryland

Stuart J. Murphy
Visual Learning Specialist
Boston, Massachusetts

Jane F. Schielack
Professor Emerita
Department of Mathematics
Texas A&M University
College Station, Texas

Jennifer M. Suh
Associate Professor for
Mathematics Education
George Mason University
Fairfax, Virginia

Jonathan A. Wray
Mathematics Supervisor
Howard County Public Schools
Ellicott City, Maryland

SAVVAS
LEARNING COMPANY

Mathematicians

Roger Howe
Professor of Mathematics
Yale University
New Haven, Connecticut

Gary Lippman
Professor of Mathematics and
Computer Science
California State University, East Bay
Hayward, California

ELL Consultants

Janice R. Corona
Independent Education Consultant
Dallas, Texas

Jim Cummins
Professor
The University of Toronto
Toronto, Canada

Reviewers

Katina Arnold
Teacher
Liberty Public School District
Kansas City, Missouri

Christy Bennett
Elementary Math and Science
Specialist
DeSoto County Schools
Hernando, Mississippi

Shauna Bostick
Elementary Math Specialist
Lee County School District
Tupelo, Mississippi

Samantha Brant
Teacher
Platte County School District
Platte City, Missouri

Jamie Clark
Elementary Math Coach
Allegany County Public Schools
Cumberland, Maryland

Shauna Gardner
Math and Science Instructional Coach
DeSoto County Schools
Hernando, Mississippi

Kathy Graham
Educational Consultant
Twin Falls, Idaho

Andrea Hamilton
K-5 Math Specialist
Lake Forest School District
Felton, Delaware

Susan Hankins
Instructional Coach
Tupelo Public School District
Tupelo, Mississippi

Barb Jamison
Teacher
Excelsior Springs School District
Excelsior Springs, Missouri

Pam Jones
Elementary Math Coach
Lake Region School District
Bridgton, Maine

Sherri Kane
Secondary Mathematics
Curriculum Specialist
Lee's Summit R7 School District
Lee's Summit, Missouri

Jessica Leonard
ESOL Teacher
Volusia County Schools
DeLand, Florida

Jill K. Milton
Elementary Math Coordinator
Norwood Public Schools
Norwood, Massachusetts

Jamie Pickett
Teacher
Platte County School District
Kansas City, Missouri

Mandy Schall
Math Coach
Allegany County Public Schools
Cumberland, Maryland

Marjorie Stevens
Math Consultant
Utica Community Schools
Shelby Township, Michigan

Shyree Stevenson
ELL Teacher
Penns Grove-Carneys Point
Regional School District
Penns Grove, New Jersey

Kayla Stone
Teacher
Excelsior Springs School District
Excelsior Springs, Missouri

Sara Sultan
PD Academic Trainer, Math
Tucson Unified School District
Tucson, Arizona

Angela Waltrup
Elementary Math Content Specialist
Washington County Public Schools
Hagerstown, Maryland

ISBN-13: 978-0-13-495473-8
ISBN-10: 0-13-495473-4

5   20

> You'll be using these digital resources throughout the year!

Digital Resources

Go to SavvasRealize.com

 Interactive Student Edition
Access online or offline.

 Interactive Additional Practice Workbook
Access online or offline.

 Math Tools
Explore math with digital tools.

 Assessment
Show what you've learned.

 Visual Learning
Interact with visual learning animations.

 Videos
Watch Math Practices Animations, Another Look Videos, and clips to support 3-Act Math.

Games
Play math games to help you learn.

Activity
Solve a problem and share your thinking.

 Practice Buddy
Do interactive practice online.

A-Z Glossary
Read and listen in English and Spanish.

SAVVAS realize™ Everything you need for math anytime, anywhere

Contents

Digital Resources at SavvasRealize.com

TOPICS

And remember your Interactive Student Edition is available at SavvasRealize.com!

SavvasRealize.com

You can think about numbers in different ways. 23 is 2 groups of 10 and 3 left over.

TOPIC 8
Understand Place Value

Contents

Compare these numbers by comparing tens first.

42 is greater than 24.

42 ⊙ 24

TOPIC 9
Compare Two-Digit Numbers

For every ten you add, move down 1 row in the hundred chart.

1	2	3	4	5	6	7	8	9	10
11	12	13	14	15	16	17	18	19	20
21	22	23	24	25	26	27	28	29	30

TOPIC 10
Use Models and Strategies to Add Tens and Ones

Contents

5 tens minus
1 ten is like subtracting
5 - 1.

5 tens – 1 ten = 4 tens

TOPIC 11
Use Models and Strategies to Subtract Tens

The crayon is 2 cubes long.

TOPIC 12
Measure Lengths

Contents

The minute hand and the hour hand can help you tell time on a clock.

minute hand

hour hand

TOPIC 13
Time and Money

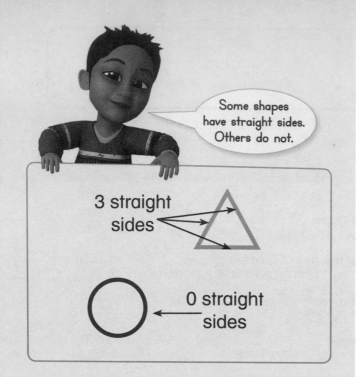

Some shapes have straight sides. Others do not.

3 straight sides

0 straight sides

TOPIC 14
Reason with Shapes and Their Attributes

Contents

This circle is divided into quarters.

TOPIC 15
Equal Shares of Circles and Rectangles

SavvasRealize.com

Grade 1 Common Core Standards

Dear Families,

The standards on the following pages describe the math that students will learn this year.

DOMAIN 1.OA
OPERATIONS AND ALGEBRAIC THINKING

MAJOR CLUSTER 1.OA.A
Represent and solve problems involving addition and subtraction.

1.OA.A.1 Use addition and subtraction within 20 to solve word problems involving situations of adding to, taking from, putting together, taking apart, and comparing, with unknowns in all positions, e.g., by using objects, drawings, and equations with a symbol for the unknown number to represent the problem.

1.OA.A.2 Solve word problems that call for addition of three whole numbers whose sum is less than or equal to 20, e.g., by using objects, drawings, and equations with a symbol for the unknown number to represent the problem.

MAJOR CLUSTER 1.OA.B
Understand and apply properties of operations and the relationship between addition and subtraction.

1.OA.B.3 Apply properties of operations as strategies to add and subtract. *Examples: If 8 + 3 = 11 is known, then 3 + 8 = 11 is also known. (Commutative property of addition.) To add 2 + 6 + 4, the second two numbers can be added to make a ten, so 2 + 6 + 4 = 2 + 10 = 12. (Associative property of addition.)*

1.OA.B.4 Understand subtraction as an unknown-addend problem. *For example, subtract 10 – 8 by finding the number that makes 10 when added to 8.*

Common Core Standards

MAJOR CLUSTER I.OA.C
Add and subtract within 20.

I.OA.C.5 Relate counting to addition and subtraction (e.g., by counting on 2 to add 2).

I.OA.C.6 Add and subtract within 20, demonstrating fluency for addition and subtraction within 10. Use strategies such as counting on; making ten (e.g., $8 + 6 = 8 + 2 + 4 = 10 + 4 = 14$); decomposing a number leading to a ten (e.g., $13 - 4 = 13 - 3 - 1 = 10 - 1 = 9$); using the relationship between addition and subtraction (e.g., knowing that $8 + 4 = 12$, one knows $12 - 8 = 4$); and creating equivalent but easier or known sums (e.g., adding $6 + 7$ by creating the known equivalent $6 + 6 + 1 = 12 + 1 = 13$).

MAJOR CLUSTER I.OA.D
Work with addition and subtraction equations.

I.OA.D.7 Understand the meaning of the equal sign, and determine if equations involving addition and subtraction are true or false. *For example, which of the following equations are true and which are false? $6 = 6$, $7 = 8 - 1$, $5 + 2 = 2 + 5$, $4 + 1 = 5 + 2$.*

I.OA.D.8 Determine the unknown whole number in an addition or subtraction equation relating three whole numbers. *For example, determine the unknown number that makes the equation true in each of the equations $8 + ? = 11$, $5 = \square - 3$, $6 + 6 = \square$.*

DOMAIN I.NBT
NUMBER AND OPERATIONS IN BASE TEN

MAJOR CLUSTER I.NBT.A
Extend the counting sequence.

I.NBT.A.1 Count to 120, starting at any number less than 120. In this range, read and write numerals and represent a number of objects with a written numeral.

MAJOR CLUSTER I.NBT.B
Understand place value.

I.NBT.B.2 Understand that the two digits of a two-digit number represent amounts of tens and ones. Understand the following as special cases:

I.NBT.B.2a 10 can be thought of as a bundle of ten ones — called a "ten."

I.NBT.B.2b The numbers from 11 to 19 are composed of a ten and one, two, three, four, five, six, seven, eight, or nine ones.

I.NBT.B.2c The numbers 10, 20, 30, 40, 50, 60, 70, 80, 90 refer to one, two, three, four, five, six, seven, eight, or nine tens (and 0 ones).

I.NBT.B.3 Compare two two-digit numbers based on meanings of the tens and ones digits, recording the results of comparisons with the symbols $>$, $=$, and $<$.

Common Core Standards

MAJOR CLUSTER 1.NBT.C
Use place value understanding and properties of operations to add and subtract.

1.NBT.C.4 Add within 100, including adding a two-digit number and a one-digit number, and adding a two-digit number and a multiple of 10, using concrete models or drawings and strategies based on place value, properties of operations, and/or the relationship between addition and subtraction; relate the strategy to a written method and explain the reasoning used. Understand that in adding two-digit numbers, one adds tens and tens, ones and ones; and sometimes it is necessary to compose a ten.

1.NBT.C.5 Given a two-digit number, mentally find 10 more or 10 less than the number, without having to count; explain the reasoning used.

1.NBT.C.6 Subtract multiples of 10 in the range 10–90 from multiples of 10 in the range 10–90 (positive or zero differences), using concrete models or drawings and strategies based on place value, properties of operations, and/or the relationship between addition and subtraction; relate the strategy to a written method and explain the reasoning used.

DOMAIN 1.MD
MEASUREMENT AND DATA

MAJOR CLUSTER 1.MD.A
Measure lengths indirectly and by iterating length units.

1.MD.A.1 Order three objects by length; compare the lengths of two objects indirectly by using a third object.

1.MD.A.2 Express the length of an object as a whole number of length units, by laying multiple copies of a shorter object (the length unit) end to end; understand that the length measurement of an object is the number of same-size length units that span it with no gaps or overlaps. *Limit to contexts where the object being measured is spanned by a whole number of length units with no gaps or overlaps.*

ADDITIONAL CLUSTER 1.MD.B
Tell and write time.

1.MD.B.3 Tell and write time in hours and half-hours using analog and digital clocks.

SUPPORTING CLUSTER 1.MD.C
Represent and interpret data.

1.MD.C.4 Organize, represent, and interpret data with up to three categories; ask and answer questions about the total number of data points, how many in each category, and how many more or less are in one category than in another.

Common Core Standards

DOMAIN I.G
GEOMETRY

ADDITIONAL CLUSTER I.G.A
Reason with shapes and their attributes.

I.G.A.I Distinguish between defining attributes (e.g., triangles are closed and three-sided) versus non-defining attributes (e.g., color, orientation, overall size); build and draw shapes to possess defining attributes.

I.G.A.2 Compose two-dimensional shapes (rectangles, squares, trapezoids, triangles, half-circles, and quarter-circles) or three-dimensional shapes (cubes, right rectangular prisms, right circular cones, and right circular cylinders) to create a composite shape, and compose new shapes from the composite shape.

I.G.A.3 Partition circles and rectangles into two and four equal shares, describe the shares using the words *halves*, *fourths*, and *quarters*, and use the phrases *half of*, *fourth of*, and *quarter of*. Describe the whole as two of, or four of the shares. Understand for these examples that decomposing into more equal shares creates smaller shares.

MATHEMATICAL PRACTICES

MP.I Make sense of problems and persevere in solving them.

MP.2 Reason abstractly and quantitatively.

MP.3 Construct viable arguments and critique the reasoning of others.

MP.4 Model with mathematics.

MP.5 Use appropriate tools strategically.

MP.6 Attend to precision.

MP.7 Look for and make use of structure.

MP.8 Look for and express regularity in repeated reasoning.

Math Practices and Problem Solving Handbook

The **Math Practices and Problem Solving Handbook** is available at SavvasRealize.com.

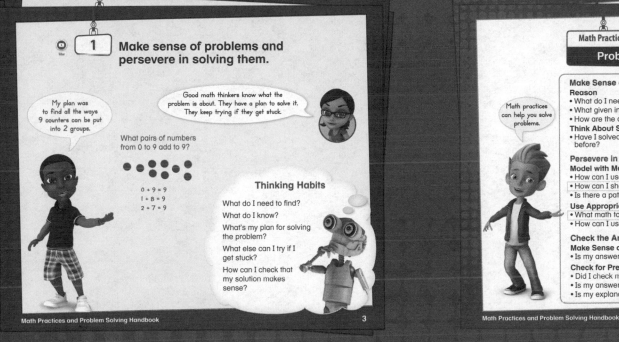

Math Practices

Problem Solving Guide
Problem Solving Recording Sheet

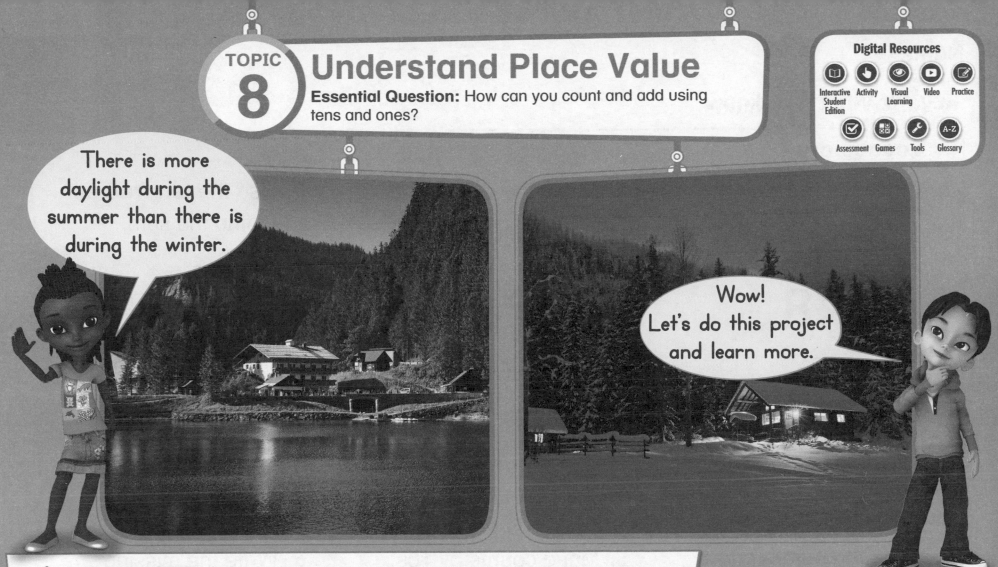

TOPIC 8 Understand Place Value

Essential Question: How can you count and add using tens and ones?

Digital Resources

Interactive Student Edition · Activity · Visual Learning · Video · Practice

Assessment · Games · Tools · Glossary

There is more daylight during the summer than there is during the winter.

Wow! Let's do this project and learn more.

enVision STEM Project: Daylight Throughout the Year

Find Out Talk to friends and relatives about why there is more daylight in summer than in winter. Ask them to help you find information about the changes in daylight each season.

Journal: Make a Book Draw pictures of the tilting globe and the sun at different times of the year. In your book, also:

• Add labels to show summer and winter.

• Write a sentence to describe the pattern of the seasons in your own words.

Review What You Know

Vocabulary

1. Circle the **tens digit**.

48

2. Circle the **ones digit**.

76

3. Use the **ten-frames** to find the sum.

$7 + 9 =$ _____

Counting to 120

4. Write the number that comes next when counting forward by 1s. Use a hundred chart to help you.

110, 111, 112, _____

5. Maria counts by 10s. She starts at 30. Write the missing numbers.

30, _____, _____,

60, _____

Hundred Chart

6. Write the missing numbers in this part of the hundred chart.

42		44		46
	53	54		

Name _____

PROJECT 8A

What do you put on your hot dog?

Project: Act Out Serving Up Hot Dogs

PROJECT 8B

What is your favorite color?

Project: Make a Color Poster

Can you eat a tiger?

Project: Play a Cracker Stack Game

Which sea creatures have 10 legs?

Project: Make a Finger Painting

Name _____

☆ ☆
Solve & Share

Use cubes. Show two different ways to make 28. Draw each way in the spaces below.

Way 1

Way 2

Visual Learning | A-Z Glossary

You can **break apart** 43 into tens and ones in different ways.

Tens	Ones

43 is 4 tens and 3 ones.

Here is one way.

Or break apart a ten to make 10 more ones.

Tens	Ones

43 is 3 tens and 13 ones.

Both ways show the same number! Use cubes to show another way!

Convince Me! How could you break apart 24 using only 1 ten? Explain.

☆ **Guided Practice** ☆ Count the tens and ones. Write different ways to show the number.

1. Write two ways to break apart 34.

Tens	Ones

34 is ___3___ tens and ___4___ ones.

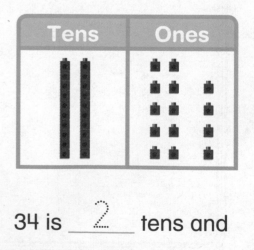

Tens	Ones

34 is ___2___ tens and _____ ones.

Topic 8 | Lesson 6

Independent Practice Count the tens and ones. Write different ways to show each number.

2. Write two ways to break apart 21.

Tens	Ones

21 is _____ tens and _____ one.

Tens	Ones

21 is _____ ten and _____ ones.

3. Draw models and write two ways to break apart 59.

59 is _____ tens and _____ ones.

59 is _____ tens and _____ ones.

Write each number in two different ways. Use cubes to help if needed.

4. Show two ways to break apart 44.

44 is _____ tens and _____ ones.

44 is _____ tens and _____ ones.

5. Show two ways to break apart 25.

25 is _____ tens and _____ ones.

25 is _____ tens and _____ ones.

6. **Explain** Nate says 5 tens and 3 ones shows the same number as 3 tens and 13 ones. Do you agree? Explain.

_____

_____

_____

7. **Number Sense** Nancy shows a number as 4 tens and 16 ones. What number does she show?

_____

8. What number is shown on the mat?

Tens	Ones

_____

9. Jeff picks 36 apples. He puts some of the apples in bags. Each bag holds 10 apples. Show two ways Jeff can put the apples in bags.

10 APPLES

_____ bags and _____ apples left over

_____ bags and _____ apples left over

10. **Higher Order Thinking** Meg breaks apart the number 80 three ways. What could be those ways?

_____ tens and _____ ones

_____ tens and _____ ones

_____ tens and _____ ones

11. ☑ **Assessment Practice** Which is a way to break apart 38? Choose two that apply.

☐ 2 tens and 18 ones

☐ 2 tens and 8 ones

☐ 1 ten and 28 ones

☐ 8 tens and 3 ones

Name _____

Solve & Share

Barry showed the number 42 with cubes. What are some of the ways he could have shown 42?

Write the tens and ones to show the ways. Describe any patterns you see in the table.

I can ...
use patterns and structure to solve problems.

© **Mathematical Practices** MP.7
Also MP.2, MP.3
Content Standard I.NBT.B.2

Tens	Ones

Thinking Habits

Is there a pattern to the answers?

How does the pattern help me?

What do the answers have in common?

How many ways can you show the number 38 with tens and ones?

38

Is there a pattern?

I can make a list of all the different ways. Then I can look for patterns in my list.

Tens	Ones

The answers all show ways to make 38 with tens and ones.

Tens	Ones
3	8
2	18
1	28
0	38

Look for a pattern. How can it help you?

I see a pattern in the table. As the number of tens goes down by 1, the number of ones goes up by 10. This helps me check my answers.

Convince Me! How can you use patterns to show all the ways to break apart a number into tens and ones?

☆ **Guided Practice** ☆ Make a list to solve. You can use cubes to help you. Talk to a partner about patterns you see in your list.

1. Carly lists all the ways to show 25 as tens and ones. What ways does she list?

Tens	Ones
2	5

2. Andy wants to show 31 as tens and ones. What are all the ways?

Tens	Ones

Topic 8 | Lesson 7

Name _____

Tools   Assessment

3. Alma lists all the ways to show 46 as tens and ones. What ways does she list?

Tens	Ones

4. Seth wants to show 33 as tens and ones. What are all the ways?

Tens	Ones

5. Higher Order Thinking Dana says there are 4 ways to show 25 using tens and ones. Is she right? How do you know?

_____

_____

_____

Make a list to help you.

Problem Solving

Bake Sale Rose brings 48 muffins to a bake sale. She only uses trays for groups of 10 muffins.
Each plate holds only 1 muffin.

How many trays and plates could Rose use to display the muffins?

Trays	Plates

6. **Look For Patterns** Fill in the table to show how many trays and plates Rose could use to display the muffins. Describe a pattern you see in the table.

_____

_____

_____

_____

7. **Reasoning** Is there any way Rose can display her muffins using only trays? Explain how you know.

_____

_____

_____

_____

_____

_____

_____

Point & Tally

Find a partner. Get paper and a pencil.
Each partner chooses a different color: light blue or dark blue.

Partner 1 and Partner 2 each point to a black number at the same time. Both partners add those numbers.

If the answer is on your color, you get a tally mark.
Work until one partner gets twelve tally marks.

I can ...
add and subtract within 10.

© **Content Standard** 1.OA.C.6
Mathematical Practices MP.3, MP.6, MP.7, MP.8

Partner 1							Partner 2
5	7	6	10	9	8	1	4
4							3
1							5
3	2	3	0	4	3	5	1
2							3
1							2

Tally Marks for Partner 1

Tally Marks for Partner 2

A-Z
Glossary

Word List
- break apart
- fewer
- more
- ones
- tens

Understand Vocabulary

1. Write the number word that is one more than fourteen.

_____

2. Write the number word that is one fewer than eighteen.

_____

3. Circle the cubes that make 2 tens.

4. Circle the cubes that make 1 ten and 5 ones.

5. Circle the cubes that make 3 tens and 3 ones.

Use Vocabulary in Writing

6. Ben shows 33 as 3 tens and 3 ones. Show 33 a different way. Use tens and ones. Explain using a word from the Word List.

Name _____

Set A

You can group objects by 10 to count.

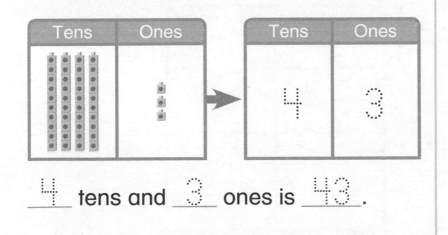

_34_ is _3_ groups of 10

and _4_ ones left over.

Circle groups of 10.
Write the numbers.

1. _____ is _____ groups of 10
    and _____ ones left over.

2. _____ is _____ group of 10
    and _____ ones left over.

Set B

You can show a two-digit number as tens and ones.

Tens	Ones

Tens	Ones
4	3

_4_ tens and _3_ ones is _43_.

Count the tens and ones.
Then write the number.

3.
Tens	Ones

Tens	Ones

_____ tens and _____ ones is _____.

You can draw a model to show tens and ones.

There are ___3___ tens and ___6___ ones in 36.

Draw a model to show tens and ones.

4. There are _____ tens and _____ ones in 78.

Thinking Habits

Look For and Use Structure

Is there a pattern to the answers?

How does the pattern help me?

What do the answers have in common?

Use patterns and make a list to solve.

5. Lupita wants to show all the ways to break apart 54 as tens and ones. What are all the ways?

54

Tens	Ones
5	

Name _____

1. **A.** Which of these is a way to show 16?

Ⓐ 1 ten and 11 ones

Ⓑ 1 ten and 6 ones

Ⓒ 16 tens and 0 ones

Ⓓ 9 tens and 5 ones

B. Which equation shows why your answer for **A** is correct?

Ⓐ $10 + 11 = 21$ Ⓒ $10 + 6 = 16$

Ⓑ $16 + 2 = 18$ Ⓓ $9 + 5 = 14$

2. **A.** Write a way to show 42.

_____ groups of ten

and _____ ones

B. Write another way to show 42.

_____ groups of ten and _____ ones

---

3. Count the tens and ones. Then write the numbers.

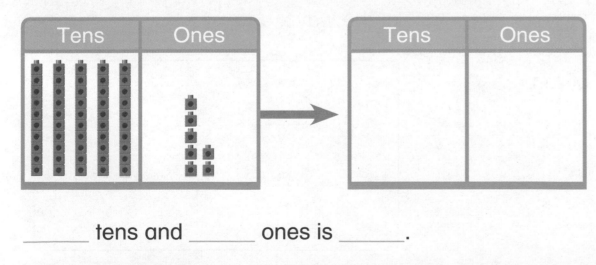

_____ tens and _____ ones is _____.

4. Write two ways to show 11.

5. A. What number does 5 groups of ten represent?

_____

B. What is another way to write 5 groups of ten?

_____ groups of ten and _____ ones

6. A. Which of these is another way to show 4 groups of ten and 9 ones?

Ⓐ 3 tens and 19 ones

Ⓑ 5 tens and 0 ones

Ⓒ 3 tens and 9 ones

Ⓓ 5 tens and 8 ones

B. What number is 4 groups of ten and 9 ones?

_____

7. Nicole found 2 ways to make 41. Complete the list to show all of the ways. Then draw a model to show one of the ways.

Tens	Ones
4	1
2	21

Topic 8 | Assessment Practice

Name _____

Snack Time

Manuel's class has a snack every day.

1. On Monday, Manuel and Ryan share 19 crackers. 10 crackers are in one bag. How many crackers are in the other bag?

   Draw counters to solve.
   Write the word and numbers.

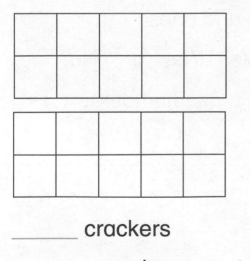

   _____ crackers

   _____ is _____ ten

   and _____ ones.

2. On Tuesday, Manuel's class has 3 packages of juice boxes. There are 10 juice boxes in each package.

   How many juice boxes does his class have?

   _____ juice boxes

   Explain your answer. Use pictures, numbers, or words.

3. On Wednesday, Manuel's class has 28 bottles of water.

Manuel starts drawing a model for the bottles. Use lines and dots to finish his drawing.

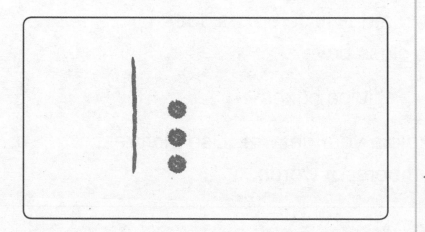

Explain what the drawing shows.

_____

_____

_____

4. On Thursday, Manuel's class had 34 packages of raisins. How many ways could the packages of raisins be grouped as tens and ones? Make a list to show all of the ways.

Tens	Ones

_____ ways

5. On Friday, Manuel's class had 26 bags of grapes. Manuel said that there are 2 ways to group the 26 bags as tens and ones.

Do you agree? Circle **Yes** or **No**.

Explain your answer. Use numbers, pictures, or words.

Compare Two-Digit Numbers

Essential Question: What are ways to compare numbers to 120?

Digital Resources

Interactive Student Edition | Activity | Visual Learning | Video | Practice

Assessment | Games | Tools | Glossary

Light changes when it shines on different objects.

When light shines on stained glass, the light that passes through is the same color as the glass.

Wow! Let's do this project and learn more.

enVision STEM Project: Light and Objects

Find Out Talk to friends and relatives about light. Discuss how light changes when it shines on different kinds of objects.

Journal: Make a Book Show what you found out. In your book, also:

• Draw pictures showing light shining on objects that are see-through and not see-through.

• Make up and solve number stories about shining light on different objects.

Name _____

Review What You Know

1. Circle the group of cubes that has **more**.

2. Circle the group of cubes that has **less**.

3. How many **tens** are in the number?

50

_____ tens

Number Lines

4. Use the number line to count by 10s. Write the missing numbers.

5. Pat sees 5 bugs. Erin sees 6 bugs. How many bugs did they see in all?

Use the number line to count.

_____ bugs

Hundred Chart

6. Use the part of the hundred chart to count.

11	12	13	14	15	16	17	18	19	20
21	22	23	24	25	26	27	28	29	30
31	32	33	34	35	36	37	38	39	40

18, 19, _____, _____, _____

Name _____

PROJECT 9A

How hot can it get?

Project: Create a Temperature Drawing

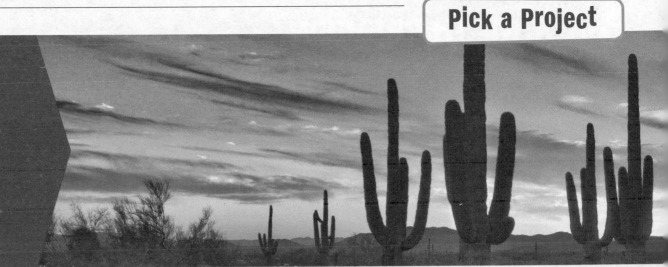

PROJECT 9B

Where did they all come from?

Project: Make a Shorebird Comparison Model

PROJECT 9C

How was that made?

Project: Make a Sponge Stamp Picture

Before watching the video, think:

Have you ever played a card game? What were some of the rules? How did someone win the game?

I can ...
model with math to solve a problem that involves comparing two-digit numbers.

© **Mathematical Practices** MP.4 Also MP.7, MP.8
Content Standards 1.NBT.B.3 Also 1.NBT.B.2, 1.MD.C.4

Name _____

Solve & Share

Sarah has 12 marbles.

Chris has one more marble than Sarah.

Lucia has 10 more marbles than Sarah.

How many marbles does Chris have?

How many marbles does Lucia have?

Show how you know.

I can ...
find numbers that are more
or less than a given number.

Ⓒ **Content Standards** I.NBT.C.5
Also I.NBT.B.3
Mathematical Practices MP.2,
MP.5, MP.8

Think about breaking
apart the numbers into
tens and ones.

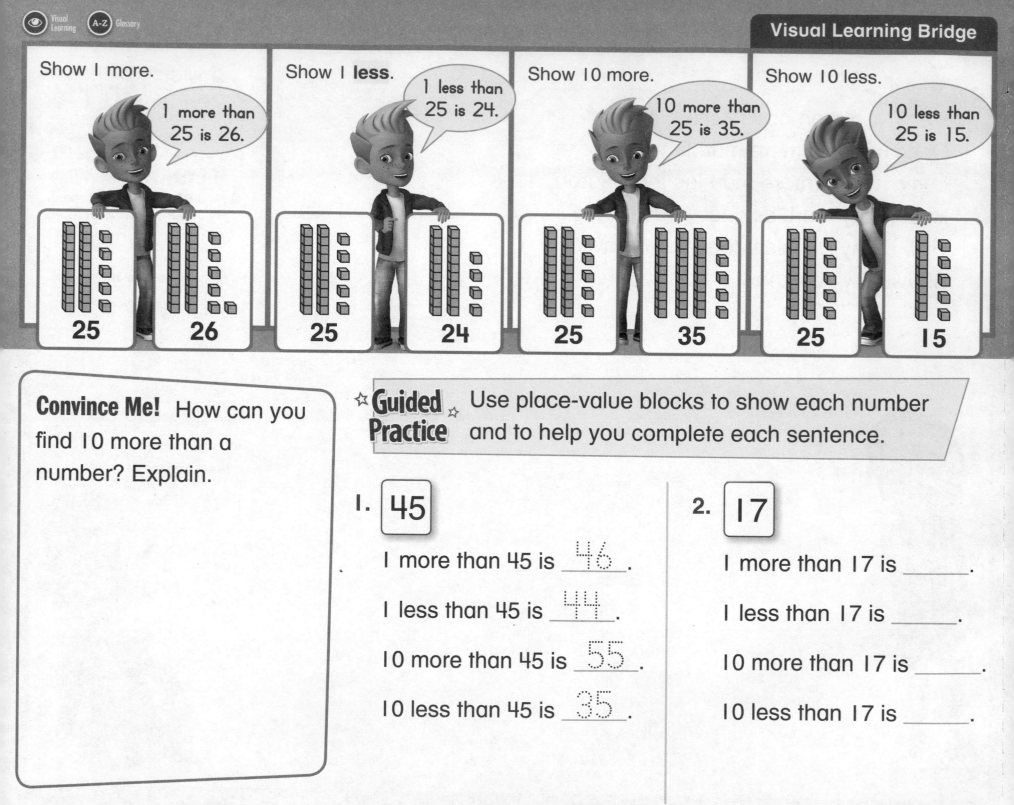

Show 1 more.

1 more than 25 is 26.

25   26

Show 1 **less**.

1 less than 25 is 24.

25   24

Show 10 more.

10 more than 25 is 35.

25   35

Show 10 less.

10 less than 25 is 15.

25   15

Convince Me! How can you find 10 more than a number? Explain.

☆ **Guided Practice** ☆ Use place-value blocks to show each number and to help you complete each sentence.

1. 45

1 more than 45 is ___46___.

1 less than 45 is ___44___.

10 more than 45 is ___55___.

10 less than 45 is ___35___.

2. 17

1 more than 17 is _____.

1 less than 17 is _____.

10 more than 17 is _____.

10 less than 17 is _____.

Topic 9 | Lesson 1

Name _____

Tools   Assessment

Independent Practice Use place-value blocks to show each number and to help you complete each sentence.

3. ☐ 11

1 more than 11 is _____.

1 less than 11 is _____.

10 more than 11 is _____.

10 less than 11 is _____.

4. ☐ 40

1 more than 40 is _____.

1 less than 40 is _____.

10 more than 40 is _____.

10 less than 40 is _____.

5. ☐ 81

1 more than 81 is _____.

1 less than 81 is _____.

10 more than 81 is _____.

10 less than 81 is _____.

6. ☐ 19

1 more than 19 is _____.

1 less than 19 is _____.

10 more than 19 is _____.

10 less than 19 is _____.

7. ☐ 65

1 more than 65 is _____.

1 less than 65 is _____.

10 more than 65 is _____.

10 less than 65 is _____.

8. ☐ 43

1 more than 43 is _____.

1 less than 43 is _____.

10 more than 43 is _____.

10 less than 43 is _____.

9. **Higher Order Thinking** Circle the picture that shows 10 more than 24. Explain how you know.

10. **Generalize** Sheila wants to write instructions to tell her friend how to find 10 more than any number. What instructions should Sheila write?

_____

_____

_____

11. **Number Sense** Fill in the missing numbers. Use place-value blocks to help you.

10 Less

I Less   73   I More

10 More

12. **Higher Order Thinking** Write and solve a riddle for a number greater than 40 and less than 60. Use "I more than" and "I less than" or "10 more than" and "10 less than" as clues.

Clues: _____

_____

My number is _____.

13. ☑ **Assessment Practice** Match each number with its description.

22   10 more than 23

9   I less than 18

17   I more than 21

33   10 less than 19

45   10 more than 35

Name _____

Solve & Share

How can you use a hundred chart to help you find 1 more than 36? What about 1 less, 10 more, and 10 less than 36? Write the numbers.

I can …
use a hundred chart to find 1 more, 1 less, and 10 more, 10 less.

Content Standards I.NBT.C.5 Also I.NBT.B.3
Mathematical Practices MP.3, MP.5, MP.7

21	22	23	24	25	26	27	28	29	30
31	32	33	34	35	(36)	37	38	39	40
41	42	43	44	45	46	47	48	49	50
51	52	53	54	55	56	57	58	59	60

1 more than 36 is _____.   10 more than 36 is _____.

1 less than 36 is _____.   10 less than 36 is _____.

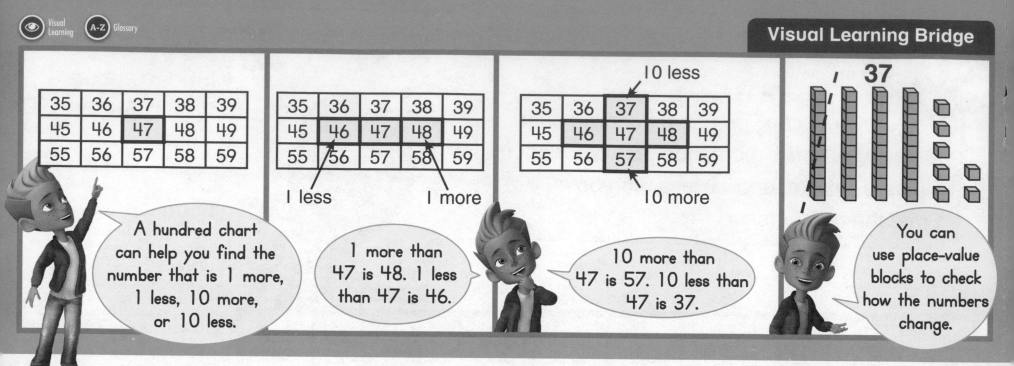

35	36	37	38	39
45	46	47	48	49
55	56	57	58	59

A hundred chart can help you find the number that is 1 more, 1 less, 10 more, or 10 less.

35	36	37	38	39
45	46	47	48	49
55	56	57	58	59

1 less   1 more

1 more than 47 is 48. 1 less than 47 is 46.

10 less

35	36	37	38	39
45	46	47	48	49
55	56	57	58	59

10 more

10 more than 47 is 57. 10 less than 47 is 37.

37

You can use place-value blocks to check how the numbers change.

Convince Me! How could you use a hundred chart to find what number is 10 more than 86? What number is that?

☆ **Guided Practice** ☆ Complete the part of the hundred chart. Use place-value blocks if needed.

1.

	23	
32	33	34
	43	

2.

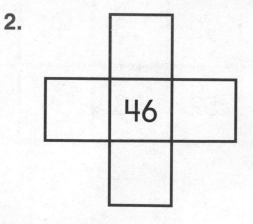

	46	

Topic 9 | Lesson 2

Independent Practice   Use a hundred chart to complete each sentence. Use place-value blocks if needed.

3. I more than 37 is _____.

   I less than 37 is _____.

   10 more than 37 is _____.

   10 less than 37 is _____.

4. I more than 22 is _____.

   I less than 22 is _____.

   10 more than 22 is _____.

   10 less than 22 is _____.

5. I more than 54 is _____.

   I less than 54 is _____.

   10 more than 54 is _____.

   10 less than 54 is _____.

6. I more than 78 is _____.

   I less than 78 is _____.

   10 more than 78 is _____.

   10 less than 78 is _____.

7. I more than 82 is _____.

   I less than 82 is _____.

   10 more than 82 is _____.

   10 less than 82 is _____.

8. I more than 16 is _____.

   I less than 16 is _____.

   10 more than 16 is _____.

   10 less than 16 is _____.

Algebra Use a hundred chart to find each student's number.

9. Alex's number is 27. Kendra's number is I less than Alex's number. Devon's number is 10 more than Kendra's number. Finish the equations to find each friend's number.

_____ – I = _____

_____ + 10 = _____

Alex   27

Kendra [ ]

Devon   [ ]

10. Look for Patterns Use the clues to find the missing number of marbles in each bag. Write the number.

Ben has 1 more than 54 marbles.

Anna has 10 more marbles than Ben.

Todd has a number that is 1 less than the number Anna has.

Anna   Todd   Ben

11. Higher Order Thinking Write a clue a partner could use to find how many marbles are in a bag. Then use the clue to tell how many marbles are in the bag.

12. ☑ **Assessment Practice**

Try to break the problem into simpler parts.

Which are true? Choose two.

☐ 10 more than 23 is 32.

☐ 1 more than 23 is 24.

☐ 10 less than 23 is 13.

☐ 1 less than 23 is 20.

Name _____

Solve & Share

How can place-value blocks help you decide which number is larger? Circle the number that is larger.

I can ...
use place-value blocks to compare 2 two-digit numbers.

© **Content Standards** I.NBT.B.3
Also I.NBT.A.I
Mathematical Practices MP.I,
MP.2, MP.6

37   73

Which is greater?
Compare the numbers.

98   94

First, compare the tens.
Both have 9 tens.
Compare the ones.

is **greater than (>)**

98   94.

is **less than (<)**

8 ones is greater
than 4 ones.
So, 98 is greater
than 94.

Now compare
these numbers.

Tens	Ones		Tens	Ones

32   35

First, compare the tens.
Both have 3 tens.
Compare the ones.

is greater than

32   35.

is less than

2 ones is less
than 5 ones.
So, 32 is less
than 35.

Convince Me! Which number
is greater, 38 or 26?
How do you know?

☆ **Guided Practice** ☆ Write a number to match each model.
Then circle **is greater than** or **is less than**.

1.

is greater than

is less than

78   53.

2.

is greater than

is less than

____   ____.

Independent Practice   Write a number to match each model.
Then circle **is greater than** or **is less than**.

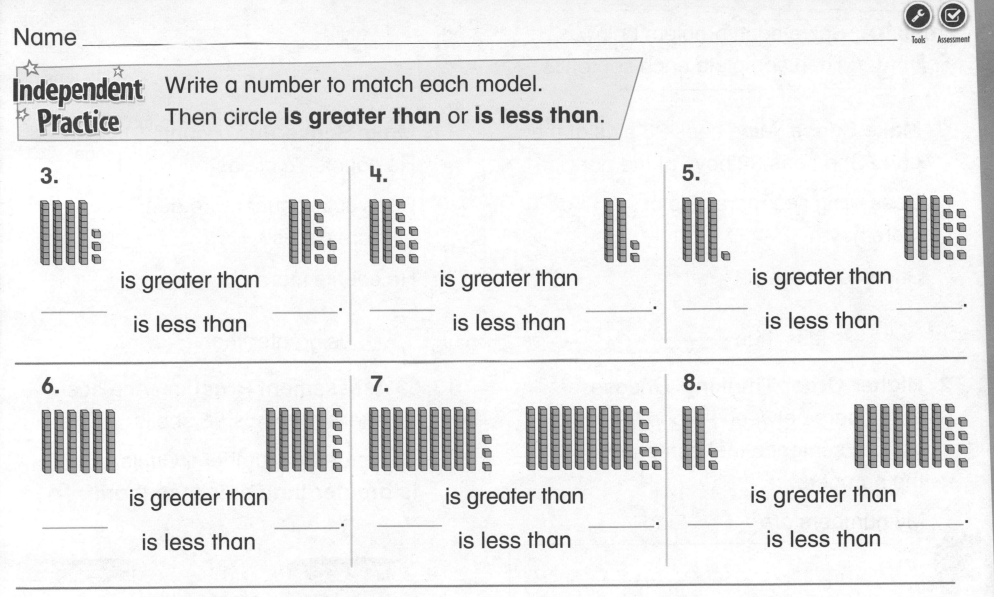

3.

_____ is greater than

_____ is less than _____.

4.

_____ is greater than

_____ is less than _____.

5.

_____ is greater than

_____ is less than _____.

6.

_____ is greater than

_____ is less than _____.

7.

_____ is greater than

_____ is less than _____.

8.

_____ is greater than

_____ is less than _____.

9. **Number Sense** Laura counts 36 stars. Andy counts 7 more stars than Laura.
Write the number of stars Andy counted. Then complete the sentence.

_____ stars

_____ is less than _____.

Problem Solving Solve each problem below. Then complete each sentence.

10. **Make Sense** Ming sees 28 girls at the park. She sees 32 boys at the park.

Does Ming see more girls or more boys?

She sees more _____.

_____ is less than _____.

11. **Make Sense** Julio counts 81 pennies. He counts 76 dimes.

Does Julio count more pennies or more dimes?

He counts more _____.

_____ is greater than _____.

12. **Higher Order Thinking** Choose 2 numbers between 40 and 99. Write a sentence that compares the numbers.

My numbers are _____ and _____.

_____

_____

I can draw a picture to show a number as tens and ones.

13. ☑ **Assessment Practice** Ann has 46 shells. Ben has 43 shells.

Compare the numbers. Circle **is greater than** or **is less than**.

is greater than

is less than

376 three hundred seventy-six

Solve & Share

Write a two-digit number inside the TV. Write a different two-digit number inside the radio. Then write the numbers and circle the words to complete the sentence below. Explain how you know.

I can ...
compare two numbers using greater than, less than, or an equal to sign.

© **Content Standard** I.NBT.B.3
Mathematical Practices MP.2, MP.3, MP.6

is greater than

_____ _____.

is less than

You can use blocks to compare 24 and 42. Compare the tens first.

24 is less than 42.

24 $<$ 42

24 has fewer tens than 42.

You can talk about 24 and 42 in a different way.

42 is greater than 24.

42 $>$ 24

42 has more tens than 24.

Now look at 35 and 38. Compare the ones when the tens are the same.

35 is less than 38.

35 $<$ 38

35 has fewer ones.

Sometimes the numbers are equal.

26 is equal to 26.

26 $=$ 26

The tens are the same. The ones are the same.

Convince Me! How do you know that 48 is greater than 40?

☆ **Guided Practice** ☆ Complete each sentence. Write **greater than**, **less than**, or **equal to**. Then write >, <, or =.

1.

28 is _less than_ 41.

28 $<$ 41

2.

53 is _____ 35.

53 ◯ 35

Topic 9 | Lesson 4

Name _____

Independent Practice Complete each sentence. Write **greater than**, **less than**, or **equal to**. Then write >, <, or =.

3.

19 is _____ 19.

19 ◯ 19

4.

62 is _____ 37.

62 ◯ 37

5.

86 is _____ 89.

86 ◯ 89

6. 34 ◯ 43

7. 95 ◯ 90

8. 74 ◯ 74

Higher Order Thinking Choose 2 number cards for each problem. Compare the numbers. Write >, <, or = in the circle. Use each number card one time.

| 19 | 99 | 42 | 72 | 56 | 19 |

9. _____ ◯ _____

10. _____ ◯ _____

11. _____ ◯ _____

12. Be Precise Mary has 21 red ribbons. She has 12 yellow ribbons. Does Mary have more red ribbons or yellow ribbons?

Write >, <, or = to compare the numbers.

21 ◯ 12

She has more _____ ribbons.

13. **Vocabulary** Write a sentence using **greater than (>)**.

[ ] ◯ [ ]

14. Higher Order Thinking Write a story that compares 2 numbers. Then complete the sentence to compare the numbers.

15. ☑ **Assessment Practice** Jake has 92 stickers. Brian has 97 stickers.

Which sentences show the correct way to compare Jake's stickers and Brian's stickers? Choose two that apply.

- [ ] 92 = 97
- [ ] 97 > 92
- [ ] 92 > 97
- [ ] 92 < 97

Name _____

Solve & Share

Nick skipped rope 24 times. Look at the number line below. Find a number that is greater than 24 and a number that is less than 24. Show your numbers on the number line and explain how you know.

I can …
compare and write two-digit numbers that are greater than or less than other two-digit numbers.

Ⓒ **Content Standard** I.NBT.B.3
Mathematical Practices MP.1, MP.4, MP.5

24

_____ is greater than 24.

_____ is less than 24.

You can use a number line to compare numbers. Find a number that is less than 55.

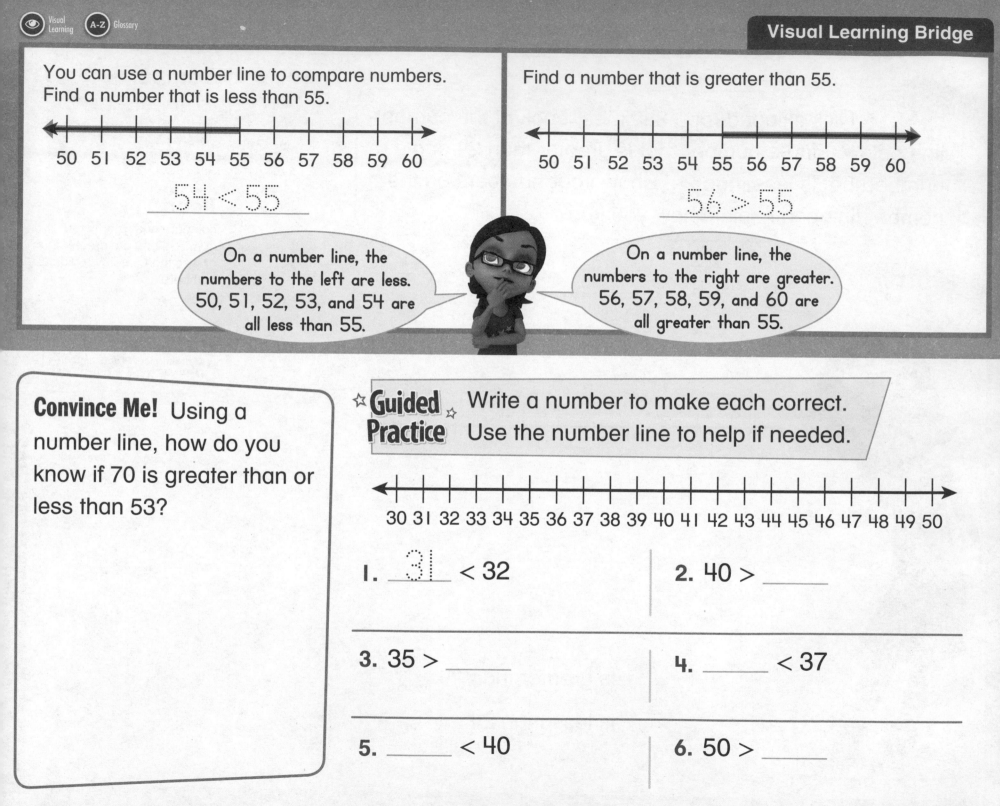

50 51 52 53 54 55 56 57 58 59 60

54 < 55

On a number line, the numbers to the left are less. 50, 51, 52, 53, and 54 are all less than 55.

Find a number that is greater than 55.

50 51 52 53 54 55 56 57 58 59 60

56 > 55

On a number line, the numbers to the right are greater. 56, 57, 58, 59, and 60 are all greater than 55.

Convince Me! Using a number line, how do you know if 70 is greater than or less than 53?

☆ **Guided Practice** ☆   Write a number to make each correct. Use the number line to help if needed.

30 31 32 33 34 35 36 37 38 39 40 41 42 43 44 45 46 47 48 49 50

1. __31__ < 32

2. 40 > _____

3. 35 > _____

4. _____ < 37

5. _____ < 40

6. 50 > _____

Topic 9 | Lesson 5

Name _____

Independent Practice

Write the number or symbol > or < to make each correct. Draw a number line to help if needed.

7. _____ < 26

8. 75 > _____

9. 33 > _____

10. _____ < 95

11. _____ > 50

12. 90 < _____

13. 39 ◯ 48

14. 47 ◯ 35

15. 29 ◯ 72

Higher Order Thinking Write numbers to make each correct. Place the numbers on the number lines.

16. _____ > 70 > _____

17. _____ < 64 < _____

70

64

18. 3 friends wrote a number on paper. Paul wrote a number that is greater than Nicole's number and less than Tina's number. Nicole's number is 42. Tina's number is 44.

What is Paul's number? _____

19. enVision® STEM Jay covers some windows with cardboard to block the sunlight from shining through. The number of windows he covers is less than 28 and more than 26. How many windows does Jay cover?

_____ windows

20. Higher Order Thinking How can you find a number that is greater than 90? Explain.

You can use a number line or draw a picture to help you.

21. ☑ **Assessment Practice** The number on Taylor's mailbox is **less than (<)** 70. Which numbers could be on Taylor's mailbox? Choose two.

☐ 60

☐ 69

☐ 70

☐ 71

Name _____

Activity

Problem Solving

Lesson 9-6
Make Sense and Persevere

I can ...
make sense of a problem and
find the best way to solve it.

© **Mathematical Practices** MP.I
Also MP.2, MP.3
Content Standard I.NBT.B.3

☆ **Solve & Share** ☆

I am thinking of a secret number.

The number is greater than 20 and less than 30.

The number is inside a shape with 4 sides.

What is the secret number?

What strategy did you use to find it?

25

31

22

56

6

Thinking Habits

What am I asked
to find?

What is a good
plan for solving
this problem?

41

19

27

14

38

The secret number is _____.

Visual Learning · A-Z Glossary

Carl has a secret number. It is greater than 40 and less than 50.
His number is red.
What is Carl's secret number?

| 29 | 50 | 22 | 46 | 24 |
| 45 | 41 | 58 | 57 | |

How can you make sense of this problem?

I can look at what I know in the problem and what I am asked to find.

My strategy is to make a list of numbers and use the clues that I know.

Number List
41
45
46

Check the next clue with the numbers that are left.

The second clue says the number is red.

Number List
~~41~~
~~45~~
46

So, 46 is the only number that fits both clues.

Convince Me! How does making a list help you make sense of a problem?

☆ **Guided Practice** ☆ Use the numbers above to solve each riddle. Write the secret number. Explain your work.

1. I am a green number.
   I am greater than 45 and less than 60.
   Which number am I?

   57

2. I am a blue number.
   You say my name when you count by 10s.
   Which number am I?

   _____

Name _____

Independent Practice

Make sense of each riddle to find the secret number. Show and explain your work.

 55 — Greg
 90 — Joan
 75 — Ben
 92 — Carla
 82 — Molly
 95 — Jay
 96 — Lisa
 48 — Yao
 64 — Katie
 98 — Peg

3. The number of pages in my book is less than 96 and greater than 90.

Who could I be?

_____

I have 3 letters in my name.
Who am I?

_____

4. The number of pages in my book is greater than 92.

Who could I be?

_____

I have the greatest number of pages.
Who am I?

_____

5. The number of pages in my book is less than 65.

Who could I be?

_____

I have 10 more than 54 pages.
Who am I?

_____

Problem Solving

Missing Numbers Akayla has to find a secret number missing from the chart. She gets some clues to help her.

What is the secret number?

61	62		64	65	66	67	68	69	70
	72	73	74	75	76	77		79	80
81	82		84	85	86	87		89	90

Akayla's Clues:

- The secret number is greater than 75.
- The number does **NOT** have an 8 in the ones place.

6. **Make Sense** What is your plan for solving this problem? Explain.

_____

_____

_____

Check that your solution makes sense.

7. **Explain** What is the secret number? How do you know your answer is correct?

_____

_____

_____

_____

_____

_____

Secret number: _____

Name _____

Find a Match

Find a partner. Point to a clue. Read the clue.

Look below the clues to find a match. Write the clue letter in the box next to the match.

Find a match for every clue.

I can …
add and subtract within 10.

© **Content Standard** 1.OA.C.6
Mathematical Practices MP.3,
MP.6, MP.7, MP.8

Clues

A $6 + 2$

B $5 + 5$

C $9 - 3$

D $5 - 1$

E $8 - 6$

F $5 + 4$

G $7 - 2$

H $1 + 2$

☐ $10 - 0$

☐ $2 + 2$

☐ $10 - 1$

☐ $9 - 7$

☐ $2 + 3$

☐ $7 - 4$

☐ $4 + 4$

☐ $3 + 3$

Understand Vocabulary

1. Compare the numbers. Circle the number that is more.

26 29

2. Compare the numbers. Circle the number that is less.

58 68

Word List
- compare
- greater than (>)
- less
- less than (<)
- more

3. Choose a term from the Word List. Fill in the blank to make it true.

_____ is _____

_____ is 10 _____ than _____

Use Vocabulary in Writing

4. Write a problem using the terms from the Word List. Use place-value blocks to help solve your problem.

Answers to Find a Match *on page 389.*

C	A	G
E	F	B
C	H	G
E	D	B

Name _____

Set A

You can use blocks to show
1 more, 1 less, 10 more,
and 10 less than a number.

34

1 less than 34 is 33.

10 more than 34 is 44.

Use blocks. Write the numbers
to complete each sentence.

1. 87

1 more than 87 is _____.

1 less than 87 is _____.

10 more than 87 is _____.

10 less than 87 is _____.

Set B

You can use a hundred chart
to find the number that is
1 more than, 1 less than,
10 more than, and 10 less than.

35	36	37	38	39
45	46	47	48	49
55	56	57	58	59

1 more than 48 is 49.

10 less than 48 is 38.

Write the number that is 1 more, 1 less,
10 more, or 10 less. You can use a
hundred chart to help you.

2. 1 less than 37

_____, 37

3. 1 more than 37

37, _____

4. 10 less than 55

_____, 55

5. 10 more than 55

55, _____

You can compare numbers using >, <, or =.

> means greater than.
33 is greater than 24.

33 24

< means less than.
24 is less than 33.

24 ◁ 33

Write **greater than**, **less than**, or **equal to**. Then write >, <, or =.

6. 46 is _____ 26.

46 ◯ 26

7. 25 is _____ 52.

25 ◯ 52

Thinking Habits

Make Sense and Persevere

What am I asked to find?

What is a good plan for solving this problem?

How can I check that my solution makes sense?

Look at the numbers below. Find the secret number.

42 73 91 7 13 63 50

8. I am a number greater than 65. What numbers could I be?

_____

9. I am 10 less than 83. What number am I? _____

392 three hundred ninety-two

Name _____

1. Trina's house number is 54. Frank's house number is greater than Trina's house number.

Which is Frank's house number? How do you know?

54

Ⓐ 52; because 52 > 50   Ⓒ 54; because 54 > 50

Ⓑ 53; because 53 < 54   Ⓓ 55; because 55 > 54

2. Choose two ways to compare the place-value blocks. Explain.

☐ 82 < 87; 82 has fewer ones than 87.

☐ 87 = 82; 87 and 82 have the same number of tens.

☐ 87 < 82; 82 has more ones than 87.

☐ 87 > 82; 87 has more ones than 82.

☐ 82 > 87; 82 has more ones than 87.

3. Find 10 more than 37 without having to count. Explain how you know.

Ⓐ 36; 36 has one fewer one than 37.   Ⓒ 38; 38 has one more one than 37.

Ⓑ 47; 47 has one more ten than 37.   Ⓓ 27; 27 has one fewer ten than 37.

4. Use the clues to find the secret number from the choices on the right.

I am less than 48.
What numbers could I be? _____

I have a 0 in the ones place. What number am I? _____

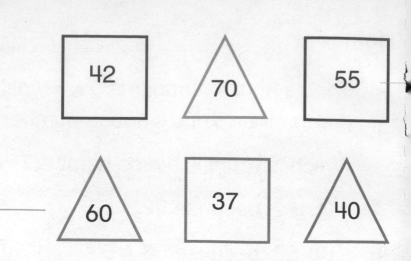

---

5. Write the number to complete the part of the hundred chart. Explain how you know.

6. What number is 10 more than 74?
What number is 10 less than 74?

10 more than 74 is _____.

10 less than 74 is _____.

---

7. Look at the place-value blocks. Write the numbers to make the sentences true. Explain how you know which number is greater.

_____ is greater than _____.

_____ is less than _____.

Mailbox Mysteries

Meg sees these mailboxes in her neighborhood.
Each mailbox has a different number.

60 25 58 17 89 35 73 34

1	2	3	4	5	6	7	8	9	10
11	12	13	14	15	16	17	18	19	20
21	22	23	24	25	26	27	28	29	30
31	32	33	34	35	36	37	38	39	40
41	42	43	44	45	46	47	48	49	50
51	52	53	54	55	56	57	58	59	60
61	62	63	64	65	66	67	68	69	70
71	72	73	74	75	76	77	78	79	80
81	82	83	84	85	86	87	88	89	90
91	92	93	94	95	96	97	98	99	100

1. Write the mailbox number for each clue.
   You can use the hundred chart to help you.

   1 more than 59 _____   1 less than 26 _____

   10 more than 7 _____   10 less than 83 _____

2. Use these clues to figure out each student's
   mailbox number.

   Show your work on the hundred chart.

   Larry's number is 10 less than Sue's number.
   Sue's number is 1 more than Bill's number.
   Bill's number is 34.

   Larry: _____

   Sue: _____

   Bill: _____

3. Fill in the missing numbers. You can use the number lines to help you.

Write a mailbox number
that is greater than 50.

_____ > 50

Write a mailbox number
that is less than 30.

_____ < 30

---

4. Meg describes her mailbox number.
She uses these clues.

What is her mailbox number? _____

Explain how you know.

Clues
• The number is greater than 40.
• The number is **NOT** on a red mailbox.
• The number has more ones than tens.

_____

_____

_____

_____

_____

Use Models and Strategies to Add Tens and Ones

Essential Question: What are ways to use tens and ones to add?

Digital Resources

Interactive Student Edition | Activity | Visual Learning | Video | Practice

Assessment | Games | Tools | Glossary

Everyone can see some stars from where they live.

The stars you see one night might be different than the stars you see another night.

Wow! Let's do this project and learn more.

enVision STEM Project: Watch the Stars

Find Out Talk to friends and relatives about stars. Discuss why the stars you see in the sky change from night to night.

Journal: Make a Book Show what you found out. In your book, also:

• Draw the stars you can see from where you live.

• Make up and solve addition problems about the stars.

Name _____

Review What You Know

A-Z Vocabulary

1. Circle the digit that shows how many **ones**.

   91

2. Circle the digit that shows how many **tens**.

   13

3. Circle the symbol that tells you **add**.

   + − =

Understanding Addition

4. Write an addition equation to match the picture.

   _____ + _____ = _____

5. Noah mows 7 lawns. Mari mows 13 lawns. How many lawns did the two friends mow in all?

   Write an addition equation to solve.

   _____ + _____ = _____

Hundred Chart

6. Fill in the missing numbers on the part of the hundred chart.

41		43	44	45	46	47	48	49	50
51	52	53	54		56	57		59	60
61	62		64	65	66	67	68	69	

   Topic 10

Name _____

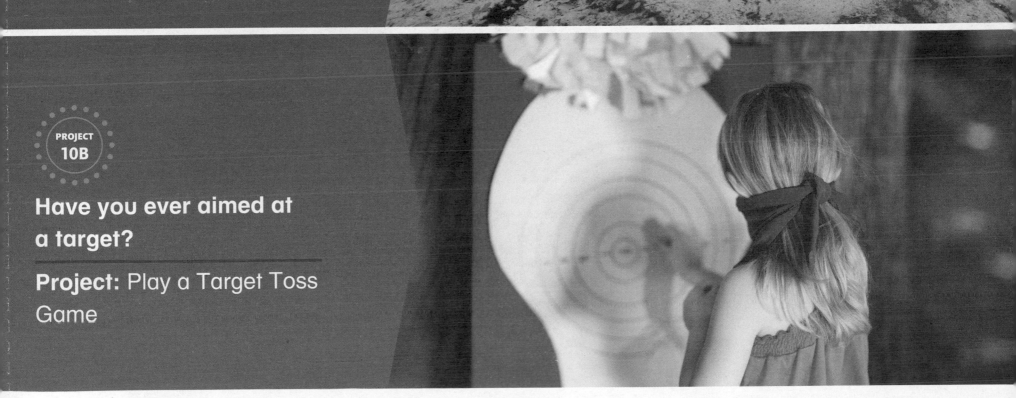

PROJECT
10A

Has anyone ever called you the wrong name?

Project: Make a Manatee Facts Book

PROJECT
10B

Have you ever aimed at a target?

Project: Play a Target Toss Game

PROJECT
10C

What is as colorful as a butterfly?

Project: Make a Leaf and Egg Model

PROJECT
10D

What would life be like without bones?

Project: Write and Draw an Octopus Story

Name _____

Solve & Share

How are these addition problems alike?

Talk to a partner about how you can use the first sum to help you find the second.

I can ...
add 2 multiples of ten.

© **Content Standards** I.NBT.C.4
Also I.NBT.B.2c
Mathematical Practices MP.1,
MP.2, MP.8

3 + 5 = _____

30 + 50 = _____

You know how to add ones.

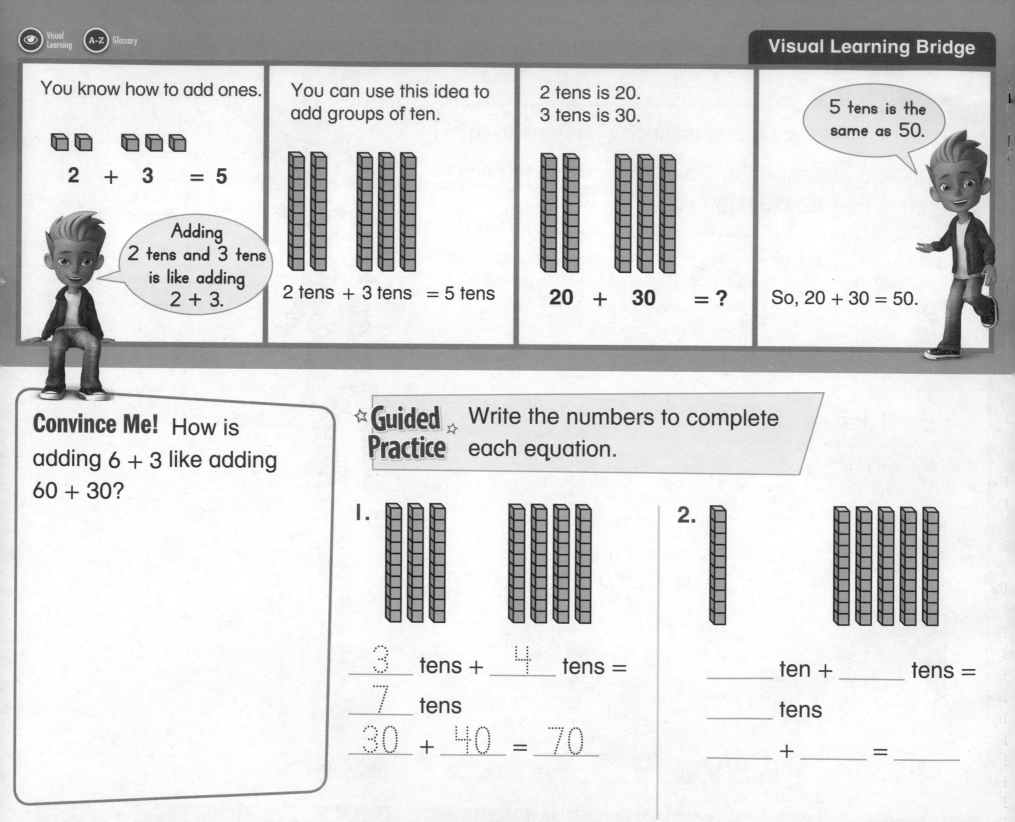

$2 + 3 = 5$

Adding 2 tens and 3 tens is like adding $2 + 3$.

You can use this idea to add groups of ten.

2 tens + 3 tens = 5 tens

2 tens is 20.
3 tens is 30.

$20 + 30 = ?$

5 tens is the same as 50.

So, $20 + 30 = 50$.

Convince Me! How is adding $6 + 3$ like adding $60 + 30$?

☆ **Guided Practice** ☆ Write the numbers to complete each equation.

1.

___3___ tens + ___4___ tens = ___7___ tens

$30 + 40 = 70$

2.

_____ ten + _____ tens = _____ tens

_____ + _____ = _____

Independent Practice ✫ Write the numbers to complete each equation.

3. ____ + ____ = ____

4. ____ + ____ = ____

5. ____ + ____ = ____

6. ____ + ____ = ____

7. ____ + ____ = ____

8. ____ + ____ = ____

9. ____ + ____ = ____

10. ____ + ____ = ____

11. ____ + ____ = ____

12. Make Sense Alex and Annie each have 5 boxes of crayons. Each box has 10 crayons.

How many crayons do Alex and Annie have in all?

_____ + _____ = _____

_____ crayons

13. Make Sense Becky and Dan buy some bottles of juice. Becky buys 6 bottles. Dan buys 2 bottles. Each bottle of juice is enough for 10 people.

How many people do Dan and Becky have enough juice for?

_____ + _____ = _____

_____ people

14. Higher Order Thinking Bree says that she knows $4 + 3 = 7$, so she also knows that $30 + 40 = 70$. Is she correct? Explain how you know.

_____

_____

_____

_____

15. ☑ Assessment Practice Which equation matches the picture?

Ⓐ $2 + 3 = 5$

Ⓑ $3 + 2 = 5$

Ⓒ $20 + 3 = 23$

Ⓓ $20 + 30 = 50$

Name _____

Solve & Share

Solve each problem. What pattern do you see in the totals?

I can ...
use mental math to add tens to two-digit numbers.

© **Content Standards** I.NBT.C.5 Also I.NBT.B.2a
Mathematical Practices MP.2, MP.3, MP.4

15 + 10 = _____

25 + 10 = _____

55 + 10 = _____

You have used place-value blocks to add 10. You can also use mental math to add 10. Find 23 + 10.

How can I add 10 mentally?

When adding 10, you should look at the tens digit.

I know 2 + 1 = 3. So, 23 + 10 = 33.

Use mental math to add.

Think about the digit in the tens place and the ones place.

33 + 10 = __43__

43 + 10 = __53__

53 + 10 = __63__

Convince Me! Explain how you can use mental math to add 10 to 47.

⭐ **Guided Practice** ⭐ Use mental math to solve the problems.

1. __25__ + __10__ = __35__

2. _____ + _____ = _____

Tools   Assessment

✰ Independent Practice ✰   Use mental math to solve each equation.

3. $58 + 10 =$ _____

4. $44 + 10 =$ _____

5. $35 + 10 =$ _____

6. $10 + 72 =$ _____

7. $87 + 10 =$ _____

8. $31 + 10 =$ _____

9. $18 + 10 =$ _____

10. $10 + 26 =$ _____

11. $9 + 10 =$ _____

12. **Number Sense** Winnie used place-value blocks to show $29 + 10$. She said the answer is 30. Is Winnie correct? Explain how you know.

_____

_____

13. **Reasoning** Sam makes 15 dollars mowing lawns one day.
He makes 10 dollars the next day.

How many dollars did Sam make in all?

_____ dollars

14. **Reasoning** Tess solves 22 math problems.
Then she solves 10 more math problems.

How many math problems did Tess solve in all?

Think about the numbers in the tens digit and the ones digit.

_____ math problems

15. **Higher Order Thinking** Roger collects
75 cans. Ella collects some cans. Roger
and Ella have 85 cans together.

How many cans did Ella collect?

_____ cans

16. ☑**Assessment Practice** Match each
pair of addends with their sum.

27   33 + 10

86   41 + 10

43   59 + 10

51   76 + 10

69   17 + 10

Name _____

Solve & Share

Use a hundred chart to find these sums.

$8 + 40 = ?$ $30 + 40 = ?$ $80 + 12 = ?$

Show your work and tell how you found each sum.

I can ...
use a hundred chart to add tens and ones.

© **Content Standards** I.NBT.C.4
Also I.NBT.B.2
Mathematical Practices MP.5, MP.7

1	2	3	4	5	6	7	8	9	10
11	12	13	14	15	16	17	18	19	20
21	22	23	24	25	26	27	28	29	30
31	32	33	34	35	36	37	38	39	40
41	42	43	44	45	46	47	48	49	50
51	52	53	54	55	56	57	58	59	60
61	62	63	64	65	66	67	68	69	70
71	72	73	74	75	76	77	78	79	80
81	82	83	84	85	86	87	88	89	90
91	92	93	94	95	96	97	98	99	100

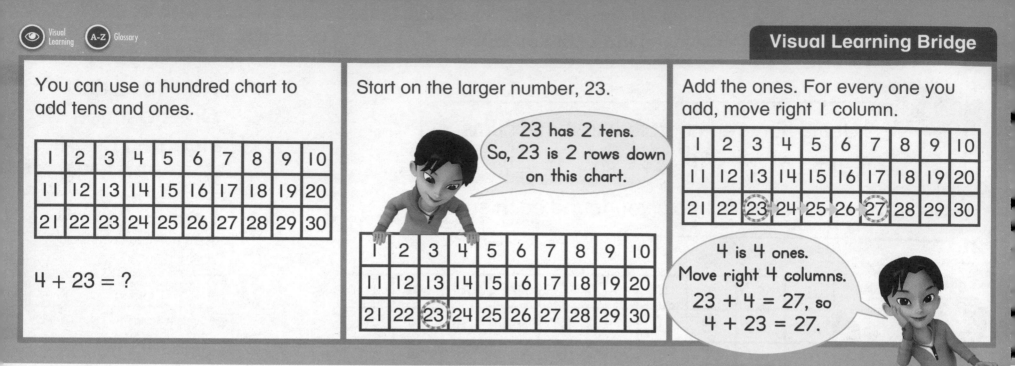

You can use a hundred chart to add tens and ones.

1	2	3	4	5	6	7	8	9	10
11	12	13	14	15	16	17	18	19	20
21	22	23	24	25	26	27	28	29	30

4 + 23 = ?

Start on the larger number, 23.

23 has 2 tens. So, 23 is 2 rows down on this chart.

Add the ones. For every one you add, move right 1 column.

4 is 4 ones. Move right 4 columns.
23 + 4 = 27, so
4 + 23 = 27.

Convince Me! How could you use the hundred chart to find the sum of 6 and 50?

☆ **Guided Practice** ☆   Use the part of the hundred chart to add.

1. 2 + 12 = ___14___

2. 5 + 40 = _____

3. 13 + 20 = _____

4. 10 + 31 = _____

5. 32 + 6 = _____

1	2	3	4	5	6	7	8	9	10
11	12	13	14	15	16	17	18	19	20
21	22	23	24	25	26	27	28	29	30
31	32	33	34	35	36	37	38	39	40
41	42	43	44	45	46	47	48	49	50

Name _____

Tools Assessment

Independent Practice ☆ Use the hundred chart to add.

1	2	3	4	5	6	7	8	9	10
11	12	13	14	15	16	17	18	19	20
21	22	23	24	25	26	27	28	29	30
31	32	33	34	35	36	37	38	39	40
41	42	43	44	45	46	47	48	49	50
51	52	53	54	55	56	57	58	59	60
61	62	63	64	65	66	67	68	69	70
71	72	73	74	75	76	77	78	79	80
81	82	83	84	85	86	87	88	89	90
91	92	93	94	95	96	97	98	99	100

6. $7 + 60 =$ _____

7. $33 + 20 =$ _____

8. $20 + 18 =$ _____

9. $5 + 13 =$ _____

10. $3 + 26 =$ _____

11. $1 + 41 =$ _____

12. $4 + 32 =$ _____

13. $56 + 2 =$ _____

14. $10 + 85 =$ _____

15. $7 + 12 =$ _____

16. $50 + 13 =$ _____

17. $71 + 5 =$ _____

18. **Higher Order Thinking** Sue had some stickers in a book. She bought 30 more stickers. Now she has 36 stickers in her book. How many stickers did Sue have in the book at the start?

_____ stickers

Start with the number that will make it easier to add on the hundred chart.

Problem Solving ☆ Use the hundred chart to solve each problem below.

1	2	3	4	5	6	7	8	9	10
11	12	13	14	15	16	17	18	19	20
21	22	23	24	25	26	27	28	29	30
31	32	33	34	35	36	37	38	39	40
41	42	43	44	45	46	47	48	49	50
51	52	53	54	55	56	57	58	59	60
61	62	63	64	65	66	67	68	69	70
71	72	73	74	75	76	77	78	79	80
81	82	83	84	85	86	87	88	89	90
91	92	93	94	95	96	97	98	99	100

19. Use Tools Some hens lay 40 eggs. Then they lay 45 more eggs. How many eggs did the hens lay in all?

_____ eggs

20. Use Tools 22 students are at the book fair. More students came to the book fair later. There are 72 students in all at the book fair. How many students came later?

_____ students

21. Higher Order Thinking Write a number story for $3 + 42$.

22. ☑ Assessment Practice Use the hundred chart. Which equations show the correct sum for $50 + 8$? Choose two that apply.

- ☐ $8 + 50 = 85$
- ☐ $50 + 8 = 13$
- ☐ $8 + 50 = 58$
- ☐ $50 + 8 = 58$

Name _____

Solve & Share

Use the open number lines to find the sums.

$43 + 6 = ?$ $5 + 19 = ?$ $10 + 32 = ?$

Activity

I can ...
use a number line to solve addition problems.

© **Content Standards** 1.NBT.C.4
Also 1.NBT.B.2
Mathematical Practices MP.2, MP.4, MP.5

43

Use an open number line to find 25 + 4.

I can count on by ones.

+1   +1   +1   +1

25   26   27   28   29

$25 + 4 = \underline{29}$

Use an open number line to find 25 + 30.

I can count on by tens.

+10   +10   +10

25   35   45   55

$25 + 30 = \underline{55}$

Convince Me! Think about the problem 20 + 17. Would it be easier to start with 20 or 17 on the number line to solve the problem?

★ **Guided Practice**   Add using the number lines.

1.

+10   +10   +10

37   47   57   67

$37 + 30 = \underline{67}$

2.

$26 + 50 = \underline{}$

Independent Practice ☆   Add using the number lines.

3.

$11 + 8 = $ _____

4.

$40 + 16 = $ _____

5.

$48 + 20 = $ _____

6.

$22 + 7 = $ _____

7. Higher Order Thinking Write an addition equation using a two-digit and one-digit number. Then solve by showing your work on the number line.

_____ + _____ = _____

8. **Use Tools** Danny writes 20 pages of his paper on Monday. He writes 32 pages on Tuesday. How many pages did Danny write in all? Use the number line to solve.

$20 + 32 =$ _____ _____ pages

9. **Use Tools** Last year, Leah watched 41 movies. This year, she has watched 30 movies. How many movies has Leah watched in all? Use the number line to solve.

$41 + 30 =$ _____ _____ movies

10. **Higher Order Thinking** Explain how you would solve $57 + 7$ on a number line.

_____

_____

11. ☑ **Assessment Practice** Add $60 + 26$ on a number line. Show your work.

$60 + 26 =$ _____

Name _____

☆ **Solve & Share**

Maddy has 50 stickers.
Jill gives Maddy 5 more stickers.
Use place-value blocks to show how many
stickers Maddy has now.
Then use numbers and pictures to show your work.

I can ...
solve addition problems by
using blocks or drawings.

© **Content Standards** I.NBT.C.4
Also I.NBT.B.2
Mathematical Practices MP.3,
MP.4, MP.5

Find 21 + 7.
First, use blocks.

21 + 7 = 28

Then, draw what you did to solve.

I added the ones first.

21 + 7 = 28

Find 21 + 20.

21 + 20 = 41

I added the tens and then the one.

21 + 20 = 41

Convince Me! Could you count on by 10s to add 21 + 20?

Guided Practice Use blocks to add. Then draw what you did.

1. 24 + 4 = 28

2. 16 + 30 = ____

3. 32 + 20 = ____

4. 33 + 6 = ____

Name _____

Independent Practice ✩   Add. Draw blocks to show your work.

5.

$37 + 2 =$ _____

6.

$21 + 40 =$ _____

7.

$42 + 10 =$ _____

8.

$4 + 33 =$ _____

9.

$50 + 14 =$ _____

You can add in any order to make it easier!

Look for a pattern to help you find the missing numbers.

10. Algebra Write the missing numbers. Then write the last addition problem in the pattern.

```
    4   0          ☐ ☐          4   0          4   0          ☐ ☐
  +     5        +     6        +     7        +   ☐
  ────────       ────────       ────────       ────────       ─────
  ☐ ☐              4   6        ☐ ☐              4   8         ☐ ☐
```

Write an equation to solve each problem below. Use blocks to help if needed.

11. **Model** Jamal has 32 coins in his piggy bank. Jamal's dad gives him 4 more coins. How many coins does Jamal have now?

_____ + _____ = _____

_____ coins

12. **Model** Julie sells 18 muffins on Monday. She sells 20 muffins on Friday. How many muffins did Julie sell in all?

_____ + _____ = _____

_____ muffins

13. **Higher Order Thinking** Jake has 9 marbles. He gets some more marbles. Now Jake has 79 marbles. How many marbles did Jake get? Draw a picture to solve.

_____ marbles

14. ☑ **Assessment Practice** Which is the sum for 40 + 37?

Ⓐ 47

Ⓑ 57

Ⓒ 67

Ⓓ 77

Name _____

Solve & Share

What strategy can you use to find 8 + 5?

How can you use the sum for 8 + 5 to help you find 28 + 5? Show your work and be ready to explain your thinking.

I can ...
use my knowledge of ten to help make addition problems easier to solve.

© **Content Standards** 1.NBT.C.4 Also 1.NBT.B.2a
Mathematical Practices MP.4, MP.6

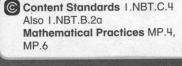

You can use blocks or an open number line to help.

Sometimes, you can make a 10 when you add.

Let's try with 28 + 6.

You can add ones to ones to make a 10.

28 + 6
28 + 2 + 4

Now, I have 3 tens and 4 ones.

30 + 4 = 34
So, 28 + 6 = 34

Sometimes, you can't make a 10 when you add.

21 + 5 = 26

Convince Me! When you add two numbers, how do you know if you can make a 10?

☆ **Guided Practice** ☆ Draw blocks and make a 10 to add.

1. Find 37 + 7.

Think: 37 + 3 = 40

Think: 7 = 3 + 4

Think: 40 + 4 = 44

So, 37 + 7 = 44.

I can break apart 7 into 3 and 4. So I still need to add 4 more.

Name _____

Tools Assessment

Independent Practice ✩ Draw blocks and make a 10 to add.

2. 17 + 7

Think: 17 + ____ = 20

So, break apart 7 into ____ + ____.

20 + ____ = ____

So, 17 + 7 = ____.

Add. Use or draw blocks to help.

4. 42 + 8 = ____

3. 38 + 4

Think: 38 + ____ = 40

So, break apart 4 into ____ + ____.

40 + ____ = ____

So, 38 + 4 = ____.

Use what you know about place value to help!

5. 29 + 5 = ____

Algebra Write each missing number. Use place-value blocks if you need to.

6. 23 + ☐ = 32

7. 35 + ☐ = 40

8. **Model** Jamie has 28 cards.

   His sister gives him 6 more cards.

   How many cards does Jamie have now?

   Draw blocks to show your work.

   _____ cards

9. **Model** Lisa knits 15 scarves.

   Then she knits 8 more.

   How many scarves does Lisa knit in all?

   Draw blocks to show your work.

   _____ scarves

10. **Higher Order Thinking** Explain how to find $19 + 6$.

    Use equations to show your thinking.

    _____

    _____

    _____

11. ☑ **Assessment Practice** Explain how to use the make a 10 strategy to find $37 + 5$.

    _____

    _____

    _____

    _____

Solve & Share

Grace is solving 35 + 8.

First she adds 35 + 5 = 40.

What should she do next to find the answer?

Draw a model to explain.

I can ...
add 2 two-digit numbers.

© **Content Standards** 1.NBT.C.4
Also 1.NBT.B.2a
Mathematical Practices MP.2,
MP.3, MP.4

Find 27 + 15.

You can draw blocks to help you add. Draw the tens and the ones.

Add the ones.
See if you can make a ten.

7 ones + 5 ones = 12 ones
7 + 5 = 12

Add the tens.

2 tens + 1 ten = 3 tens
20 + 10 = 30

Find the sum.

7 + 5 = 12
20 + 10 = 30

27 + 15 = 42

So we have 4 tens and 2 ones. That's 42!

Convince Me! Do you need to make a 10 to add 23 + 15? How do you know?

⋆ **Guided Practice** Add. Draw blocks to help.

1. Find 36 + 24.

6 + 4 = __10__

30 + 20 = ____

So, 36 + 24 = ____

2. Find 19 + 25.

9 + 5 = __14__

10 + 20 = __30__

So, 19 + 25 = ____

Name _____

Independent Practice   Add. Draw blocks or an open number line to help.

3. Find 19 + 42.

9 + 2 = _____

10 + 40 = _____

19 + 42 = _____

4. Find 27 + 25.

7 + 5 = _____

20 + 20 = _____

27 + 25 = _____

Add. You can draw blocks or an open number line to help.

5. 37 + 33 = _____

6. 28 + 44 = _____

7. 25 + 26 = _____

8. 56 + 33 = _____

9. Reasoning Sara mows 15 lawns. Bill mows 12 lawns. How many lawns did they mow in all? Write an addition equation to show the problem.

_____ lawns

10. Reasoning Jon reads 24 pages. Then he reads 27 more pages. How many pages does he read in all? Write an addition equation to show the problem.

_____ pages

11. Higher Order Thinking Explain how to find 27 + 15 by adding the tens first. Use equations to show your thinking.

12. ☑ Assessment Practice For which addition equations can you make a 10 to add? Choose two that apply.

☐ 12 + 29 = ___?___

☐ 61 + 26 = ___?___

☐ 33 + 35 = ___?___

☐ 34 + 18 = ___?___

Name _____

☆ Solve & Share

A puzzle has 59 green pieces and 25 orange pieces. Solve 59 + 25 to find how many pieces in all. Use any of the strategies you have learned.

I can ...
solve addition problems using different strategies.

© **Content Standards** I.NBT.C.4
Also I.NBT.C.5
Mathematical Practices MP.2, MP.3, MP.4

59 + 25 = _____ pieces

Find 25 + 17 in different ways.

I used blocks. I made a 10.

25 + 17 = 42

You can draw tens and ones to find 25 + 17.

25 + 17 = 42

You can add 25 + 17 on an open number line.

Add 10 and then break apart the 1s as easier numbers.

+10   +5 +2

25   35   40 42   25 + 17 = 42

Convince Me! Why can you use different strategies to solve the same problem?

☆ **Guided Practice** ☆ Find each sum. Solve any way you choose. Draw or explain what you did.

1. 37 + 24 = 61

2. 48 + 10 = _____

Independent Practice   Find each sum. Solve any way you choose.
Draw or explain what you did.

3.

27 + 9 = _____

4.

50 + 23 = _____

5.

32 + 28 = _____

6.

62 + 19 = _____

7. **Reasoning** Lilly makes necklaces. She has 43 blue beads. She has 20 pink beads. How many beads does Lilly have in all?

_____ beads

8. **Reasoning** Jay has a hat collection. He has 27 hats from football teams. He has 33 hats from baseball teams. How many hats does Jay have in all?

_____ hats

9. **Higher Order Thinking** Connie's soccer team has a bake sale. The team sells 18 banana muffins and 24 oat muffins. They sell 12 granola bars. How many muffins did Connie's team sell? Draw a picture and write an equation to show your work.

_____ muffins

10. ☑ **Assessment Practice** Garret uses place-value blocks to show 53 + 18. Which of the following model this problem? Choose two that apply.

☐   ☐   ☐   ☐

Solve & Share

Pam has 13 buttons. Julie gives her some more. Now Pam as 30 buttons. Use blocks or a number line to figure out how many buttons Julie gave Pam.

I can ...
model with math by drawing a picture and writing an equation to help me solve a problem.

© **Mathematical Practices** MP.4
Also MP.2, MP.3, MP.5
Content Standards 1.NBT.C.4
Also 1.NBT.B.2a

Thinking Habits

How can I use numbers and symbols to solve this problem?

How can I use the math I know to show this problem?

Miko has 23 green marbles and 18 blue marbles. How many marbles does he have in all?

How can I show the problem?

> I could use blocks, a number line, an equation, or drawings to show the problem.

$23 + 18 = ?$

> This is an addition story. I can draw tens and ones to show $23 + 18$.

$23 + 18 = \underline{41}$

> I can make a 10. I have 4 tens and 1 one. Miko has 41 marbles in all.

Convince Me! If Miko has 23 green marbles and 30 blue marbles, how many marbles does he have in all? Draw a picture to solve the problem.

☆**Guided Practice**☆ Use drawings to show and solve the problem. Then write the equation.

1. Ellen has 27 stickers. Her brother gives her 26 stickers. How many stickers does Ellen have in all?

_____ + _____ = _____

Name _____

Independent Practice

Use drawings to show and solve the problem.
Then write the equation.

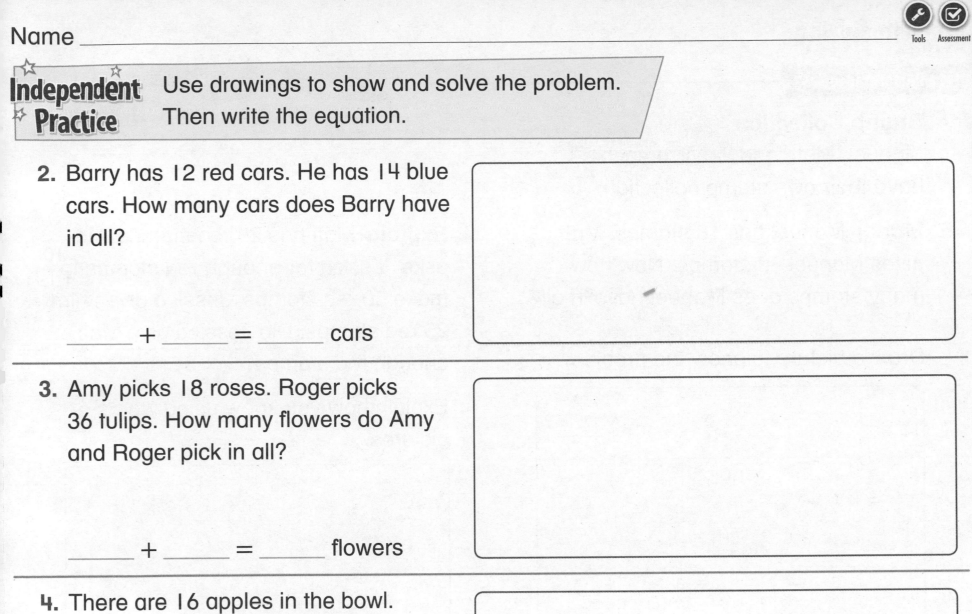

2. Barry has 12 red cars. He has 14 blue
cars. How many cars does Barry have
in all?

_____ + _____ = _____ cars

3. Amy picks 18 roses. Roger picks
36 tulips. How many flowers do Amy
and Roger pick in all?

_____ + _____ = _____ flowers

4. There are 16 apples in the bowl.
George buys 15 more apples.
How many apples are there in all?

_____ + _____ = _____ apples

Problem Solving

Stamp Collection

Manuel, Matt, and Jessica each have their own stamp collection.

5. **Model** Manuel has 18 stamps. Matt gives Manuel 30 stamps. Now how many stamps does Manuel have in all?

Draw a picture to show the problem.

6. **Model** Write an equation that matches the story.

_____ ◯ _____ = _____

7. **Explain** Matt has 24 red stamps. He asks Jessica for enough red stamps to make 50 red stamps. Jessica gives him 25 red stamps. Did Jessica give Matt enough red stamps?

Explain how you know using words or pictures.

Can you make a 10? Why or why not.

_____

_____

Show the Word

Color these sums and differences. Leave the rest white.

| 8 | 6 | 9 |

I can ...
add and subtract within 10.

© **Content Standard** 1.OA.C.6
Mathematical Practices MP.3, MP.6, MP.7, MP.8

4 + 2	9 − 3	0 + 6	10 − 2	3 + 1	5 + 3	5 + 4	10 − 1	9 + 0
6 − 0	8 − 7	8 − 2	4 + 4	1 + 2	8 − 0	6 + 1	8 + 1	5 − 5
3 + 3	6 + 0	7 − 1	3 + 5	5 − 3	2 + 6	0 + 2	9 − 0	2 + 8
2 + 4	4 + 3	3 + 2	8 + 0	4 − 4	7 + 1	2 − 1	4 + 5	1 + 1
10 − 4	2 + 2	6 − 6	6 + 2	9 − 1	0 + 8	4 + 0	0 + 9	8 − 3

The word is

_____   _____   _____

Vocabulary Review

Word List
- add
- ones
- open number line
- tens

Understand Vocabulary

1. Use the models to add the tens.

_____ tens + _____ tens = _____ tens

2. Use the models to add the tens.

_____ tens + _____ tens = _____ tens

3. Find 19 + 12.

   Add the ones.
   Then add the tens.

   Draw blocks to help.

   9 + 2 = _____

   10 + 10 = _____

   19 + 12 = _____

Use Vocabulary in Writing

4. Solve 20 + 6 using an open number line.
   Explain how you solved it using terms from the Word List.

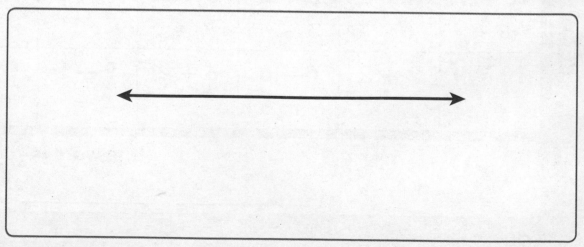

Name _____

Set A

You can add groups of 10.

Write the numbers to complete each equation.

__2__ tens + __4__ tens = __6__ tens

$20 + 40 = 60$

1.

____ + ____ = ____

2.

____ + ____ = ____

Set B

You can also use mental math to add 10. When you add 10, the tens digit goes up by 1. The ones digit stays the same.

2 tens + 1 ten = 3 tens

$24 + 10 =$ __34__

Use mental math to solve the problems below.

3. $36 + 10 =$ _____

4. $53 + 10 =$ _____

5. $71 + 10 =$ _____

Set C

You can use part of a hundred chart to add tens and ones.

$$3 + 40 = ?$$

1	2	③	4	5	6	7	8	9	10
11	12	13	14	15	16	17	18	19	20
21	22	23	24	25	26	27	28	29	30
31	32	33	34	35	36	37	38	39	40
41	42	㊸	44	45	46	47	48	49	50

$$3 + 40 = \underline{43}$$

Use the part of the hundred chart to add tens and ones.

1	2	3	4	5	6	7	8	9	10
11	12	13	14	15	16	17	18	19	20
21	22	23	24	25	26	27	28	29	30
31	32	33	34	35	36	37	38	39	40
41	42	43	44	45	46	47	48	49	50
51	52	53	54	55	56	57	58	59	60

6. $4 + 50 = $ _____   7. $8 + 30 = $ _____

Set D

You can use an open number line to add.

$$34 + 20 = \underline{54}$$

Use an open number line to add.

8.

$$11 + 6 = $$ _____

Name _____

Set E _____

You can use blocks to add tens to a number.

22 + 30 = 52

Add the tens and the ones. Use blocks to help you.

9. 44 + 30 = _____

10. 20 + 5 = _____

11. 30 + 28 = _____

12. 19 + 60 = _____

Set F _____

Sometimes you can make 10 when you add.

27 + 6 = ?

27 + 3 + 3

30 + 3 = 33

So, 27 + 6 = 33.

Draw blocks and make a 10 to add.

13. 33 + 9

Think: 33 + _____ = 40

So, break apart 9 into _____ + _____.

40 + _____ = _____

So, 33 + 9 = _____.

$24 + 19 = ?$

You can draw blocks to help you add.
First add the ones. Then add the tens.

There are 4 tens and 3 ones.

$24 + 19 = 43$

Add. Draw blocks to help.

14. Find $67 + 16$.

$7 + 6 = \underline{\hspace{2cm}}$

$60 + 10 = \underline{\hspace{2cm}}$

$67 + 16 = \underline{\hspace{2cm}}$

Thinking Habits

Model with Math

Can I use a drawing, diagram, table, or graph to model the problem?

Can I write an equation to show the problem?

Use drawings to show and solve the problem. Then write the equation.

15. Sally sees 15 birds. Then she sees 17 more. How many birds did Sally see in all?

$\underline{\hspace{1.5cm}} + \underline{\hspace{1.5cm}} = \underline{\hspace{1.5cm}}$

Name _____

1. Write an equation that matches the place-value blocks below.

_____

2. Find the sum.
Draw place-value blocks to show how you found it.

50 + 3 = _____

3. Find the sum of 16 and 18.

Use words, pictures, or a model to solve.
Write the equation.

_____ + _____ = _____

4. Which equation matches the place-value blocks shown below?
Choose two that apply.

☐ 60 + 30 = 90
☐ 6 tens + 3 tens = 9 tens
☐ 60 + 10 = 70
☐ 4 tens + 3 tens = 7 tens
☐ 6 tens + 3 ones = 9 ones

5. Find the sum of 18 and 11.
Explain how you solved the problem.
Did you need to make a 10?

_____

_____

_____

6. Solve the problem.
Use place-value blocks if needed.

$28 + 13 =$ _____

Can you make a 10? Explain.

Circle **Yes** or **No**.

Yes   No

7. Use the part of the hundred chart to add.
Choose the possible explanation for how to
find $46 + 20$.

31	32	33	34	35	36	37	38	39	40
41	42	43	44	45	46	47	48	49	50
51	52	53	54	55	56	57	58	59	60
61	62	63	64	65	66	67	68	69	70

Ⓐ I start at 46 and then move two rows up
to get 26. So, $46 + 20 = 26$.

Ⓑ I start at 46 and then move one row down
and four columns to the right to get 60.
So, $46 + 20 = 60$.

Ⓒ I start at 46 and then move two rows down
to get 66. So, $46 + 20 = 66$.

Ⓓ I start at 46 and then move two rows down
to get 68. So, $46 + 20 = 68$.

 Topic 10 | Assessment Practice

Name _____

Use the part of the hundred chart to solve each problem. What is one way to explain your answer?

1	2	3	4	5	6	7	8	9	10
11	12	13	14	15	16	17	18	19	20
21	22	23	24	25	26	27	28	29	30
31	32	33	34	35	36	37	38	39	40

8. $10 + 27 = ?$

Ⓐ 17; I started at 27 and subtracted 1 ten.

Ⓑ 28; I started at 27 and added 1 ten.

Ⓒ 37; I started at 27 and added 1 ten.

Ⓓ 40; I started at 10 and added 3 tens.

9. $4 + 35 = ?$

Ⓐ 95; I started at 35 and added 4 tens.

Ⓑ 39; I started at 35 and added 4 ones.

Ⓒ 31; I started at 35 and subtracted 4 ones.

Ⓓ 12; I started at 32 and subtracted 2 tens.

Use mental math to solve. Then explain how you found your answer.

10. $53 + 10 =$ _____

_____

11. $48 + 10 =$ _____

_____

12. $64 + 10 =$ _____

_____

Find the correct number to complete each equation.

13. $20 + 70 =$ _____

14. $30 +$ _____ $= 60$

15. _____ $+ 20 = 40$

16. Use the open number line to find $40 + 23$. Show your work.

$40 + 23 =$ _____

17. Find $43 + 8$. Do the models correctly show the sum? Explain how you know.

_____

_____

_____

Solve each problem. Can you make a 10? Use place-value blocks if needed.

	Show	Add	Can you make a 10?		Find the sum
18.	42	37	Yes	No	
19.	16	35	Yes	No	
20.	14	16	Yes	No	

Name _____

Pet Survey

Maria asked other students what kind of pet they have. She made this chart.

Number of Pets	
Fish	27
Cats	30
Birds	8
Dogs	39

1. How many **Fish** and **Cats** in all?
   Use the open number line to solve.

<——————————————————————————>

_____ fish and cats

2. How many **Dogs** and **Birds** in all?
   Use the hundred chart to add.

1	2	3	4	5	6	7	8	9	10
11	12	13	14	15	16	17	18	19	20
21	22	23	24	25	26	27	28	29	30
31	32	33	34	35	36	37	38	39	40
41	42	43	44	45	46	47	48	49	50
51	52	53	54	55	56	57	58	59	60
61	62	63	64	65	66	67	68	69	70
71	72	73	74	75	76	77	78	79	80
81	82	83	84	85	86	87	88	89	90
91	92	93	94	95	96	97	98	99	100

_____ + _____ = _____

_____ dogs and birds

3. Maria asks 18 students about their pets on Monday. She asks 17 students about their pets on Tuesday. How many students did she ask on both days?

Use place-value blocks to solve. Draw the blocks you used.

_____ students

Did you need to make a 10 when you added the ones?

Explain your answer.

_____

_____

_____

4. Maria adds other pets to her chart. 19 students in first grade have a rabbit. 24 students in second grade have a rabbit. How many students in all have rabbits?

Part A

Draw blocks to help you solve the problem.

Part B

Write an equation that matches the story.

_____ ◯ _____ = _____ students

Use Models and Strategies to Subtract Tens

Essential Question: How can I use what I know about subtraction to subtract tens?

Digital Resources

Interactive Student Edition · Activity · Visual Learning · Video · Practice

Assessment · Games · Tools · Glossary

People develop all kinds of tools to solve problems and make our lives easier.

Sometimes they just take a tool that already exists and make it better.

Wow! Let's do this project and learn more.

enVision STEM Project: Tools Solve Problems

Find Out Talk to friends and relatives about different tools we use to solve problems. Ask them about tools they use in their everyday lives.

Journal: Make a Book Show what you found out. In your book, also:

• Draw some tools that solve simple problems. Make sure to describe the simple problems they solve.

• Make up and solve subtraction problems about tools.

Name _____

Review What You Know

Vocabulary

1. How many **tens** are in this number?

23

_____ tens

2. Use the **hundred chart** to count by 10s.

1	2	3	4	5	6	7	8	9	10
11	12	13	14	15	16	17	18	19	20
21	22	23	24	25	26	27	28	29	30
31	32	33	34	35	36	37	38	39	40
41	42	43	44	45	46	47	48	49	50
51	52	53	54	55	56	57	58	59	60
61	62	63	64	65	66	67	68	69	70
71	72	73	74	75	76	77	78	79	80
81	82	83	84	85	86	87	88	89	90
91	92	93	94	95	96	97	98	99	100

30, 40, 50, _____, _____

3. Use the **open number line** to add.

⟵————————————⟶

$7 + 9 =$ _____

Count Back to Subtract

4. Mark takes 8 pictures. Julia takes 3 fewer pictures than Mark. Count back to find how many pictures Julia took.

8, _____, _____, _____

_____ pictures

5. Katie picks 15 flowers. Max picks 13 flowers. Count back to find how many fewer flowers Max picked than Katie.

15, _____, _____

_____ fewer flowers

Subtraction Facts

6. Find each difference.

$12 - 4 =$ _____

$14 - 7 =$ _____

$19 - 9 =$ _____

Name _____

PROJECT
11A

Have you ever looked closely at money?

Project: Study Penny Collections

PROJECT
11B

Where are baby sea turtles born?

Project: Tell Sea Turtle Subtraction Stories

PROJECT
11C

What's your favorite flavor of smoothie?

Project: Set Up a Smoothie Stand

Math Modeling

So Many Colors

▶ Video

Before watching the video, think:

When you clean up, how many toys can you clean up at the same time? How can you tell how many toys fit in a container?

I can ...

model with math to solve a problem that involves adding and subtracting with groups of tens.

© **Mathematical Practices** MP.4
Also MP.2, MP.3
Content Standards I.NBT.C.6
Also I.NBT.C.4, I.NBT.C.5

Topic 11 | 3-Act Math

Name _____

Solve & Share

How can thinking about 4 − 1 help you to find 40 − 10? Use place-value blocks to help you.

I can ...
use models to subtract tens.

Content Standards 1.NBT.C.6
Also 1.NBT.B.2c, 1.NBT.C.5
Mathematical Practices MP.2, MP.5, MP.6

You know how to subtract ones.

$5 - 1 =$ ___4___

So, you can subtract 1 ten from groups of 10.

5 tens – 1 ten = ___4___ tens

5 tens minus 1 ten is like subtracting 5 – 1.

5 tens is 50.
1 ten is 10.

$50 - 10 =$ ___?___

5 tens minus 1 ten equals 4 tens.

4 tens is 40, so

$50 - 10 =$ ___40___.

Convince Me! When you solve 40 – 10, how does the tens digit change? How does the ones digit change?

☆ **Guided Practice** ☆ Write the numbers to complete each equation.

1. ___7___ tens – ___1___ ten = ___6___ tens.

$70 - 10 = 60$

2. ___ tens – ___ tens = ___ tens

___ – ___ = ___

Independent Practice ☆   Write the numbers to complete each equation.

3.

_____ tens − _____ tens = _____ tens

_____ − _____ = _____

4.

_____ tens − _____ ten = _____ tens

_____ − _____ = _____

5.

Look at the tens digit!

_____ tens − _____ tens = _____ tens

_____ − _____ = _____

6.

_____ tens − _____ tens = _____ tens

_____ − _____ = _____

7. Ethan has 30 crayons. He gives 10 crayons away. How many crayons does Ethan have now?

Write the equation.

_____ – _____ = _____   _____ crayons

8. Algebra Jacob solved these problems. Did Jacob subtract 1 or 10?

Finish the equations.

$50 - \boxed{} = 40$ $60 - \boxed{} = 59$

9. Higher Order Thinking Write and solve a story problem for $90 - 10$.

_____

_____

_____

10. ☑ **Assessment Practice** 20 teddy bears are for sale at the store. Then, 10 teddy bears are sold.

How many teddy bears are on sale at the store now?

30   50   10   0

Ⓐ   Ⓑ   Ⓒ   Ⓓ

Solve & Share

Use a hundred chart to find these differences.

50 − 30 = ?   30 − 20 = ?   80 − 10 = ?

Explain.

I can ...

use a hundred chart to subtract multiples of 10 from 2-digit numbers.

© **Content Standards** I.NBT.C.6
Also I.NBT.B.2, I.NBT.C.5
Mathematical Practices MP.3, MP.5, MP.6

1	2	3	4	5	6	7	8	9	10
11	12	13	14	15	16	17	18	19	20
21	22	23	24	25	26	27	28	29	30
31	32	33	34	35	36	37	38	39	40
41	42	43	44	45	46	47	48	49	50
51	52	53	54	55	56	57	58	59	60
61	62	63	64	65	66	67	68	69	70
71	72	73	74	75	76	77	78	79	80
81	82	83	84	85	86	87	88	89	90
91	92	93	94	95	96	97	98	99	100

👁 Visual Learning   A-Z Glossary

You can use a hundred chart to subtract tens. Find 70 – 20.

41	42	43	44	45	46	47	48	49	50
51	52	53	54	55	56	57	58	59	60
61	62	63	64	65	66	67	68	69	70

70 – 20 = ___?___

Start on 70.

For every ten you subtract, move up 1 row.

41	42	43	44	45	46	47	48	49	50
51	52	53	54	55	56	57	58	59	60
61	62	63	64	65	66	67	68	69	70

70 – 20 = __50__

20 is 2 tens. Move up 2 rows.

Check your work. Start at 70. Count back by 10s.

__70__, 60, 50

Counting back by 10 is like subtracting 10.

Convince Me! Find 80 – 50. Explain how you found the difference.

☆ **Guided Practice** ☆   Use the chart to subtract. Be ready to explain your work.

1	2	3	4	5	6	7	8	9	10
11	12	13	14	15	16	17	18	19	20
21	22	23	24	25	26	27	28	29	30
31	32	33	34	35	36	37	38	39	40

1. 40 – 10 = __30__

2. 40 – 20 = _____

3. 30 – 20 = _____

4. 10 – 10 = _____

Tools Assessment

Independent Practice

Use the chart to subtract.
Be ready to explain your work.

1	2	3	4	5	6	7	8	9	10
11	12	13	14	15	16	17	18	19	20
21	22	23	24	25	26	27	28	29	30
31	32	33	34	35	36	37	38	39	40
41	42	43	44	45	46	47	48	49	50
51	52	53	54	55	56	57	58	59	60
61	62	63	64	65	66	67	68	69	70
71	72	73	74	75	76	77	78	79	80
81	82	83	84	85	86	87	88	89	90
91	92	93	94	95	96	97	98	99	100

5. $50 - 30 =$ _____   6. $80 - 60 =$ _____

7. $30 - 30 =$ _____   8. $90 - 30 =$ _____

9. $70 - 20 =$ _____   10. $20 - 10 =$ _____

11. $60 - 30 =$ _____   12. $90 - 50 =$ _____

13. $90 - 40 =$ _____   14. $80 - 40 =$ _____

Algebra Find the missing numbers.

You can think addition to subtract!

15. $30 -$ _____ $= 20$ 16. _____ $- 30 = 10$

17. _____ $- 50 = 20$ 18. $20 -$ _____ $= 0$

19. _____ $- 20 = 30$ 20. $70 -$ _____ $= 30$

Problem Solving

Use the chart to solve each problem. Show your work.

31	32	33	34	35	36	37	38	39	40
41	42	43	44	45	46	47	48	49	50
51	52	53	54	55	56	57	58	59	60
61	62	63	64	65	66	67	68	69	70

1	2	3	4	5	6	7	8	9	10
11	12	13	14	15	16	17	18	19	20
21	22	23	24	25	26	27	28	29	30
31	32	33	34	35	36	37	38	39	40

21. **Use Tools** Colvin throws a dart at a target 70 times. 10 times, he misses the target. How many times did he hit the target?

_____ – _____ = _____

_____ times

22. **Use Tools** Mal's basketball team scores 40 points. They score 10 more points than the other team.
How many points did the other team score?

_____ – _____ = _____

_____ points

23. **Higher Order Thinking** Circle any number in the last row of the partial hundred chart above. Subtract 30. Write your equation.

_____ – _____ = _____

24. ☑ **Assessment Practice** Leo makes 50 muffins for his class bake sale. He sells 10 muffins. How many muffins are left?

Ⓐ 10

Ⓑ 20

Ⓒ 30

Ⓓ 40

Name _____

Solve & Share

Solve 50 − 20 by showing it on this open number line. Be ready to explain your work.

I can ...
use an open number line to solve subtraction problems.

© **Content Standards** I.NBT.C.6
Also I.NBT.B.2c, I.NBT.C.5
Mathematical Practices MP.4, MP.5

⟵—————————————————————⟶

50 − 20 = _____

You can use an open number line to subtract tens. Find 70 − 30.

Start by marking 70 on an open number line.

70

Use place value. Think of 30 as 3 groups of 10.

−10 −10 −10

40   50   60   70

30 is 3 tens.

Subtracting 3 tens is the same as subtracting 30.

− 30

40   70

I landed on 40.
70 − 30 = 40

Convince Me! How can you use an open number line to subtract tens?

☆**Guided Practice**☆ Use the open number line to subtract. Be ready to explain your work.

1.   30 − 20 = _____

−10   −10

10   20   30

2.   90 − 50 = _____

Name _____

Independent Practice

Use the open number lines to subtract.
Be ready to explain your work.

3. 70 − 20 = _____

4. 60 − 10 = _____

5. 80 − 30 = _____

6. 40 − 40 = _____

7. **Model** Dexter has 40 toothpicks. He uses 20 of them. How many toothpicks does he have left to use? Show your work.

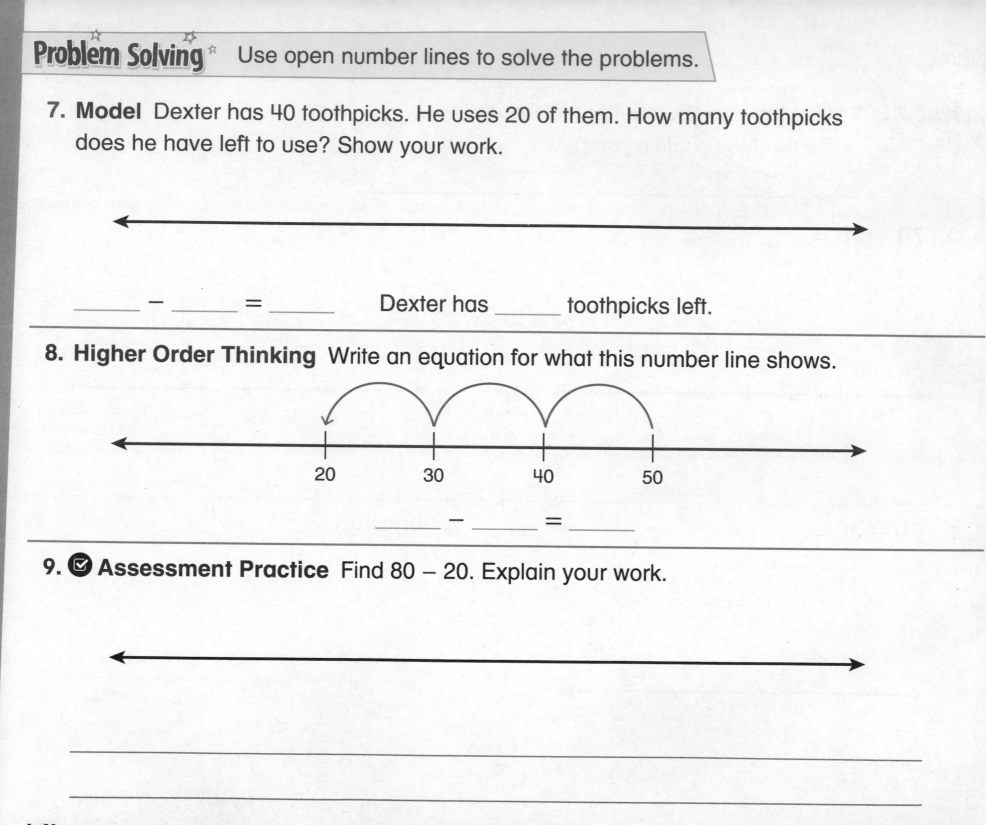

_____ − _____ = _____   Dexter has _____ toothpicks left.

8. **Higher Order Thinking** Write an equation for what this number line shows.

20   30   40   50

_____ − _____ = _____

9. ☑ **Assessment Practice** Find 80 − 20. Explain your work.

_____

_____

Name _____

Solve & Share

Mia has 70 stickers. Jack has 30 stickers. How many more stickers does Mia have than Jack has?

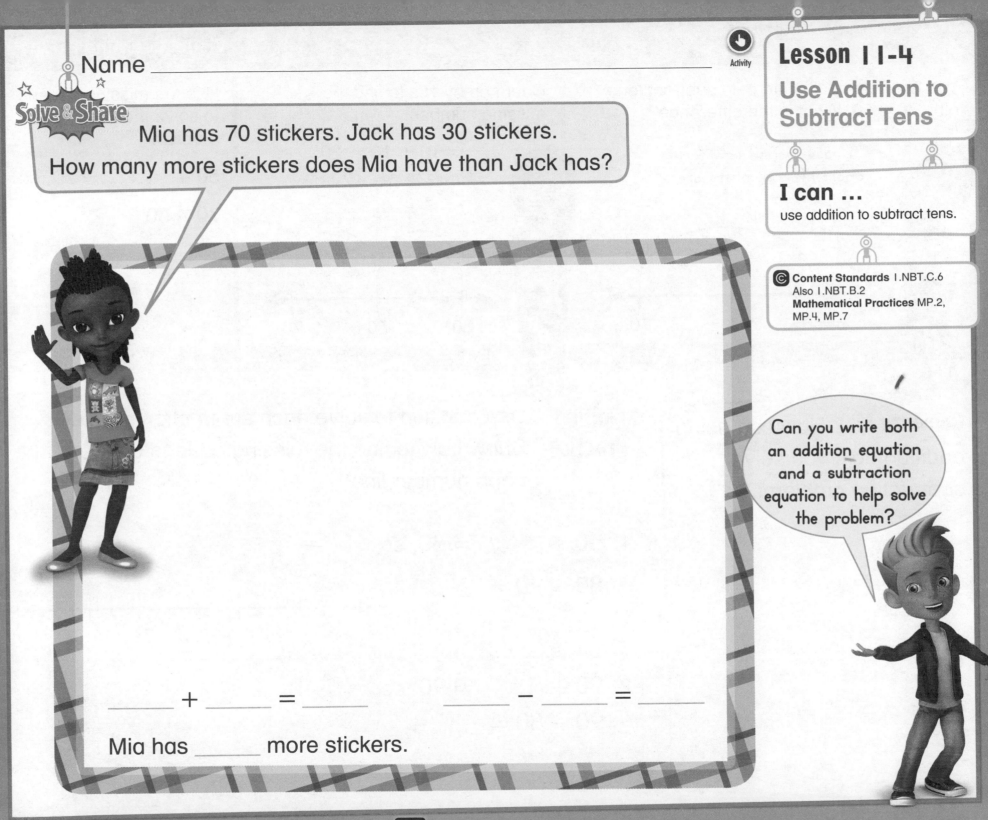

I can ...
use addition to subtract tens.

© **Content Standards** I.NBT.C.6 Also I.NBT.B.2
Mathematical Practices MP.2, MP.4, MP.7

Can you write both an addition equation and a subtraction equation to help solve the problem?

____ + ____ = ____   ____ − ____ = ____

Mia has ____ more stickers.

You can use addition to help subtract tens. Find 70 – 50. What is the difference?

I need to find how far apart these numbers are.

?

50   70

Count on by 10s to find the missing number.

*10 + 10 = 20
I need to add 20 to 50.*

+10   +10

50   60   70

Use the missing addend to solve the subtraction problem.

$50 + \underline{20} = 70$, so

$70 - 50 = \underline{20}$.

Convince Me! How can using addition help you solve subtraction problems?

★**Guided Practice**★ Use addition to solve each subtraction problem. Show how to find the missing addend on the open number line.

1. $40 + \underline{40} = 80$, so
$80 - 40 = \underline{40}$.

+10 +10 +10 +10

40   50   60   70   80

2. $30 + \underline{} = 90$, so
$90 - 30 = \underline{}$.

Name _____

Independent Practice Use addition to solve each subtraction problem. Show how to find the missing addend on the open number line.

3. $20 +$ _____ $= 60$, so $60 - 20 =$ _____ .

4. $30 +$ _____ $= 80$, so $80 - 30 =$ _____ .

Use addition to solve each subtraction problem. Draw a picture to show your thinking.

5. $30 +$ _____ $= 50$, so $50 - 30 =$ _____ .

I can draw tens to show the addend I know and the missing addend.

6. $60 +$ _____ $= 80$, so $80 - 60 =$ _____ .

Topic 11 | Lesson 4

four hundred sixty-seven **467**

Problem Solving ☆ Write an equation and solve the problems below.

7. **Reasoning** Mr. Andrews collects 90 papers from his students. He has already graded 40 papers. How many papers does Mr. Andrews have left to grade?

_____ ◯ _____ = _____

_____ papers

8. **Reasoning** Stacy drives 40 miles to work. She has already driven some miles. Stacy has 20 miles left to drive. How many miles has Stacy already driven?

_____ ◯ _____ = _____

_____ miles

9. **Higher Order Thinking** Sam has 4 cases of juice boxes. There are 10 juice boxes in each case. He brings 3 cases to share with his class.

Write and solve an equation to show how many juice boxes Sam has left.

_____ – _____ = _____

_____ juice boxes

10. ☑**Assessment Practice** Dr. Tess had 20 patients to see today. She has already seen 10 of them. How many patients does Dr. Tess have left to see?

Ⓐ 40

Ⓑ 30

Ⓒ 20

Ⓓ 10

 Topic 11 | Lesson 4

Name _____

Solve & Share

Suppose you have 89 trading cards.

How many cards would 10 more cards be?

How many cards would 10 less cards be?

I can ...
use mental math to subtract ten from a two-digit number.

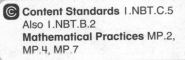

© **Content Standards** I.NBT.C.5
Also I.NBT.B.2
Mathematical Practices MP.2,
MP.4, MP.7

Be ready to explain how you know.

You have used different ways to subtract tens. Find 35 − 10.

I can use a model to help.

1	2	3	4	5	6	7	8	9	10
11	12	13	14	15	16	17	18	19	20
21	22	23	24	25	26	27	28	29	30
31	32	33	34	35	36	37	38	39	40

You can also use mental math to subtract ten. When you subtract 10, the tens digit goes down by 1.

I know 3 − 1 = 2. So, 35 − 10 = 25.

$$35 - 10 = \underline{25}$$

Subtract 10 from these numbers.

$$46 - 10 = \underline{36}$$

$$78 - 10 = \underline{68}$$

$$95 - 10 = \underline{85}$$

Remember, when subtracting tens, only the tens digit changes.

Convince Me! Explain why only the tens digit changes when you subtract 10 from 76.

Guided Practice Use mental math to subtract. Use ten-frames if needed.

1.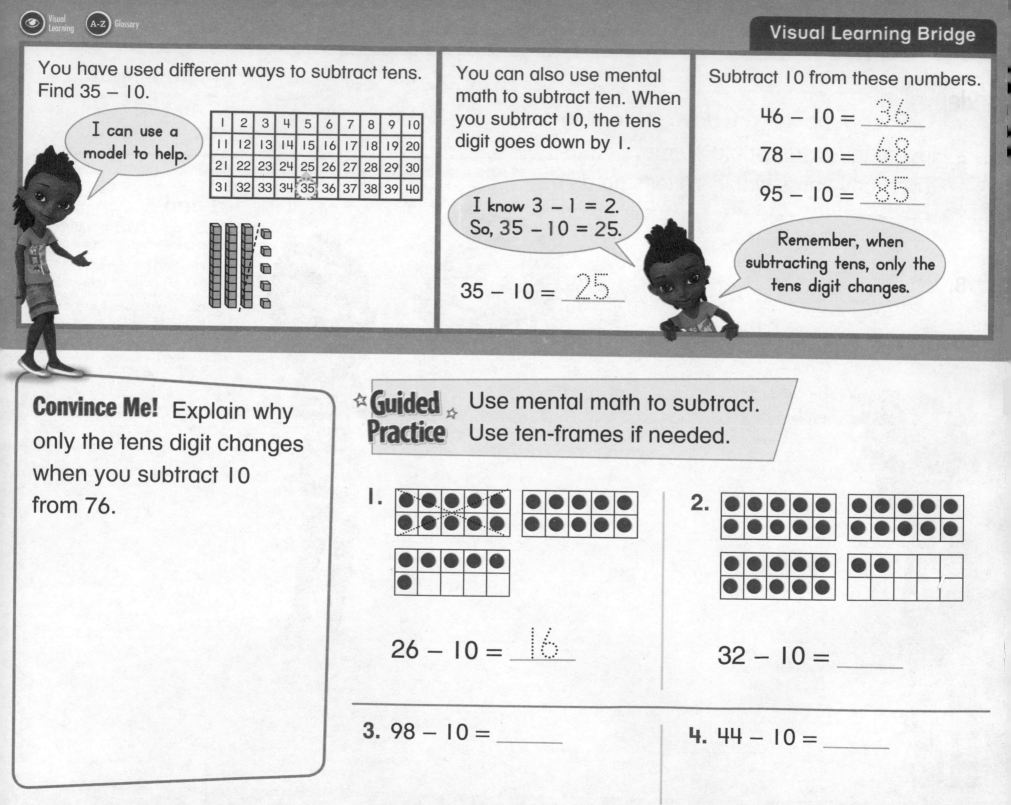

$$26 - 10 = \underline{16}$$

2.

$$32 - 10 = \underline{}$$

3. $98 - 10 = \underline{}$

4. $44 - 10 = \underline{}$

Name _____

☆ Independent Practice ☆   Use mental math to solve.

5. $53 - 10 =$ _____

6. $20 - 10 =$ _____

7. $32 - 10 =$ _____

8. $80 - 10 =$ _____

9. $17 - 10 =$ _____

10. $60 - 10 =$ _____

11. $47 - 10 =$ _____

12. $85 - 10 =$ _____

13. $11 - 10 =$ _____

14. Number Sense Subtract using ten-frames and mental math. Complete the related addition equation.

Think about how the digits change when you subtract tens.

$39 - 10 =$ _____

_____ $+ 10 = 39$

15. Reasoning Jamal has 43 stamps on his desk. He puts 10 stamps in a notebook. How many stamps are left?

_____ stamps

16. Vocabulary Ed brings 27 oranges home. His family eats 10 of them. How many oranges does Ed have left? Find the **difference**.

$27 - 10 =$ _____

_____ oranges

17. Higher Order Thinking Write a subtraction story about 56 − 10. Then solve your story.

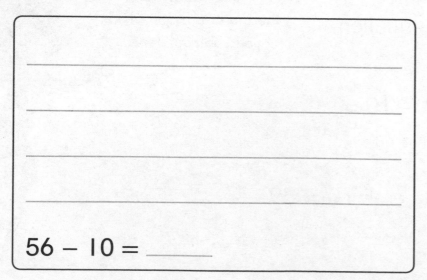

$56 - 10 =$ _____

18. Assessment Practice Use mental math to find 44 − 10.

Ⓐ 54

Ⓑ 45

Ⓒ 43

Ⓓ 34

Name _____

Solve & Share

Make up a story about 60 − 40.
Then solve the subtraction problem.
Use the strategy you think works best.

I can ...
use different strategies to
subtract.

© **Content Standards** I.NBT.C.6
Also I.NBT.C.5
Mathematical Practices MP.3,
MP.4, MP.5

60 − 40 = _____

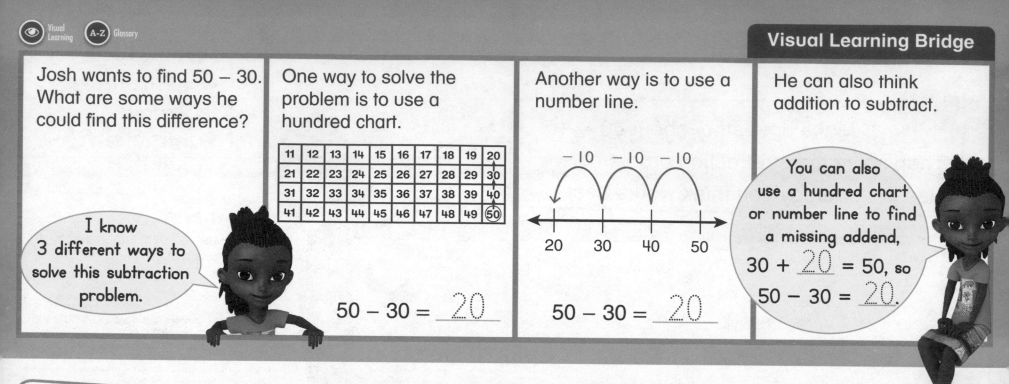

Josh wants to find 50 − 30. What are some ways he could find this difference?

I know 3 different ways to solve this subtraction problem.

One way to solve the problem is to use a hundred chart.

50 − 30 = 20

Another way is to use a number line.

50 − 30 = 20

He can also think addition to subtract.

You can also use a hundred chart or number line to find a missing addend,

30 + 20 = 50, so

50 − 30 = 20.

Convince Me! Which strategy would you use to solve 50 − 40? Explain why.

☆**Guided Practice**☆ Use the partial hundred chart or another strategy to solve each subtraction problem.

31	32	33	34	35	36	37	38	39	40
41	42	43	44	45	46	47	48	49	50
51	52	53	54	55	56	57	58	59	60
61	62	63	64	65	66	67	68	69	70

1. 70 − 10 = 60

2. 60 − 20 = _____

3. 43 − 10 = _____

4. 70 − 30 = _____

Tools Assessment

Independent Practice Use the strategy you think works best to solve each subtraction problem. Explain your reasoning.

5. 90 − 40 = _____

6. 40 − 20 = _____

7. 80 − 60 = _____

8. 50 − 20 = _____

9. 74 − 10 = _____

10. 80 − 40 = _____

11. enVision® STEM Students at a school plant flowers in a garden.
They plant 50 flowers in a part that gets a lot of sunshine.
They plant 30 flowers in a part that is shaded from the sun.
How many fewer flowers did they plant in a shaded spot than in a sunny spot?
Write an equation to show your work.

_____ − _____ = _____   _____ fewer flowers

12. Use Tools Charlie puts baseball cards into an album. He already put 10 cards in the album. He has 83 cards in all.

How many baseball cards does Charlie have left to put in the album?

_____ cards

13. Use Tools Pearl's basketball team scores 50 points in one game. They score some points in the first half. They score 20 points in the second half.

How many points did Pearl's team score in the first half?

_____ points

14. Higher Order Thinking Write a subtraction problem for which you would think addition to subtract. Explain why this would be a good strategy to use to solve this problem.

_____

_____

_____

15. ☑ Assessment Practice Explain how you would use a hundred chart to solve 60 − 20.

_____

_____

_____

_____

Name _____

Solve & Share

Val picks 40 strawberries. She shares 20 of them with her brother. How many strawberries did Val keep for herself?

How can modeling your thinking help you solve this problem?

I can ...
model my thinking to solve problems.

© **Mathematical Practices** MP.4
Also MP.1, MP.5
Content Standards 1.NBT.C.6
Also 1.NBT.C.5

Thinking Habits

Can I use a drawing, diagram, graph, or table to model this problem?

How can I make my model better if it doesn't work?

Nate has 70 green apples. He has 30 red apples. How many more green apples does Nate have than red ones?

How can I model this problem?

I can use pictures, objects, and equations to show and solve this problem. Then I can decide if my model makes sense.

I will draw a picture and write an equation.

10
10
10
10
10   10
10   10
10   10

$70 - 30 = \underline{40}$

7 tens − 3 tens = 4 tens

Nate has _40_ more green apples.

I can show my work in another way!

Convince Me! In the example above, how do the boxes of 10 help model the problem?

⭐ **Guided Practice** ⭐ Use drawings, models, or equations to solve.

1. A store has 60 muffins. It sells 30 of the muffins. How many muffins does the store have now?

   10 | 10 | 10 | 10 | 10 | 10

   _30_ muffins

2. Andy has 84 baseball cards. He has 10 more cards than Tia has. How many cards does Tia have?

   _____ cards

Name _____

Independent Practice ✭ Use drawings, models, or equations to solve. Explain your work.

3. Viola has 80 stickers.
Dean has 60 stickers.
How many more stickers
does Viola have than Dean?

_____ more stickers

4. Carla reads some pages in
a book. She reads 20 pages
less than Mary reads. Mary
reads 50 pages. How many
pages did Carla read?

_____ pages

5. A store has 72 toy cars.
It sells 10 cars.
How many cars does the
store have left?

_____ cars

Problem Solving

Dog Walking James, Emily, and Simon walk dogs after school.

On Monday, they have 40 dogs to walk. James and Emily take 20 of the dogs for a walk. How many dogs are left for Simon to walk?

6. Make Sense What problem do you need to solve?

_____

_____

_____

7. Use Tools What tool or tools can you use to solve this problem?

_____

_____

_____

_____

8. Model Write an equation to show the problem. Then use pictures, words, or symbols to solve.

_____ ◯ _____ = _____

_____ dogs

Name _____

Point & Tally

Find a partner. Get paper and a pencil.

Each partner chooses a different color: light blue or dark blue.

Partner 1 and Partner 2 each point to a black number at the same time. Subtract Partner 2's number from Partner 1's number.

If the answer is on your color, you get a tally mark.

Work until one partner gets twelve tally marks.

I can ...
add and subtract within 10.

© Content Standard 1.OA.C.6
Mathematical Practices MP.3, MP.6, MP.7, MP.8

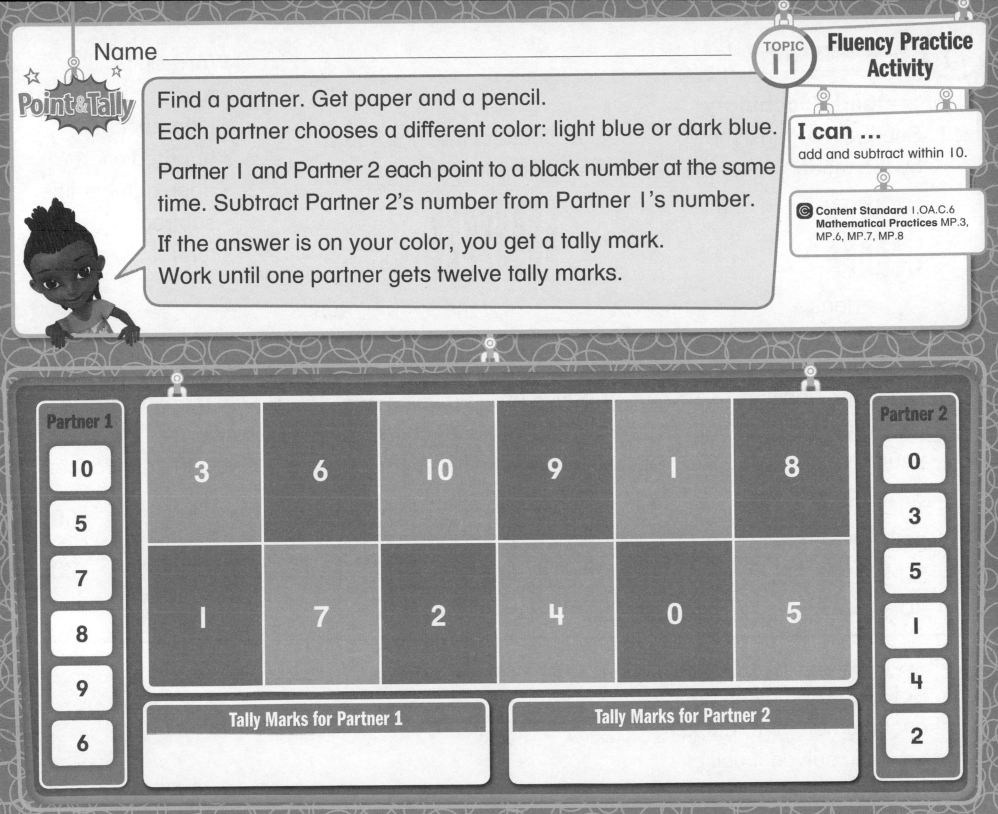

Partner 1							Partner 2
10	3	6	10	9	1	8	0
5							3
7							5
8	1	7	2	4	0	5	1
9							4
6							2

Tally Marks for Partner 1

Tally Marks for Partner 2

A-Z Glossary

Word List
- add
- difference
- hundred chart
- open number line
- subtract
- tens

Understand Vocabulary

1. Subtract the tens shown by the model.

_____ tens – _____ tens

= _____ tens

2. Subtract the tens shown by the model.

_____ tens – _____ tens

= _____ tens

3. Circle the addition problem that could help you solve 50 – 30.

$10 + 40 = 50$

$25 + 25 = 50$

$30 + 20 = 50$

$40 + 10 = 50$

4. Solve 40 – 20 using a partial hundred chart. Circle the difference.

1	2	3	4	5	6	7	8	9	10
11	12	13	14	15	16	17	18	19	20
21	22	23	24	25	26	27	28	29	30
31	32	33	34	35	36	37	38	39	40
41	42	43	44	45	46	47	48	49	50

5. Use mental math to solve 70 – 10. Circle the difference.

40   50

60   70

Use Vocabulary in Writing

6. Solve 80 – 50 using an open number line. Explain how you solved it using terms from the Word List.

Name _____

Set A

You can subtract tens.

$$40 - 30 = \underline{\quad ? \quad}$$

You need to subtract 30, which is 3 tens.

Cross out that many tens.

Count the tens and ones that are left.

$$40 - 30 = 10$$

Cross out the tens. Write the difference.

1. $60 - 40 = \underline{\qquad}$

2. $50 - 20 = \underline{\qquad}$

Set B

You can use a hundred chart to subtract tens.

$$80 - 20 = \underline{\quad ? \quad}$$

51	52	53	54	55	56	57	58	59	60
61	62	63	64	65	66	67	68	69	70
71	72	73	74	75	76	77	78	79	80

$$80 - 20 = \underline{60}$$

Use this partial hundred chart to subtract tens.

41	42	43	44	45	46	47	48	49	50
51	52	53	54	55	56	57	58	59	60
61	62	63	64	65	66	67	68	69	70

3. $70 - 20 = \underline{\qquad}$

4. $60 - 10 = \underline{\qquad}$

You can use mental math to subtract tens. Find 46 − 10.

4 tens − 1 ten = 3 tens.
So, 46 − 10 = 36.

Subtract. Use mental math.

5. 62 − 10 = _____

6. 89 − 10 = _____

7. 27 − 10 = _____

Thinking Habits

Model with Math

Can I use a drawing, diagram, table, or graph to model the problem?

How can I make my model better if it doesn't work?

Write an equation to solve. Use drawings or models to show your work.

8. A store has 50 toy boats. They sell 10 boats. How many toy boats does the store have now?

_____ toy boats

484 four hundred eighty-four

Topic 11 | Reteaching

Name _____

1. Use the partial hundred chart to subtract tens.

41	42	43	44	45	46	47	48	49	50
51	52	53	54	55	56	57	58	59	60
61	62	63	64	65	66	67	68	69	70

$70 - 20 =$ _____

Ⓐ 70   Ⓑ 60   Ⓒ 50   Ⓓ 40

---

2. Use the place-value blocks. Find the difference.

$40 - 30 =$ _____

Ⓐ 10   Ⓑ 20   Ⓒ 30   Ⓓ 40

---

3. Use the open number line to solve. Show your work.
Explain how you used the number line to find the answer.

$60 - 20 =$ _____

_____

_____

_____

4. Solve the problem. Use any strategy. Explain why you picked the strategy. Write an addition equation to check your answer.

$$70 - 60 = \underline{\hspace{1cm}}$$

_____

_____

_____

Use mental math to solve. Then write an addition equation to check your answer.

5. $23 - 10 = $ _____

6. $94 - 10 = $ _____

7. $51 - 10 = $ _____

Use addition to solve each subtraction problem.

8. $50 + \underline{\hspace{1cm}} = 80$, so

$80 - 50 = \underline{\hspace{1cm}}$.

9. $20 + \underline{\hspace{1cm}} = 60$, so

$60 - 20 = \underline{\hspace{1cm}}$.

10. A store has 90 sleds. It sells 30 sleds. How many sleds does the store have left?

Write an equation and solve. Use drawings or models to show your work.

_____ sleds

Name _____

Fred's Farm

Fred sells different vegetables at his farm. He puts them in packages of 10.

Potatoes →

Tomatoes ←

Carrots →

Green Peppers →

1. Fred sells 3 packages of green peppers. How many green peppers does he have left to sell?
Use the open number line to solve.

⟵————————————————⟶

_____ green peppers

2. Fred feeds 10 carrots to his horse. How many carrots does he have left?

_____ carrots

3. Fred sells 30 potatoes on Monday. He sells the rest on Tuesday. How many potatoes were sold on Tuesday?
Use the partial hundred chart to solve the problem. Write the missing numbers in the equation.

21	22	23	24	25	26	27	28	29	30
31	32	33	34	35	36	37	38	39	40
41	42	43	44	45	46	47	48	49	50
51	52	53	54	55	56	57	58	59	60
61	62	63	64	65	66	67	68	69	70
71	72	73	74	75	76	77	78	79	80

_____ ◯ _____ = _____

_____ potatoes

4. Debbie buys 4 packages of carrots at the farm. She uses 10 carrots to make soup. How many carrots does she have left?

Solve the problem. Use one of the strategies you learned. Show how you solved the problem.

- number line
- hundred chart
- think addition to subtract
- blocks

_____ carrots

5. Ty buys 36 vegetables. Lee buys 10 fewer vegetables than Ty. How many vegetables does Lee buy?

- picture
- blocks
- hundred chart
- number line
- another tool

You can use these tools!

Part A

What strategy could you use to solve the problem?

_____

_____

Part B

Write an equation and solve the problem. Show how you solved it.

_____ ◯ _____ = _____

_____ vegetables

TOPIC 12 Measure Lengths

Essential Question: What are ways to measure how long an object is?

Digital Resources

Interactive Student Edition · Activity · Visual Learning · Video · Practice

Assessment · Games · Tools · Glossary

People cannot see in the dark.

Some animals can make themselves light up or glow in the dark.

Wow! Let's do this project and learn more.

enVision STEM Project: Now You See Me, Now You Don't!

Find Out Talk to friends and relatives about animals that can be seen in the dark. Ask how some animals can make themselves glow in the dark.

Journal: Make a Book Show what you found out. In your book, also:

• Draw pictures of animals that can glow in the dark.

• Think about how you could measure these animals.

Name _____

Review What You Know

Vocabulary

1. Circle the number that is **less than** the number of cubes.

3   5   8

2. Circle the number that is **greater than** the number of cubes.

1   3   5

3. Circle the symbol that is used to **compare** two numbers

+   –   >

Comparing Numbers

4. Choose two numbers to make the sentence true.

_____ is less than _____ .

5. Charlie has 9 stickers. Pearl has 5 stickers. Write these numbers and the symbol to compare the numbers.

_____ ◯ _____

Counting

6. Write the missing numbers.

6, 7, 8, _____, _____, 11, _____

PROJECT 12A

Have you ever seen a real castle?

Project: Build Castles

PROJECT 12B

Have you ever seen a leaf this big?

Project: Make a Poster About Leaves

How can you measure without using a ruler or tape measure?

Project: Collect Measurement Data

Where would you like to go camping?

Project: Draw a Campsite Map

Name _____

Solve & Share

Can you put these objects in order from longest to shortest? How can you tell if one object is longer than another object?

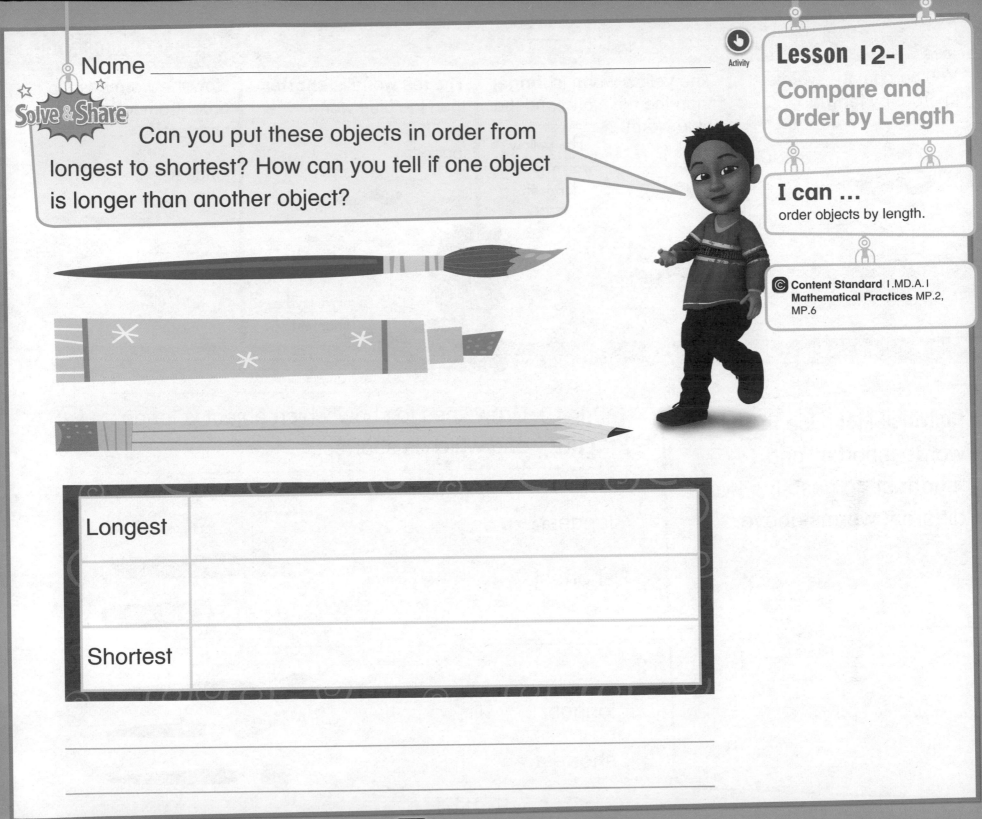

Longest	
Shortest	

You can put the worms in order by **length**.

The yellow worm is **longer** than the red worm and the blue worm.

The yellow worm is the longest.

The red worm is **shorter** than the blue worm.

longest

The red worm is the shortest.

Now the worms are in order from longest to shortest.

longest

shortest

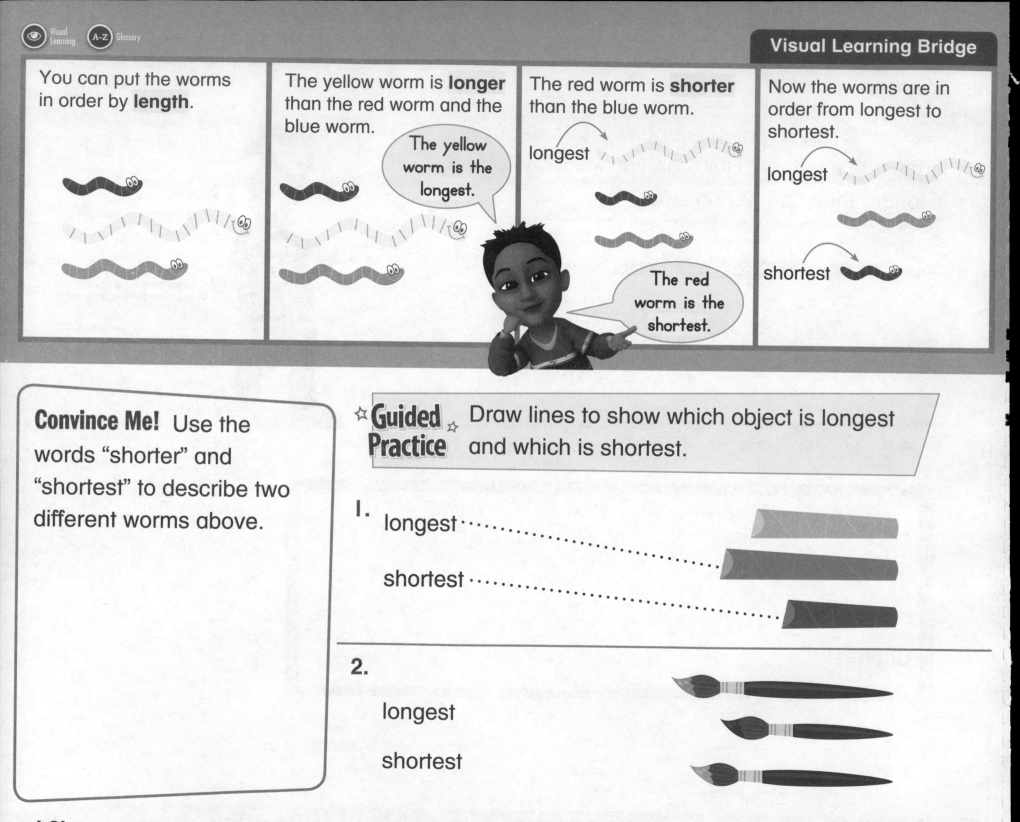

Convince Me! Use the words "shorter" and "shortest" to describe two different worms above.

☆ **Guided Practice** ☆ Draw lines to show which object is longest and which is shortest.

1.
longest ·

shortest ·

2.

longest

shortest

Independent Practice ☆ Draw lines to show which object is longest and which is shortest.

3. longest

shortest

4. longest

shortest

🅰🇿 **Vocabulary** Use the clues about **length** to color the crayons.

5. The **shortest** crayon is orange.
The blue crayon is **longer** than
the green crayon.

6. **Be Precise** Tomaz paints a line that is longer than the blue line.
What color line did he paint?
Use the picture to solve. _____

7. Compare the lengths. Write the names of these three objects from shortest to longest.

Feather

Screw

Pencil

_____   _____   _____
Shortest   Longest

8. **Higher Order Thinking** Draw 3 lines with different lengths in order from longest to shortest. Label the longest and shortest lines.

9. ☑**Assessment Practice** Which list shows the order from longest to shortest?

Ⓐ Blue pen, red pen, green pen

Ⓑ Red pen, blue pen, green pen

Ⓒ Green pen, blue pen, red pen

Ⓓ Red pen, green pen, blue pen

Name _____

Solve & Share

How can you find out whether the shoe or the pencil is longer without putting them next to each other? What can you use? Circle the longer object and explain how you found out.

I can ...
indirectly compare objects by length.

© **Content Standard** 1.MD.A.1
Mathematical Practices MP.1, MP.3, MP.7

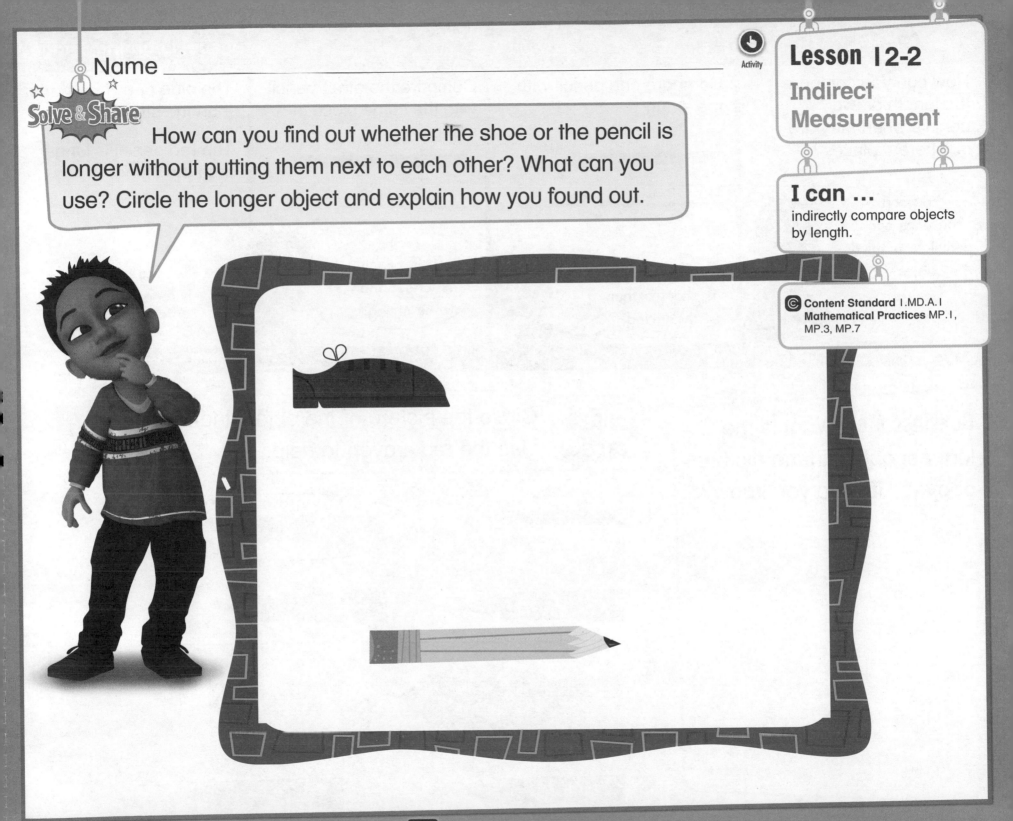

Go Online | SavvasRealize.com

four hundred ninety-seven **497**

How can you compare the length of two pencils when they are in different places?

> You can compare each pencil to a third object.

Compare one pencil with the string.

> This pencil is shorter than the string.

Compare the other pencil with the same piece of string.

> This pencil is longer than the string.

The blue pencil is shorter than the string.

The red pencil is longer than the string.

> So, the red pencil is longer than the blue pencil.

Convince Me! What is the longest object in the pictures above? How do you know?

☆ **Guided** ☆ Circle the picture of the object that is longer.
Practice   Use the red crayon to help.

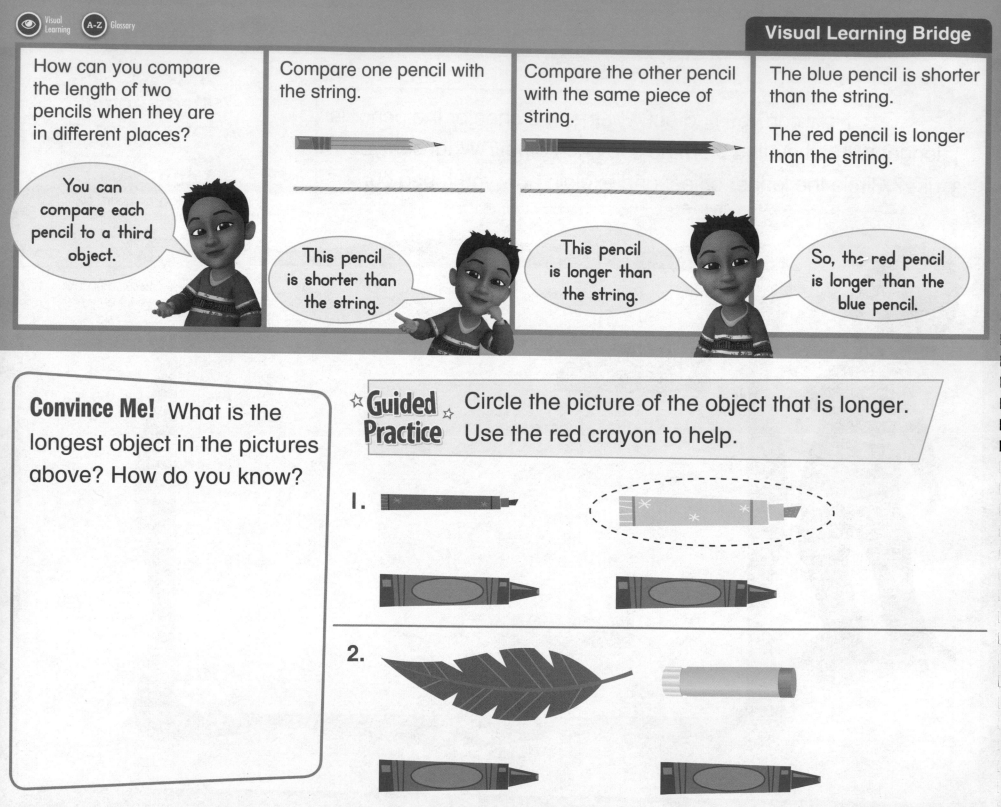

1.

2.

Topic 12 | Lesson 2

Name _____

Tools Assessment

Independent Practice Circle the picture of the object that is longer.
Use the orange string to help.

3. frog   leaf

4. scissors   stapler

5. book   toothpaste

6. toothpaste   stapler

7. **Higher Order Thinking** Use the pictures of the objects in Items 5 and 6
   to fill in the blanks.

   The book is longer than the _____.

   The toothpaste is longer than the _____.

   So, the book is _____ than the stapler.

8. **Make Sense** Use the clues to figure out the name of each dog. Write the name under the correct dog.

Clues

- Tango is taller than Bongo.
- Turbo is shorter than Bongo.

What's my plan for solving the problem? How can I check that my answer makes sense?

| Bongo |
| Turbo |
| Tango |

_____ _____ _____

9. **Higher Order Thinking** Josh has two crayons and a piece of string. Explain how he can decide which is the longer crayon without putting the crayons together.

_____

_____

10. ☑ **Assessment Practice** Circle the key that is longer. Use the blue string to help.

Name _____

☆ Solve & Share

How can you use small paper clips to tell how long the pencil is? How can you use big paper clips to tell how long the pencil is?

I can ...
use small same-sized objects to measure the length of a longer object.

© **Content Standard** I.MD.A.2
Mathematical Practices MP.2, MP.5, MP.6

The pencil is about _____ 🔗 long.

The pencil is about _____ 🔗 long.

Use objects, or length units, that are all exactly the same size. Do not leave gaps or overlap.

3

You can use a different object to measure, such as cubes that are all the same size.

4

Convince Me!

Why do you have to line up the edge of the cubes with the edge of the marker?

☆ **Guided Practice** Use cubes to measure the length.

1.

4

2.

Copyright © SAVVAS Learning Company LLC. All Rights Reserved.

Name _____

Independent Practice   Use cubes to measure the length.

3.

_____

4.

_____

5. Draw a circle around the correct way to measure. Then tell how long the crayon is.

_____

6. A piece of wood is 3 cubes thick. A screw that goes into the wood needs to be shorter than 3 cubes. Measure the length of the screw. Is the screw shorter than 3 cubes?

Circle **Yes** or **No**.

Yes   No

2

7. Draw a train that is longer than 3 cubes but shorter than 6 cubes. Then use cubes to measure.

My train is about _____ long.

8. Higher Order Thinking Kate and Tim are both using paper clips to measure the same feather. Kate says the feather is 4 paper clips long. Tim says the feather is 6 paper clips long. Explain how they could both be correct.

9. ☑ **Assessment Practice** Which is **NOT** the correct length of the marker shown? Choose three that apply.

20 ☐   10 ☐   5 ☐   1 ☐

Name _____

Solve & Share

Pick one or more of these tools to measure the length of the track. About how long is it? Circle the tools you used.

I can ...
choose an appropriate tool and use it to measure a given object.

© **Mathematical Practices** MP.5
Also MP.3, MP.6, MP.8
Content Standards 1.MD.A.2
Also 1.MD.A.1

Thinking Habits
Which tools can I use?

Is there a different tool I could use?

The track is about _____ long.

How can you measure the length of an object that is **not** straight?

Which tools can I use?

I can use string, a pipe cleaner, or something else that bends.

You can straighten the string or pipe cleaner and then thread the straws to measure its length.

The snake is about 4 straws long.

Convince Me! How does using a string help you measure the length of the snake?

Guided Practice Circle whether you need just straws or the straws and a string to measure the length of each object. Then measure.

1. straws   (string and straws)

about __3__ straws

2. straws   string and straws

about ____ straws

Topic 12 | Lesson 4

Tools   Assessment

Independent Practice

Circle whether you need just straws or the straws and a string to measure the length of each object. Then measure.

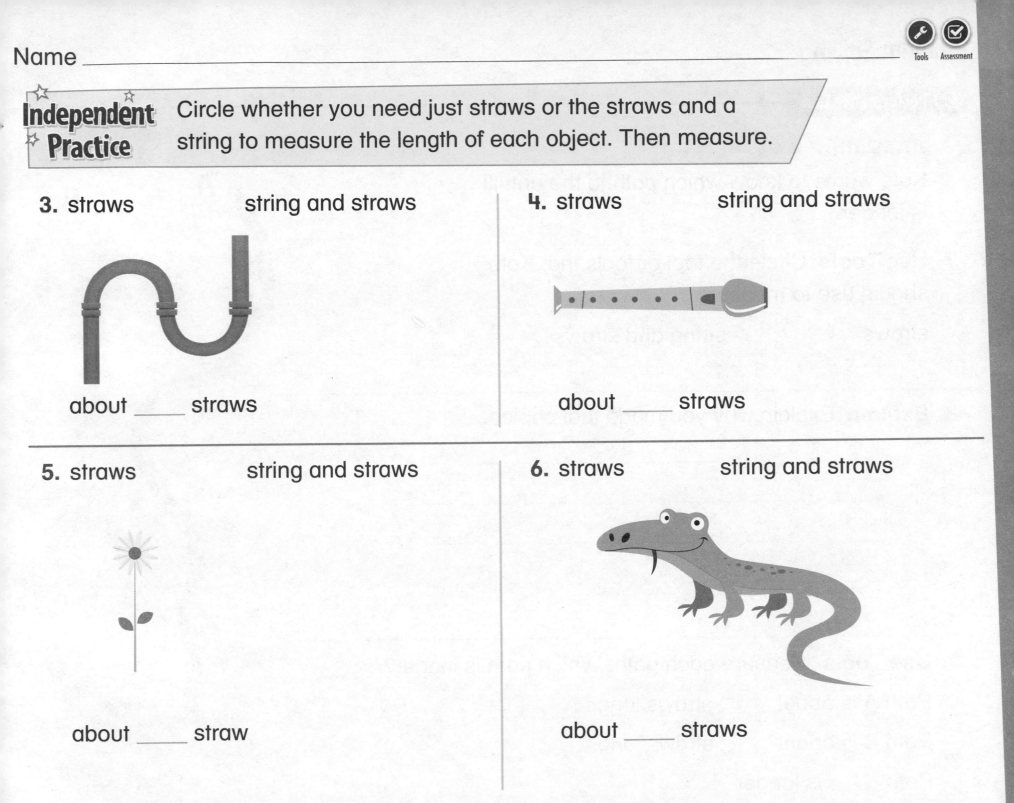

3. straws   string and straws

about _____ straws

4. straws   string and straws

about _____ straws

5. straws   string and straws

about _____ straw

6. straws   string and straws

about _____ straws

Problem Solving

Ant Paths

Kate wants to know which path to the anthill is longer.

7. **Use Tools** Circle the tool or tools that Kate should use to measure.

   straws   string and straws

8. **Explain** Explain why you made that choice.

   _____

   _____

   _____

   _____

9. **Use Tools** Measure each path. Which path is longer?

   Path A is about _____ straws long.

   Path B is about _____ straws long.

   Path _____ is longer.

Find a Match

Find a partner. Point to a clue. Read the clue.

Look below the clues to find a match. Write the clue letter in the box next to the match.

Find a match for every clue.

TOPIC 12 | **Fluency Practice Activity**

I can ...
add and subtract within 10.

© **Content Standard** 1.OA.C.6
Mathematical Practices MP.3, MP.6, MP.7, MP.8

Clues

A 8 + 1

B 4 + 4

C 8 − 3

D 8 − 7

E 8 − 1

F 1 + 1

G 4 + 2

H 1 + 3

☐ 3 + 2	☐ 7 − 5	☐ 8 − 0	☐ 9 − 3
☐ 4 + 3	☐ 6 − 2	☐ 10 − 1	☐ 5 − 4

Vocabulary Review

A-Z Glossary

Word List
- length
- longer
- longest
- measure
- shorter
- shortest

Understand Vocabulary

1. Fill in the blank.

I can use objects that are the same size to _____ to find out how long something is.

2. Fill in the blank.

The _____ of an object must be measured with units that are all the same size.

3. Circle the lines that are longer than this one.

_____

_____

_____

_____

4. Circle the shortest line.

_____

_____

_____

5. Cross out the tool that can **NOT** be used to measure length.

cubes

number chart

string and straws

Use Vocabulary in Writing

6. Write something you notice about objects in your classroom. Use at least one term from the Word List.

Name _____

Set A

You can find the object that is the longest.

← longest

← shortest

You can also find the object that is the shortest.

Circle the longest line in each group. Draw a box around the shortest line in each group.

1.

2.

Set B

You can compare the lengths of two objects that are not lined up next to each other by using a third object.

The paper clip is shorter than the eraser. The pencil is longer than the eraser. So, the pencil is longer than the paper clip.

Circle the picture of the object that is longer. Use the red object to help.

3.

4.

You can use same-size objects to measure the length of an object.

The marker is about
___4___ cubes

Use cubes to measure.

5.

about ____ cubes

6.

about ____ cubes

Make sure you line up the edge of the cubes with the edge of the marker when measuring.

Set D

Thinking Habits

Use Tools

What tool can I use to help solve the problem?

Can I use a different tool? Why or why not?

Choose the tool or tools you can use to measure the object. Then measure the length.

7. straws   string and straws

about ____ straws

Name _____

1. What tool would you use to measure the length of the picture?

_____

2. What is the length of the shoe in paper clips?

_____ paper clips

3. Which word describes the red line?

_____

_____

_____

shortest   middle   smallest   longest

Ⓐ   Ⓑ   Ⓒ   Ⓓ

4. What is the length of the notebook in cubes?

_____ cubes

5. Choose three statements that are true about the image below.

☐ The feather is 7 cubes long.

☐ The feather is being measured correctly.

☐ The feather is 8 cubes long.

☐ The right end of the feather is at 7 cubes.

☐ The right end of the feather is at 8 cubes.

6. Which sentences are true about the lines? Choose 2 that apply.

☐ The blue line is shortest.

☐ The blue line is longer than the yellow line.

☐ The red line is shortest.

☐ The yellow line is longer than the blue line.

☐ The yellow line is the longest.

Circle the object that is shorter. Use the red object to help. Explain.

7.

8.

Topic 12 | Assessment Practice

Name _____

School Supplies

Sally uses many different supplies at school.

1. Which pencil is the longest?
   Circle that color.
   Which pencil is the shortest?
   Cross out that color.

   yellow   red   blue

2. Which object is longer, the glue stick or the eraser?
   Circle that object. Use the orange crayon to help.

GLUE

3. Sally is making a bookmark. She needs a strip of paper longer than 8 cubes.

Use cubes. Could Sally use this strip of paper?

Circle **Yes** or **No**.   **Yes**   **No**

Explain your answer.

---

4. Sally uses the two ribbons below for her art project.

Part A

Which tools would you use to measure each ribbon? Explain.

Part B

Use tools to measure the length of each ribbon.

about _____ straws   about _____ straws

TOPIC **13**

Time and Money

Essential Question: What are the values of coins, and what are some different ways to tell time?

Digital Resources

Interactive Student Edition · Activity · Visual Learning · Video · Practice

Assessment · Games · Tools · Glossary

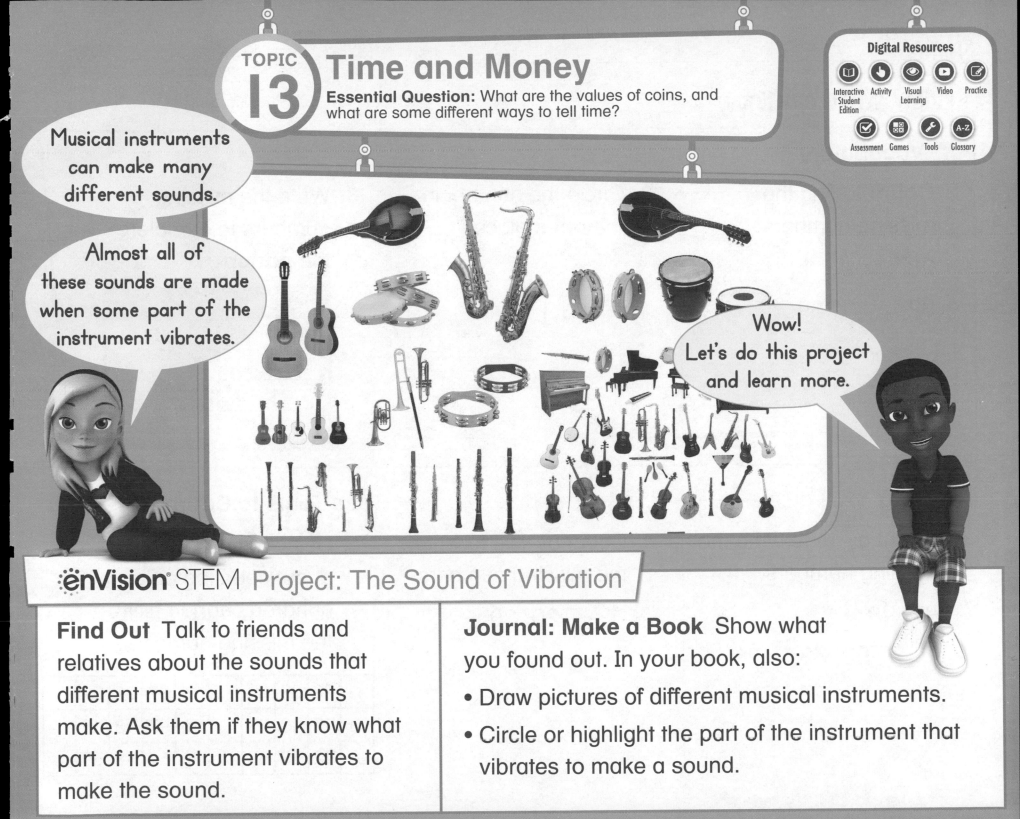

Musical instruments can make many different sounds.

Almost all of these sounds are made when some part of the instrument vibrates.

Wow! Let's do this project and learn more.

eñVision STEM Project: The Sound of Vibration

Find Out Talk to friends and relatives about the sounds that different musical instruments make. Ask them if they know what part of the instrument vibrates to make the sound.

Journal: Make a Book Show what you found out. In your book, also:

• Draw pictures of different musical instruments.

• Circle or highlight the part of the instrument that vibrates to make a sound.

Name _____

Review What You Know

A-Z Vocabulary

1. Count to find the missing numbers.

28, 29, _____, _____,

32, _____, 34, _____

2. Circle the number in the **ones** place.

1 2

3. Write the missing numbers to complete the **pattern**.

Tens	Ones
3	3
1	
	33

Counting

4. Count by 1s to write the missing numbers.

47, 48, _____, _____,

_____, 52, 53, _____

5. Count by 10s to write the missing numbers.

_____, 20, 30, _____,

_____, _____

Use Tools to Count

6. Use what you know about counting on a hundred chart to fill in the missing numbers.

31	32	33	34		36	37	38	39	
41	42	43	44		46	47	48	49	
51	52	53	54		56	57	58	59	

Name _____

PROJECT
13A

What are your favorite library books?

Project: Keep a Reading Log

PROJECT
13B

Where did all these coins come from?

Project: Make a Coin Poster

PROJECT
13C

Would you like to work in a store?

Project: Play Store

3-ACT MATH PREVIEW

Drip Dry

Video

Before watching the video, think:

What are some ways to empty a bucket? What's the fastest way? What's the slowest? How do you know?

I can ...
model with math to solve a problem about time and measurement.

Mathematical Practices MP.4
Also MP.6 MP.8
Content Standards I.MD.B.3
Also I.MD.C.4

Name _____

Solve & Share

Jennifer has 8 coins.
She wants to share them with her friend.
She says, "We each get 4 coins like this."
Do you think this is a fair way to share the coins? Explain.

I can ...
identify coins and tell their value.

© **Content Standards** Prepares for 2.MD.C.8
Also 1.NBT.A.1, 1.NBT.B.2
Mathematical Practices MP.1, MP.2, MP.3

_____

_____

_____

A **penny** is a coin.
A penny has a value of 1 **cent**.

front   back   1¢

The sign for cent is ¢.

There are 100 pennies in 1 **dollar**.

front   back

Here are three other coins.

nickel   **dime**   **quarter**

5¢   10¢   25¢

20 nickels in 1 dollar

10 dimes in 1 dollar

4 quarters in 1 dollar

Convince Me! Look at the penny and the nickel. Write 2 ways they are alike. Then write 2 ways they are different.

☆ **Guided Practice** ☆   Write the name of the coin.
Then tell its value and how many are in a dollar.

1.

Name of coin _____Dime_____

Value _10¢_

How many in a dollar?
_____10_____

2.

Name of coin _____

Value _____ ¢

How many in a dollar?

_____

Name _____

☆ Independent Practice ☆   Circle the coins. Then complete the sentences.

3. Circle every quarter.

A quarter is worth _____ ¢.

There are _____ quarters in a dollar.

What designs are on a quarter from your state?

4. Circle every coin with a value of 5¢.

A _____ is worth 5¢.

How many in a dollar? _____

5. Mark has 6 dimes. How many more dimes does he need in order to have 1 dollar?

_____ more dimes

6. Higher Order Thinking Beth has a stack of nickels worth 1 dollar. She also has a stack of quarters worth 1 dollar. How many coins does she have in all?

_____ coins in all

7. Draw lines to show which coins go in which bank.

8. Higher Order Thinking Jake has a dollar's worth of dimes. Henry has a dollar's worth of nickels. Who has more coins? How many more?

9. Number Sense Solve the riddle.

I am a coin that is worth more than a nickel and less than a quarter. What coin am I?

10. Explain Kate wants to buy a bottle of juice. It costs a dollar. Kate has 3 quarters. How many more quarters does she need?

11. ☑ **Assessment Practice** Which coins have the same value as a dollar? Choose two that apply.

☐ 50 dimes

☐ 20 nickels

☐ 100 pennies

☐ 10 quarters

Activity

Solve & Share

Julia has 1 dime and 2 pennies. How many pop beads can she buy? Use words or pictures to explain how you know.

I can ...
find the value of a group of coins.

© **Content Standards** Prepares for 2.MD.C.8
Also 1.NBT.A.1, 1.NBT.B.2
Mathematical Practices MP.1, MP.2, MP.6

POP
BEADS
1c

You can count to find the value of coins.

Start with the coin that is worth more, the dimes.

10¢   20¢   30¢

10¢   20¢   30¢   31¢   32¢

Then count the pennies to find the value.

In All

32¢

Convince Me! How is counting dimes and pennies like counting by tens and counting by ones?

☆ **Guided Practice** ☆ Count on. Then write how much money in all.

1.

10¢ 20¢ 30¢ 40¢ 50¢ 60¢   **In All** 60¢

2.

_____ _____ _____ _____ _____   **In All** _____

Name _____

 Tools   Assessment

Independent Practice ☆ Count on. Then write how much in all.

3.

In All
___

_____ _____ _____ _____ _____

4.

In All
___

_____ _____ _____ _____ _____ _____

5.

In All
___

_____ _____ _____ _____

6. Higher Order Thinking Find the total value of the coins.

Which coins will you count first? Why?

Topic 13 | Lesson 2

five hundred twenty-seven **527**

7. Sally has 45¢.

   She has dimes and pennies.

   Draw a picture to show the coins

   Sally could have.

8. **Be Precise** Jack has 5 dimes and 17 pennies. How many cents does Jack have?

9. **Higher Order Thinking** Tom has 4 dimes. He wants to buy the marker. How many more cents does he need?

54¢

10. ☑**Assessment Practice** Rita has the 2 coins below in her purse.

   Which coins does Rita need to have 31¢ exactly?

   Ⓐ   Ⓑ   Ⓒ   Ⓓ

Name _____

Solve & Share

Look at the clock.
Ria says this clock shows 12 o'clock.
Pat says this clock shows 3 o'clock.
Do you agree with Ria or Pat? Tell why.

I can ...
tell time to the hour.

© **Content Standards** I.MD.B.3
Also I.NBT.B.2
Mathematical Practices MP.3, MP.6, MP.7

The short hand is the **hour hand**.
The hour hand tells us what **hour** it is.

hour hand

The long hand is the **minute hand**.
The minute hand points to the **minute**.

minute hand

When the minute hand points to 12, we say **o'clock**.

This clock shows 3 o'clock.

The hour hand is on 3. The minute hand is on 12.

Convince Me! How is the hour hand different from the minute hand?

☆ **Guided Practice** ☆ Write the time shown on each clock.

1.

hour hand: 4

minute hand: 12

4 o'clock

2.

hour hand: ____

minute hand: ____

____ o'clock

3.

hour hand: ____

minute hand: ____

____ o'clock

530 five hundred thirty

Name _____

Tools Assessment

Independent Practice ☆ Draw the hour and minute hands to show the time.

4. 10 o'clock

5. 2 o'clock

6. 11 o'clock

7. 12 o'clock

8. 6 o'clock

9. 1 o'clock

10. 5 o'clock

11. 8 o'clock

12. **Higher Order Thinking** Write a time.

Draw the hour and minute hands to show the time.

Draw a picture to show an activity you do at that time.

_____ o'clock

13. **Look for Patterns** Sarah wakes up at 7 o'clock. Draw the hands on the clock to show 7 o'clock.

14. **enVision®** STEM Each string on a guitar makes a different sound when it vibrates. Joe starts tuning his guitar at 9 o'clock. It takes him one hour to finish. What time does he finish?

_____ o'clock

15. **Higher Order Thinking** Karen starts playing soccer one hour after 5 o'clock. Draw the hour and minute hands on the clock to show what time Karen starts playing soccer.

Then write a sentence about an activity you might do at that time.

_____

_____

16. ☑**Assessment Practice** Bill likes to read after 3 o'clock and before 5 o'clock. Which clock shows the time Bill might read?

Ⓐ   Ⓑ

Ⓒ   Ⓓ

Name _____

☆ **Solve & Share**

Both of the clocks show the same time. Tell what time is shown. Then write one way the clocks are alike and one way they are different.

Activity

Lesson 13-4

Tell and Write Time to the Hour

I can ...
tell time to the hour using 2 different types of clocks.

Ⓒ **Content Standards** I.MD.B.3 Also I.OA.C.5, I.NBT.B.2 **Mathematical Practices** MP.2, MP.7, MP.8

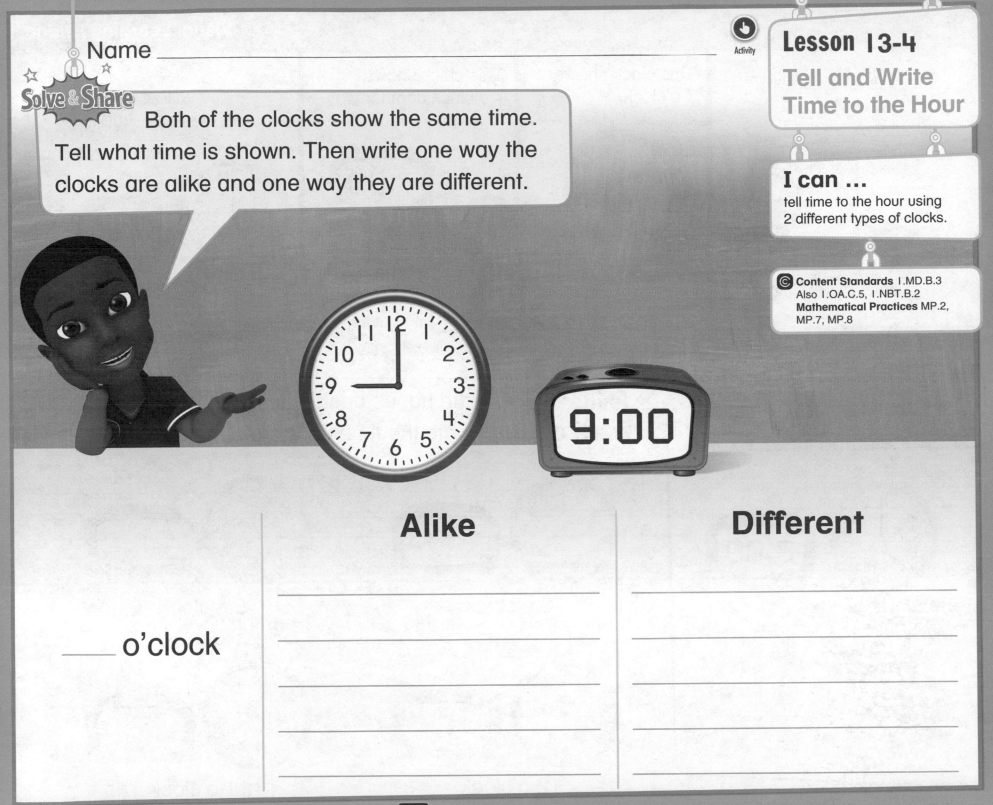

Alike   **Different**

_____ o'clock

_____   _____

_____   _____

_____   _____

_____   _____

I eat breakfast at 7 o'clock.

This clock shows 7 o'clock.

This clock shows 7 o'clock another way.

7:00

7 tells the hour. 00 tells the minutes.

7 o'clock is the same as 7:00.

7:00

Convince Me! Do the clocks show the same time? Explain.

8:00

☆ **Guided Practice** ☆ Draw the hands on the clock face. Then write the time on the other clock.

1.

3:00

3 o'clock

2.

:

5 o'clock

3.

:

12 o'clock

4.

:

11 o'clock

534 five hundred thirty-four

Topic 13 | Lesson 4

Name _____

Independent Practice Draw the hands on the clock face.
Then write the time on the other clock.

5.

2 o'clock

6.

4 o'clock

7.

6 o'clock

8.

9 o'clock

9.

10 o'clock

10.

1 o'clock

Think about how hands move on a clock
to help solve the problem.

11. **Number Sense** Mary writes a pattern.
Then she erases some of the times.
Write the missing times.   6:00, 8:00, _____:_____, 12:00, _____:_____

12. Reasoning Raul starts riding his bike at 1:00. He rides for 1 hour.
What time does Raul stop?
Draw the hands on the clock face.
Then write the time on the other clock.

13. (A-Z) **Vocabulary** Lucy reads for 1 **hour**.
She starts reading at 8:00.
What time did Lucy stop reading?
Draw the hands on the clock face.
Then write the **hour** Lucy stops reading.

 _____ o'clock

14. Higher Order Thinking David goes to bed 2 hours before his mother. David's mother goes to bed at 11:00.

Write the time David goes to bed on the clock.

15. ☑ **Assessment Practice** Maribel washes dishes after 6:00 and before 9:00. Which clocks show a time Maribel might wash dishes? Choose two that apply.

☐

☐

☐

☐

Name _____

☆ Solve & Share ☆

The minute hand travels all the way around the clock every hour. Each little mark is 1 minute of time.

Count how many minutes make up 1 hour. How many marks are there if the minute hand goes only halfway around the clock? Explain your answer.

When the minute hand is on 6, we can say 30 or half past the hour.

An hour is 60 minutes. A half hour is 30 minutes.

The hour hand is halfway between the 2 and 3.

It is half past 2, or it is two-thirty (2:30).

Convince Me! Why is the hour hand between 6 and 7 when it is 6:30?

Guided Practice Write the numbers to complete each sentence. Then write the time on the other clock.

1. The hour hand is between

   _7_ and _8_.

   The minute hand is on _6_.

   [clock showing 7:30]

2. The hour hand is between

   ____ and ____.

   The minute hand is on ____.

   [clock showing 6:00]

Name _____

Tools   Assessment

Independent Practice ✩   Write the time shown on each clock.

3.

4.

5.

Look at the pattern. Write the missing times.

6. 6:00, 6:30, 7:00, _____, 8:00, _____, _____

7. 2:30, 3:30, _____, 5:30, _____, _____

---

8. Higher Order Thinking Carlos plays basketball for 30 minutes each day. He always starts playing at half past an hour. Write times he might start and stop playing basketball. Draw the hands on each clock face to show the times.

START

STOP

____ : ____

____ : ____

9. **Be Precise** Sandy walks her dog at 3:00. She walks for 30 minutes. What time does Sandy stop walking her dog? Draw the hands on the clock face. Write the time on the other clock.

10. **Be Precise** Robin gets to school at 9:00. Her math class starts at half past 9. What time does Robin's math class start? Draw the hands on the clock face. Write the time on the other clock.

11. **Higher Order Thinking** Show 8:00 on the first clock. On the second clock, show the time 30 minutes later. Is the hour hand still at 8? Explain.

_____

_____

12. ☑**Assessment Practice** Which clock below shows the same time as the clock face?

Ⓐ 12:30   Ⓑ 1:30   Ⓒ 2:30   Ⓓ 3:30

Solve & Share

Noel has a music lesson at 3:30. At 4:30, he goes to the library. He gets ready at 5:00 so he can have dinner at 5:30. After dinner ends at 6:00, he plays a game. Organize Noel's schedule in a way that makes sense to you.

I can ...
use reasoning to tell and write time.

© **Mathematical Practices** MP.2
Also MP.3, MP.4, MP.8
Content Standard 1.MD.B.3

Thinking Habits

What do the numbers stand for?

How are the numbers in the problem related?

Mr. Diaz starts to read a story halfway between 8:00 and 9:00. What time does Mr. Diaz start the story? Show the hands on the clock.

Mr. Diaz's Class Schedule	
Time	**Activity**
8:00	Reading
9:00	Math
10:00	Recess
10:30	Art
11:30	Lunch

How can I make sense of the question?

What does "halfway" mean?

What is my thinking?

The time between 8:00 and 9:00 is one hour, or 60 minutes. A half hour is 30 minutes.

8:30 is halfway between 8:00 and 9:00. I can look back at the table to see if my answer makes sense.

Convince Me! What happens 1 hour after Art begins? Explain how you know.

☆ **Guided Practice** ☆ Use Mr. Diaz's Class Schedule above to answer the questions. Circle the activity that starts at the time shown. Then explain your reasoning.

1.

Recess

Art

Reading

2.

10:30

Art

Recess

Lunch

Name _____

Independent Practice ☆ Use the Nature Trip Schedule to answer the questions.

3. Which activity do children do just before the Bird Watch?
Explain your reasoning.

_____

_____

Nature Trip Schedule	
Time	**Activity**
10:00	🏃 Walk
11:00	🐦 Bird Watch
12:00	🥪 Lunch
12:30	Make a Birdhouse
1:30	🌼 Pick Flowers

4. Which activity or activities do children do after Lunch?
Explain your reasoning.

_____

_____

5. Which activity starts at the time shown?
Explain your reasoning.

_____

_____

_____

6. A-Z **Vocabulary** Circle the time that shows a **half hour** past 3:00.

2:00   3:00   3:30   4:00

Topic 13 | Lesson 6

Problem Solving

Family Schedule	
Time	**Activity**
10:00	Museum
12:30	Aquarium
2:00	City Tour
4:30	C Building
5:30	Dinner

Visiting the City Andrew's family takes a day trip to the city.

Help him solve the problems below using the Family Schedule.

7. **Model** The minute hand fell off this clock. What time should the clock show when Andrew's family arrives at the Aquarium?

Draw the minute hand and write the time shown.

_____

8. **Reasoning** Andrew writes down all the activities his family is doing at 30 minutes after the hour. How many activities did Andrew write? Explain how you found out.

_____

_____

_____

Name _____

Point & Tally

Find a partner. Get paper and a pencil.

Each partner chooses a different color: light blue or dark blue.

Partner 1 and Partner 2 each point to a black number at the same time. Both partners add those numbers.

If the answer is on your color, you get a tally mark.

Work until one partner gets twelve tally marks.

I can ...
add and subtract within 10.

© **Content Standard** 1.OA.C.6
Mathematical Practices MP.3, MP.6, MP.7, MP.8

Partner 1

| 8 |
| 6 |
| 0 |
| 7 |
| 3 |
| 5 |

| 0 | 6 | 10 | 9 | 3 | 8 |
| 1 | 7 | 2 | 4 | 0 | 5 |

Partner 2

| 0 |
| 1 |
| 2 |
| 1 |
| 0 |
| 2 |

| Tally Marks for Partner 1 | Tally Marks for Partner 2 |

A-Z Glossary

Word List

- cent (¢)
- dime
- dollar
- half hour
- hour
- hour hand
- minute
- minute hand
- nickel
- o'clock
- quarter

Understand Vocabulary

1. Circle the hour hand.

2. Circle the minute hand.

3. Fill in the blank.
   Use a word from the Word List.
   A 5¢ coin is called a
   _____.

4. Fill in the blank.
   Use a word from the Word List.
   A 25¢ coin is called a
   _____.

5. Fill in the blank.
   Use a word from the Word List.
   There are 10 dimes in one _____.

Use Vocabulary in Writing

6. Tell what time is shown on the clock using a word from the Word List.

Name _____

You can draw the hour and minute hands to show the time. Show 8:00.

minute hand

hour hand

This clock shows 5 o'clock.

Draw or write the time.

1.

3 o'clock

2. **6:00**

_____ o'clock

Draw the hands on the clock face. Then write the time on the other clock.

3.

10 o'clock

What time do the clocks show?

half past ___8___

or __8__ : _30_

Remember: Half past means 30 minutes after the hour.

Write the time shown on each clock.

4. 7:30   half past _____

or _____ : _____

5.   half past _____

or _____ : _____

Thinking Habits

Reasoning

What do the numbers stand for?

How are the numbers in the problem related?

Use the schedule to answer the questions.

Mr. Diaz's Class Schedule	
Time	**Activity**
8:30	Reading
9:30	Math
10:30	Recess

6. What activity starts 2 hours after Reading?

_____

7. What time does Math begin?

_____ : _____

Name _____

1. Lisa rides her bike after 2 o'clock and before 6 o'clock every Friday. Choose two clocks that show the time Lisa might ride her bike.

☐　　　☐　　　☐　　　☐　　　☐

---

2. Which clock shows the same time as the clock face?

Ⓐ 12:00　　Ⓑ 1:00　　Ⓒ 2:00　　Ⓓ 3:00

3. Draw the time on the clock.

5 o'clock

4. Draw hands on the clock face to show the time that Story Time starts.

Camp Schedule	
Time	**Activity**
11:00	Lunch
12:00	Swimming
1:30	Story Time
2:00	Snack Time
2:30	Arts and Crafts

---

5. Show the same time on both clocks. How do you know you are correct?

_____

_____

_____

_____

Name _____

A Trip to the Zoo

Carol and her class take a trip to the zoo.
The chart shows their schedule.

Zoo Schedule	
Time	**Activity**
9:00	Bird House
9:30	Train Ride
10:00	Large Animals
11:30	Lunch
12:30	Dolphin Show
1:00	Small Animals

1. Show another way to write the time
   for each activity.

   Large Animals _____

   Train Ride _____

2. Draw the hands on the clock
   to show the time for the
   Dolphin Show.

3. The class left school at half past 8.

   Draw the hands and write the time on the
   clocks to show what time they left school.

4. Carol says that this clock shows the same time that Lunch starts.

Do you agree with her?

Circle **Yes** or **No**.

Explain your answer.

_____

_____

_____

_____

_____

5. The class finishes seeing the Small Animals at 1:30. They will get back at school in 30 minutes.

What time will it be then? Choose a way to show the time.

Reason with Shapes and Their Attributes

Essential Question: How can you define shapes and compose new shapes?

Digital Resources

Interactive Student Edition | Activity | Visual Learning | Video | Practice

Assessment | Games | Tools | Glossary

Materials can be made into shapes that help do a job.

Bricks are rectangular prisms. They stack to make buildings!

Wow! Let's do this project and learn more.

enVision STEM Project: Use Shapes to Build

Find Out Talk to friends and relatives about everyday objects that have special shapes. Discuss how the shape is important for its use.

Journal: Make a Book Show what you found out. In your book, also:

• Draw different buildings using circles, squares, rectangles, cylinders, and rectangular prisms.

• In your drawings, show how shapes can be put together to make new shapes.

Name _____

Review What You Know

Vocabulary

1. Scott **sorted** these shapes. Put an X on the one that does not belong.

2. Circle the object that is a **different** shape.

3. Circle the **triangle**.

Same and Different

4. Draw a shape that is the same as the one below.

5. Draw a shape that is different from the one below.

Count by 1s

6. Write the missing numbers.

1, _____, 3, 4, _____

Name _____

PROJECT
14A

Have you ever seen a building this crooked?

Project: Build a Strong Tower

PROJECT
14B

Where can you see your reflection?

Project: Reflect Shapes

PROJECT 14C

How can lots of little tiles make one big piece of art?

Project: Design a Tile Picture

PROJECT 14D

What is a robot?

Project: Design and Build a Robot

556 five hundred fifty-six

Name _____

★ **Solve & Share**

Tell how the 4 shapes are alike.
Tell how the 4 shapes are different.
Use a measuring tool to help.

I can ...
use attributes to describe shapes.

© **Content Standards** 1.G.A.1
Also 1.MD.A.2
Mathematical Practices MP.6, MP.7, MP.8

triangle   circle   **hexagon**

Two-dimensional, or 2-D shapes, are plane shapes. You can define 2-D shapes by their attributes.

Some 2-D shapes have straight **sides** and some 2-D shapes do not.

3 straight sides

0 straight sides

Some 2-D shapes have corners called **vertices** and some 2-D shapes do not.

3 vertices

2   3

0 vertices

2-D shapes are closed. Their sides are all connected.

This is not a triangle. It is not a closed shape with 3 sides.

Convince Me! Look at the blue triangle above. How would you define it by how it looks?

★ **Guided Practice** ★   For each shape, tell how many straight sides or vertices, and if it is closed or not.

1. How many straight sides? __4__

   Closed? __Yes__

2. How many vertices? ____

   Closed? _____

3. How many straight sides? ____

   Closed? _____

558 five hundred fifty-eight

Independent Practice ☆ Draw each shape.

4. Draw a closed shape with 3 vertices.

5. Draw a closed shape with 0 straight sides.

6. Draw a closed shape with more than 3 vertices.

7. Circle the closed shapes.

8. Higher Order Thinking Look at the shapes in each group. Explain how the shapes are sorted.

_____

_____

_____

Group 1   **Group 2**

9. Be Precise Circle 3 shapes that have the same number of vertices and sides.

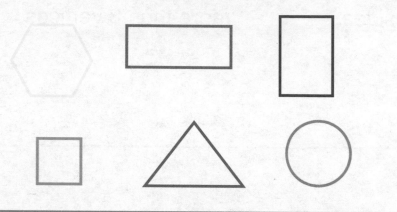

10. Be Precise Circle 3 shapes that do **NOT** have any vertices.

11. Higher Order Thinking Think about a 2-D shape. Write a riddle about the shape for a partner to solve.

_____

_____

_____

_____

12. ☑ Assessment Practice I have 6 vertices. I am a closed figure. Which shape or shapes can I **NOT** be? Choose three that apply.

Name _____

Solve & Share

Tell how the 5 shapes are alike.
Tell how the 5 shapes are different.
Use a tool to help.

I can ...
define 2-D shapes by their attributes.

© **Content Standards** 1.G.A.1
Also 1.MD.A.2
Mathematical Practices MP.3, MP.5, MP.8

How are all these shapes alike?

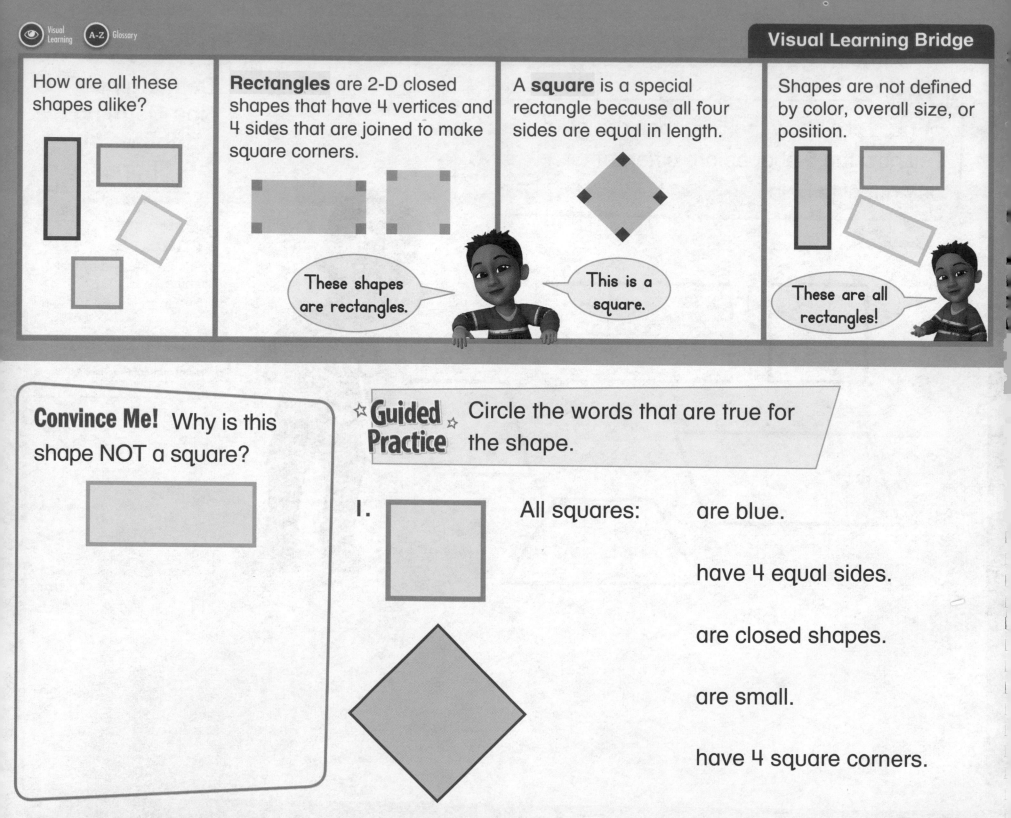

Rectangles are 2-D closed shapes that have 4 vertices and 4 sides that are joined to make square corners.

These shapes are rectangles.

A **square** is a special rectangle because all four sides are equal in length.

This is a square.

Shapes are not defined by color, overall size, or position.

These are all rectangles!

Convince Me! Why is this shape NOT a square?

☆ **Guided Practice** ☆ Circle the words that are true for the shape.

1. All squares:

are blue.

have 4 equal sides.

are closed shapes.

are small.

have 4 square corners.

Independent Practice ✩   Circle the words that are true for each shape.

2.

All triangles:
are orange.

have 3 sides.

have 3 equal sides.

are tall.

are closed figures.

3.

All circles:
are blue.

have 0 vertices.

are small.

have 0 straight sides.

4. Higher Order Thinking Tim says that this is a rectangle. Is he correct? Tell why or why not.

_____

_____

5. **Use Tools** Do all rectangles have equal sides? Circle **Yes** or **No**.

    Yes   **No**

    Choose a tool to show how you know.

6. **Higher Order Thinking** Jake says both of these shapes are hexagons because they are closed, have 6 straight sides, and are red. Do you agree? Explain.

7. ☑**Assessment Practice** Tanya says that this shape is NOT a square. Do you agree?

    Circle **Yes** or **No**.   **Yes**   **No**
    Explain why or why not.

Name _____

Solve & Share

Find square corners and rectangle shapes in the classroom. Tell your partner why a shape you find is a rectangle. Count how many square corners you find. Use the chart to help keep track.

I can ...
use different materials to make shapes.

Content Standards I.G.A.1
Also I.NBT.A.1
Mathematical Practices MP.2, MP.8

Your book has a rectangle shape. It has 4 square corners.

1	2	3	4	5	6	7	8	9	10
11	12	13	14	15	16	17	18	19	20
21	22	23	24	25	26	27	28	29	30
31	32	33	34	35	36	37	38	39	40
41	42	43	44	45	46	47	48	49	50
51	52	53	54	55	56	57	58	59	60
61	62	63	64	65	66	67	68	69	70
71	72	73	74	75	76	77	78	79	80
81	82	83	84	85	86	87	88	89	90
91	92	93	94	95	96	97	98	99	100

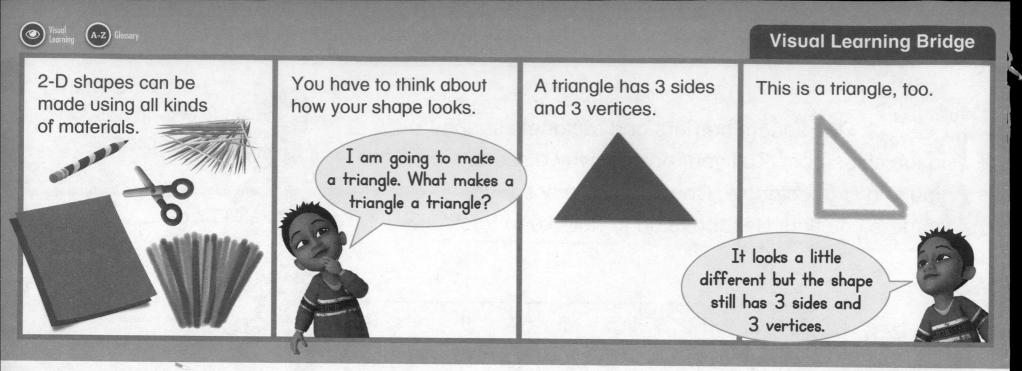

2-D shapes can be made using all kinds of materials.

You have to think about how your shape looks.

I am going to make a triangle. What makes a triangle a triangle?

A triangle has 3 sides and 3 vertices.

This is a triangle, too.

It looks a little different but the shape still has 3 sides and 3 vertices.

Convince Me! Sue made the gray shape on the right.

Is it also a hexagon?

Tell how you know.

☆ **Guided Practice** ☆ Make a square. Use materials your teacher gives you. Glue or tape the square in the box. Explain how you know it is a square.

1.

Independent Practice Use materials your teacher gives you to make each shape. Glue or tape the shape in the box. Explain how you know the shape is correct.

2. Make a circle.

3. Make a rectangle.

4. Higher Order Thinking Carlos made the shapes below. He says they are both squares. Is he correct? Explain.

_____

_____

_____

_____

5. **Reasoning** Sandy makes a closed shape with 4 equal sides. What shape did she make?

_____

Draw the shape Sandy made.

6. **Reasoning** Miguel makes a closed shape with 3 straight sides and 3 vertices. What shape did Miguel make?

_____

Draw the shape Miguel made.

7. **Higher Order Thinking** Use a piece of paper to make a square. Then turn the square into a triangle. What did you do? Explain.

8. ☑ **Assessment Practice** Mark wants to use straws to make a hexagon. Use the dots to draw straight lines that show Mark how the hexagon would look.

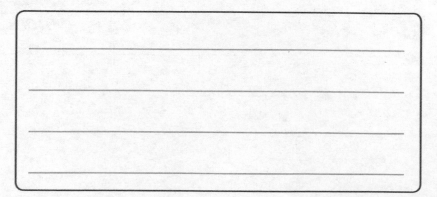

Name _____

Solve & Share

Use , , and shapes to make a .

Write how many of each shape you use. Then add the three numbers to find how many pieces in all. See if you can make the hexagon with less than 15 pieces in all!

I can ...
put shapes together to make another shape.

© **Content Standards** I.G.A.2
Also I.OA.A.2
Mathematical Practices MP.1, MP.4, MP.5

_____ pieces in all

| Use smaller shapes to make a larger shape. | Trace the larger shape. | Then use smaller shapes to cover the tracing. | Trace the smaller shapes. |

Convince Me! How can you make a large shape using smaller shapes?

☆ **Guided Practice** ☆ Use pattern blocks to make the large triangle shape.

1. Complete the chart.

Ways to Make the Large Triangle

Shapes I Used	(rhombus)	(triangle)
Way 1	0	4
Way 2		

Topic 14 | Lesson 4

Name _____

Independent Practice ☆ Use the smaller shapes to make larger shapes.

2. Complete the chart to show a list of ways you can make the hexagon. Use pattern blocks to help.

Ways to Make			
Shapes I Used			
Way 1			
Way 2			
Way 3			

3. Use to make a ⬤ .

Draw the in the space below.

4. Higher Order Thinking Use 3 pattern blocks to make a new shape. Trace the pattern blocks. What shapes did you use? What shape did you make?

5. **Make Sense** Two of which shape can make 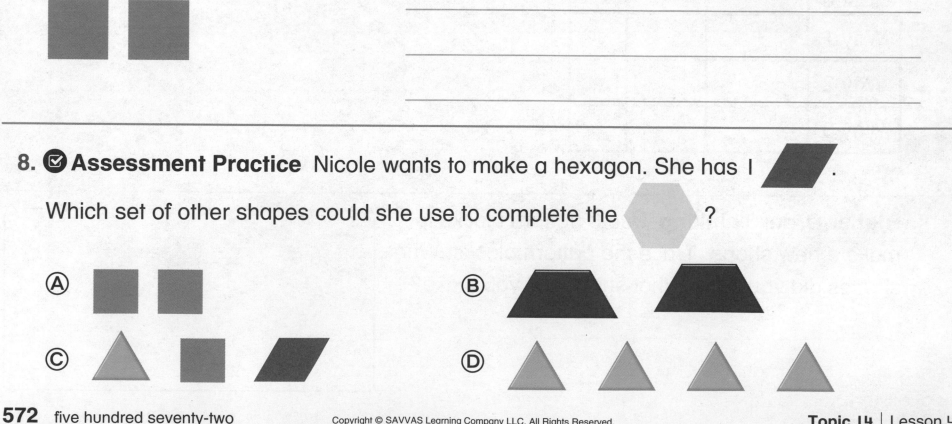 ?

6. **Make Sense** Two of which shape can make ?

7. **Higher Order Thinking** Name and draw the shape you will make if you put the orange pattern blocks together with their full sides touching. Explain how you know.

_____

_____

_____

8. ☑ **Assessment Practice** Nicole wants to make a hexagon. She has I .

Which set of other shapes could she use to complete the ?

Ⓐ

Ⓑ

Ⓒ

Ⓓ

Name _____

Solve & Share

Use exactly 10 pattern blocks to make a picture of a boat. Trace the shapes in the space below to show your boat.

Then use what you know about tens. How many pattern blocks would you need to make 6 boats?

I can ...
use shapes to make different shapes.

© **Content Standards** 1.G.A.2
Also 1.NBT.B.2a, 1.NBT.B.2c
Mathematical Practices MP.2, MP.4, MP.5

It would take _____ pattern blocks to make 6 boats.

You can use shapes to make pictures.

I can use a △ and a ▢ to make a house!

Add shapes to change the picture.

I can make a larger house! I can add a ▱ and 1 more ▢.

I can make the house even larger! I can add 2 more ▢.

Here are more pictures you can make.

Convince Me! Use pattern blocks to make a picture of a tree. What shapes did you use? Explain.

☆**Guided Practice**☆ Start with a triangle and use pattern blocks to make a picture. Trace around your shapes to show your picture. Write how many of each shape you used.

1.

_____ △

_____ ▢

_____ ▱

_____ ⬟

Topic 14 | Lesson 5

Name _____

Tools Assessment

Independent Practice

Use any of the pattern blocks shown to make pictures.
Trace around your shapes to show your pictures.
Write how many of each shape you used for each picture.

2.

_____ ▲

_____ ■

_____ ▰

_____ ▱

3.

_____ ▲

_____ ▰

_____ ╱

_____ ⬡

4. **Model** Dana started making a flower using these pattern blocks. Draw more leaves and petals to help her finish.

5. **Higher Order Thinking** Use pattern blocks to make a picture of a fish.

6. ☑ **Assessment Practice** Jeff is making a model of this arrow. Which shape does he need to add to his model to finish it?

Ⓐ   Ⓑ   Ⓒ   Ⓓ

Name _____

☆ Solve & Share

Can you find objects in the classroom that are shaped like the objects below? Find as many as you can and record the number of each shape you find. Circle the shape that you find the most.

I can ...
define 3-D shapes by their number of edges, vertices, and faces or flat surfaces.

© **Content Standards** I.G.A.I
Also I.NBT.A.I
Mathematical Practices MP.2, MP.3

cube _____

sphere _____

rectangular prism _____

cone _____

cylinder _____

Three-dimensional (3-D) shapes can be grouped in different ways.

The **flat surfaces** of these shapes are circles.

flat surfaces

These shapes have **edges** and vertices. Their flat surfaces are called **faces**.

edges

vertices

faces

A **sphere** has no flat surfaces, no edges, and no vertices.

A cylinder has 2 flat surfaces. A cone has only 1.

The faces of the cube and the rectangular prism are all rectangles.

Convince Me! Do 3-D shapes always have either faces, flat surfaces, or vertices? Explain.

☆ Guided Practice ☆ Write how many faces or flat surfaces and vertices each 3-D shape has.

3-D shape	Number of faces or flat surfaces	Number of vertices	Number of edges
1.	6	8	12
2.			

Name _____

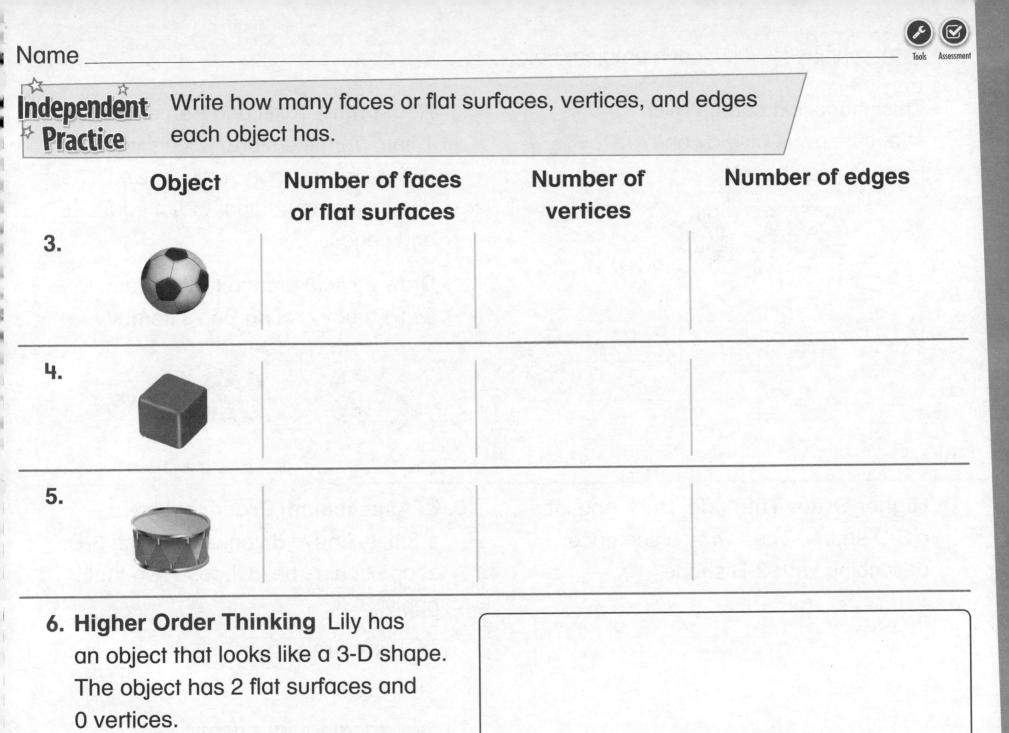

Independent Practice

Write how many faces or flat surfaces, vertices, and edges each object has.

Object	Number of faces or flat surfaces	Number of vertices	Number of edges
3.			
4.			
5.			

6. **Higher Order Thinking** Lily has an object that looks like a 3-D shape. The object has 2 flat surfaces and 0 vertices.

Draw an object that Lily could have.

7. This shape is a cone. Which shape below is also a cone? How do you know?

_____

_____

_____

8. **Reasoning** Nikki and Ben each buy 1 item from the store. Nikki's item has 4 more edges than vertices. Ben's item has the same number of flat surfaces and edges.

Draw a circle around Nikki's item. Draw a box around Ben's item.

9. **Higher Order Thinking** Draw and label a 3-D shape. Then write a sentence describing your 3-D shape.

_____

_____

10. ☑ **Assessment Practice** I have 6 faces. I have 8 vertices. Which 3-D shape could I be? Choose two that apply.

☐ sphere

☐ cube

☐ rectangular prism

☐ cylinder

Activity

Solve & Share

Measure the lengths of the cylinders. How could you make a tower 10 cubes tall using some of the cylinders? Tell what shape the tower would be.

I can ...
choose the defining attributes of 3-D shapes.

© **Content Standards** I.G.A.1
Also I.MD.A.2
Mathematical Practices MP.3, MP.8

_____ cubes

_____ cubes

_____ cubes

_____ cubes

_____ cubes

Are these all the same kind of 3-D shape?

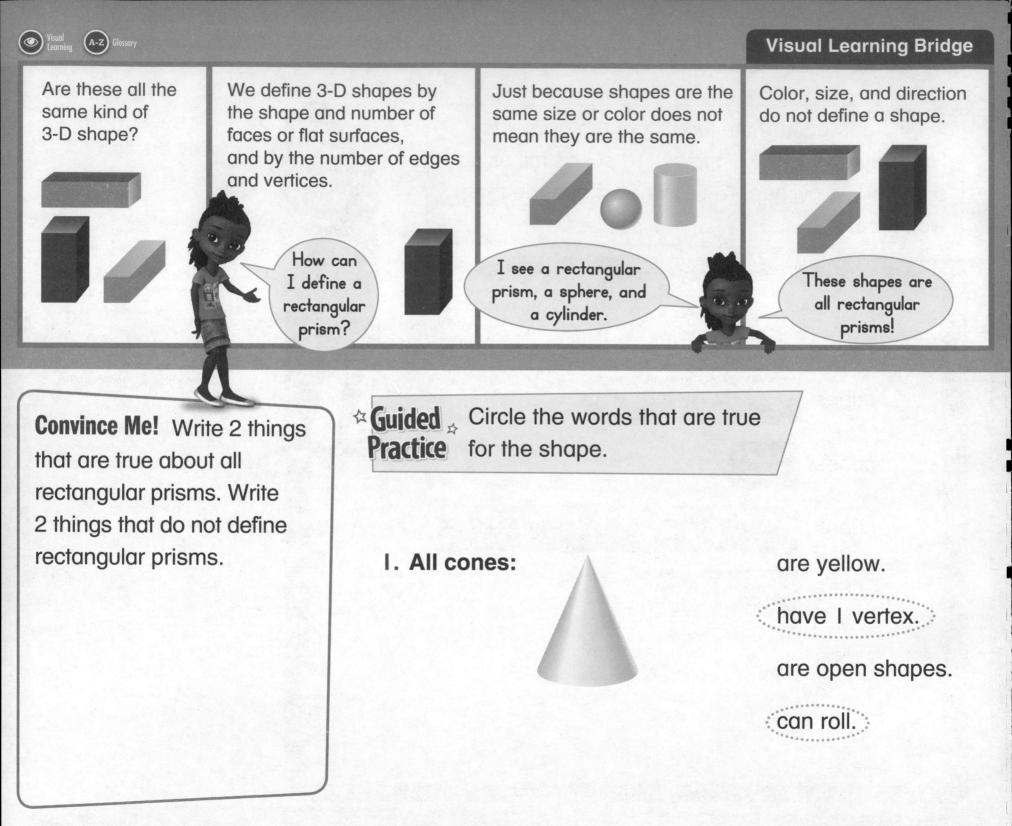

We define 3-D shapes by the shape and number of faces or flat surfaces, and by the number of edges and vertices.

How can I define a rectangular prism?

Just because shapes are the same size or color does not mean they are the same.

I see a rectangular prism, a sphere, and a cylinder.

Color, size, and direction do not define a shape.

These shapes are all rectangular prisms!

Convince Me! Write 2 things that are true about all rectangular prisms. Write 2 things that do not define rectangular prisms.

☆ **Guided Practice** ☆ Circle the words that are true for the shape.

1. **All cones:**

are yellow.

have 1 vertex.

are open shapes.

can roll.

Name _____

Independent Practice ☆   Circle the words that are true for each shape.

2. All cubes:

have 12 edges.

have 8 vertices.

cannot roll.

are blue.

3. All cylinders:

have 2 flat surfaces.

cannot roll.

are red.

can roll.

4. enVision® STEM Kevin wants to build a wall. Circle the 3-D shape or shapes he could stack to build the wall.

5. **Explain** Do all cubes have the same number of edges? Yes No

Explain or draw a picture to show how you know.

6. **Higher Order Thinking** Steve says that both of these shapes are the same because they both have 6 faces and both are purple. Do you agree? Explain.

7. ☑ **Assessment Practice** Match each shape with the words that describe it.

rectangular prism   cube   sphere   cone

6 equal faces   1 vertex   8 vertices   no flat surfaces or vertices

     Topic 14 | Lesson 7

Activity

Lesson 14-8

Compose with 3-D Shapes

Solve & Share

Use green cubes to build two different rectangular prisms. Draw and write about the shapes you made. How many cubes did you use to build both rectangular prisms?

I can ...
put 3-D shapes together to make another 3-D shape.

© **Content Standards** 1.G.A.2
Also 1.NBT.A.1
Mathematical Practices MP.1, MP.2, MP.8

You can combine 3-D shapes to make bigger 3-D shapes.

You can build a rectangular prism from cubes.

You can make a big cube from smaller cubes.

You can also use 3-D shapes to make objects that you know.

What can I make with these?

A cube, a cylinder, and a cone make a rocket!

Convince Me! How can you find the 3-D shapes that make an object?

☆**Guided Practice**☆ Circle the 3-D shapes that could be put together to make the object.

1.

2.

Independent Practice

Circle the 3-D shapes that could be put together to make the object.

3.

4.

5.

6. Higher Order Thinking Jon wants to combine 6 green cubes to make a bigger cube. Can Jon do this? Explain. Use cubes to help.

7. **Make Sense** Ralph made this shape below with 3-D shapes.

What 3-D shapes did Ralph use?

_____

_____

8. **Make Sense** Kirsten has 12 ice cubes. She wants to combine the ice cubes to make an ice sculpture.

What 3-D shape could Kirsten make with the ice cubes?

_____

9. **Higher Order Thinking** Ellen uses two of the same shape to build a bigger 3-D shape. Her new figure has 2 flat surfaces and 0 vertices.

What 2 shapes did Ellen use?

_____

What bigger shape did Ellen build?

_____

10. ☑ **Assessment Practice** Which object could be made with a ▲ and a ▮?

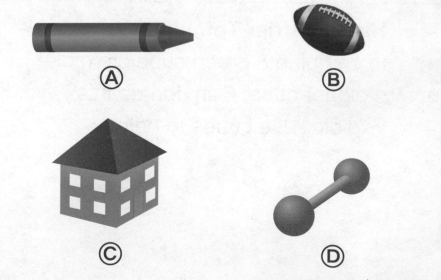

Ⓐ

Ⓑ

Ⓒ

Ⓓ

Name _____

Solve & Share

Draw an *X* on all the objects that have flat surfaces that are circles. Tell how you know the flat surfaces are circles. Make sense of the problem by circling the words that are true about the objects you crossed out.

I can ...
make sense of problems.

Ⓒ **Mathematical Practices** MP.1
Also MP.2, MP.6, MP.8
Content Standards 1.G.A.1
Also 1.G.A.2

Thinking Habits

What am I asked to find?
What else can I try if I get stuck?

The objects: are white   have 0 edges   have faces

are small   have 0 vertices   have flat surfaces

All of these shapes are triangles. Circle the words that are true of all triangles.

How can I make sense of the problem?

What's my plan for solving the problem?

All triangles:
> have 3 sides.
> are blue.
> have a flat bottom.
> are big.
> have 3 vertices.

I will only circle the words that are true of all triangles.

All triangles:
> have 3 sides.
> are blue.
> have a flat bottom.
> are big.
> have 3 vertices.

I know triangles have 3 sides and 3 vertices.

Yes, all triangles have 3 sides and 3 vertices. I have circled the correct words.

Convince Me! What words can always be used to describe a rectangular prism?

☆**Guided Practice**☆ Circle the words that are true of the shapes.

I. All of these shapes are squares.

All squares: are orange   are small

have 4 equal sides   have 4 vertices

Name _____

Independent Practice Circle the words that are true of the shapes. Then explain how you know.

2. All of these shapes are cones.

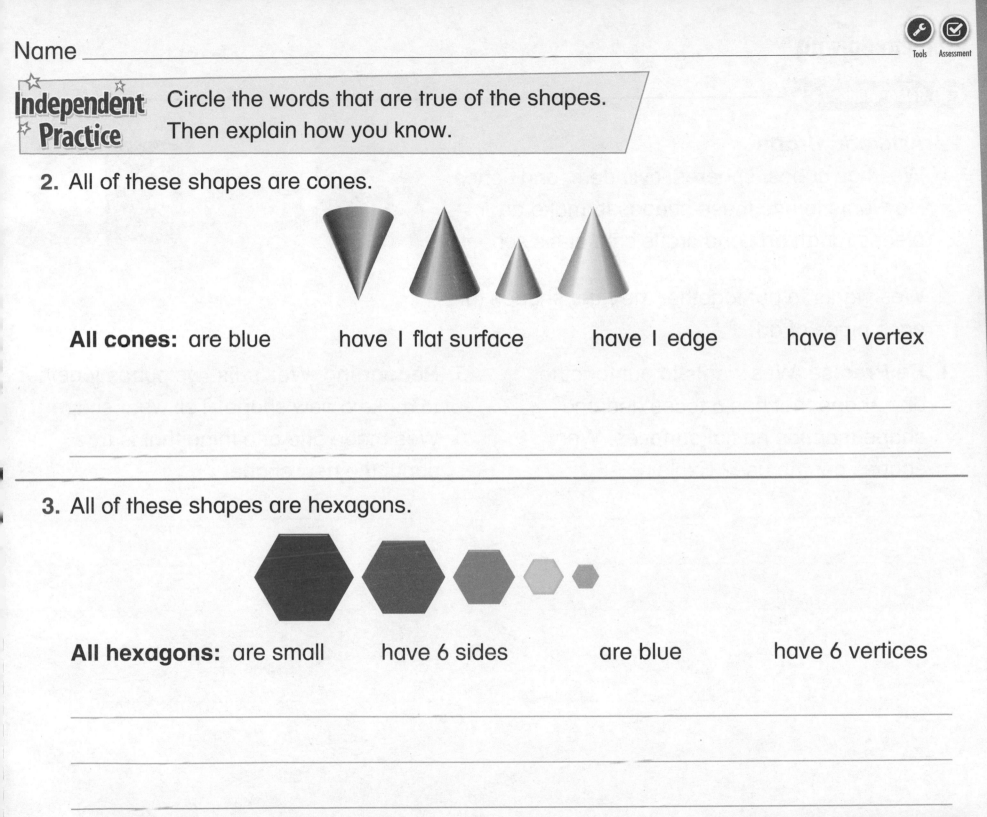

All cones: are blue   have I flat surface   have I edge   have I vertex

_____

_____

3. All of these shapes are hexagons.

All hexagons: are small   have 6 sides   are blue   have 6 vertices

_____

_____

Problem Solving

Arts and Crafts

Wes has cubes, spheres, cylinders, and cones. He wants to use these shapes to make art pieces for an arts and crafts sale at his school.

Wes wants to put together the right shapes for each piece of art.

4. **Be Precise** Wes wants to put together one shape that has 6 faces and one shape that has no flat surfaces. What shapes can he use? Explain.

_____

_____

_____

_____

5. **Reasoning** Wes puts two cubes together to make a new shape. Tell what shape Wes made and one thing that is true about the new shape.

_____

_____

_____

_____

Show the Word

Color these sums and differences. Leave the rest white.

| 3 | 2 | 1 |

I can ...
add and subtract within 10.

© **Content Standard** 1.OA.C.6
Mathematical Practices MP.3, MP.6, MP.7, MP.8

0 + 2	5 – 3	1 + 1	10 – 7	1 + 2	0 + 3	0 + 1	10 – 9	3 – 2
6 – 4	8 – 1	8 – 6	4 – 1	6 + 4	8 – 3	6 – 5	8 + 1	5 – 5
2 + 0	2 + 2	7 – 5	3 + 0	2 + 1	6 – 3	5 – 4	9 – 8	1 + 0
4 – 2	4 + 3	9 – 7	9 – 6	4 – 4	7 + 1	2 – 1	0 + 8	4 + 5
10 – 8	2 – 0	3 – 1	7 – 4	3 + 1	2 + 8	8 – 7	4 + 0	8 – 2

The word is

_____ _____ _____

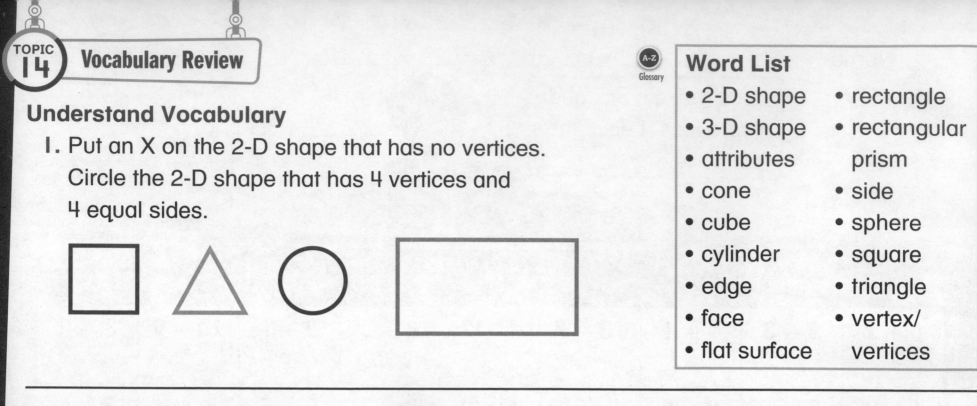

A-Z Glossary

Word List

- 2-D shape
- 3-D shape
- attributes
- cone
- cube
- cylinder
- edge
- face
- flat surface
- rectangle
- rectangular prism
- side
- sphere
- square
- triangle
- vertex/ vertices

Understand Vocabulary

1. Put an X on the 2-D shape that has no vertices.
Circle the 2-D shape that has 4 vertices and
4 equal sides.

---

2. Write what part of the shape is shown. Use the Word List.

_____

3. Complete the name of the shape. Use the Word List to help you.

_____ prism

Use Vocabulary in Writing

4. Draw some shapes. Label the shapes using words from the Word List.

Name _____

Set A _____

You can define 2-D shapes by their attributes.

A hexagon must be a closed figure. It must have 6 sides and 6 vertices.

← sides →

vertices

Color, overall size, or position do not define a shape.

Reteaching

Solve each problem below.

1. Circle the shape that has 4 straight sides and 4 vertices.

2. Circle the shape that has 0 vertices.

Set B _____

You can make 2-D shapes using different kinds of materials.

Construction paper   Toothpicks

Colored sticks   Construction paper

Use materials your teacher gives you to make a rectangle. Glue or tape it in the box.

3.

You can use pattern blocks
to make a larger shape.

Way I	I	I
Way 2	3	0

4. Make this shape in two different ways.

Way I			
Way 2			

You can use pattern blocks to
make a picture.

Write the number of blocks you
used.

4   0   0   0   I

5. Make a picture. Write how many of each
block you used.

___   ___   ___   ___   ___

Name _____

Set E

You can find faces, flat surfaces, edges, and vertices on 3-D shapes or objects.

_6_ faces
_8_ vertices
_12_ edges

_0_ flat surfaces
_0_ vertices
_0_ edges

Write how many flat surfaces, edges, and vertices for each shape.

6.

_____ flat surfaces
_____ vertices
_____ edges

7.

_____ flat surface
_____ vertex
_____ edges

Set F

You can combine 3-D shapes to make bigger 3-D shapes.
Combine 2 cubes.

2 cubes make a bigger rectangular prism.

_6_ faces   _8_ vertices   _12_ edges

Two shapes were combined to make a new shape. Write the number of flat surfaces, vertices, and edges for the new shape.

8.

flat surfaces   vertices   edges

All of these are cylinders.

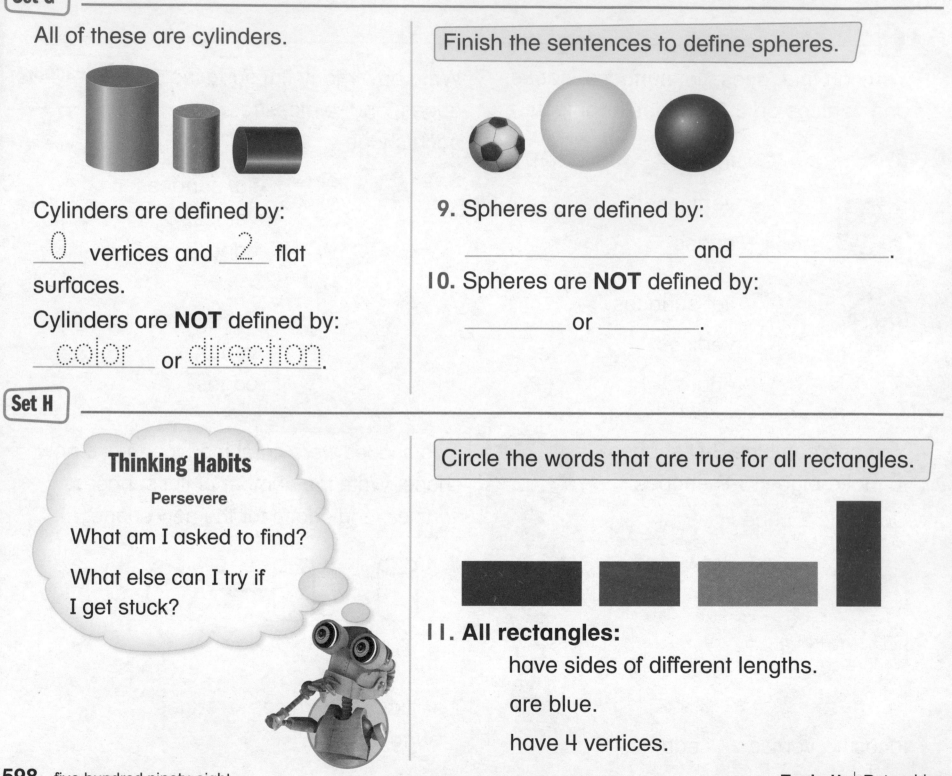

Cylinders are defined by:

__0__ vertices and __2__ flat surfaces.

Cylinders are **NOT** defined by:

__color__ or __direction__.

Finish the sentences to define spheres.

9. Spheres are defined by:

_____ and _____.

10. Spheres are **NOT** defined by:

_____ or _____.

Thinking Habits

Persevere

What am I asked to find?

What else can I try if I get stuck?

Circle the words that are true for all rectangles.

11. **All rectangles:**

have sides of different lengths.

are blue.

have 4 vertices.

Name _____

1. Which shape has exactly 3 sides?

Ⓐ rectangle   Ⓑ triangle   Ⓒ circle   Ⓓ square

2. How do you know if a shape is a square?

Ⓐ The shape has 0 edges and 0 vertices.   Ⓒ The shape has 4 edges and 4 vertices.

Ⓑ The shape has 3 edges and 3 vertices.   Ⓓ The shape has 4 edges that are the same length and 4 vertices.

3. How many flat surfaces and edges does a cone have?

_____ flat surface(s)   _____ edge(s)

4. Jaxon makes 3 triangles. Then he puts them together to make a new shape.

Draw a shape that Jaxon could have made.

5. Complete the sentence. Then explain how you know you are correct.

This 3-D shape is a _____.

6. Jazmin is making a butterfly. Use pattern blocks to draw in the pieces she is still missing.

7. Choose two sets of shapes you can use to make .

---

8. All of these shapes are triangles. Circle two ways to describe all triangles.

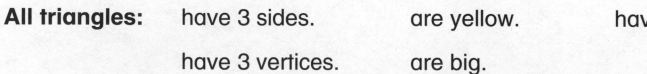

All triangles: have 3 sides.   are yellow.   have 4 sides.

have 3 vertices.   are big.

9. **A.** Which 3-D shape does **NOT** have a vertex?

Ⓐ   Ⓑ   Ⓒ   Ⓓ

B. What is the name of the shape you chose in **A**?

_____

10. Circle the two 3-D shapes that can be used to make this object.

11. A. Which 2-D shape has no straight sides?

Ⓐ Ⓑ Ⓒ Ⓓ

B. How many vertices does your answer to **A** have?

_____

12. Match each 3-D shape with one way to describe it. Use each description once.

	12 edges	1 vertex	6 square faces	no flat surface
(cone)	☐	☐	☐	☐
(sphere)	☐	☐	☐	☐
(rectangular prism)	☐	☐	☐	☐
(cube)	☐	☐	☐	☐

Name _____

Home Sweet Home!

Leslie uses shapes to make this drawing of her house.

1. Color two of the rectangles in the drawing blue.

_____

2. Explain how you know that the two shapes are rectangles.

_____

_____

3. One of the windows of the house is in the shape of a hexagon.

Show 3 ways you could make a hexagon using smaller shapes. You can use pattern blocks to help you.

4. Leslie has these tents in her backyard.

She says that the doors of both tents are the shape of a triangle because they have 3 sides and 3 vertices.

Do you agree with Leslie's reasoning? Circle **Yes** or **No**.   **Yes**   **No**

Explain your answer.

_____

_____

_____

5. Leslie has a table in her house that is this shape.

Part A

What is the shape of her table?

_____

Part B

How many of each does her table have?

faces _____

edges _____

vertices _____

Part C

What 3-D shapes could Leslie put together to make her table?

_____

_____

_____

Equal Shares of Circles and Rectangles

Essential Question: What are some different names for equal shares?

Digital Resources

Interactive Student Edition · Activity · Visual Learning · Video · Practice

Assessment · Games · Tools · Glossary

A wheel is a perfect circle.

Wheels help us move people and things much more easily than we could otherwise.

Wow! Let's do this project and learn more.

enVision STEM Project: Wheels and Shapes

Find Out Talk to friends and relatives about different objects that have wheels. Ask them how they use wheels in their everyday lives.

Journal: Make a Book Show what you found out. In your book, also:

- Draw pictures of different objects that have wheels. Describe the shapes you see. How could you divide the shapes into equal shares?

- Tell how wheels are used to move people or things.

Name _____

Review What You Know

A-Z Vocabulary

1. Put an X on the **circle**.

2. Draw a **rectangle**.

3. Draw the hands on the clock to show a time to the **half hour**.

Different Kinds of Rectangles

4. Color all the rectangles.

Then draw an X on the rectangle that is a square.

5. How many rectangles do you see?

 rectangles

What's the Time?

6. Cody gets home at 4:30. Draw the hour and minute hands on the clock to show at what time Cody gets home.

Name _____

PROJECT 15A

What games do you play at recess?

Project: Design and Play a Game

PROJECT 15B

Do you have a favorite dance?

Project: Create Your Own Square Dance

PROJECT 15C

Is every game fair?

Project: Make a Pair of Spinners

Before watching the video, think:

What shapes can you use to make a square? Can you find another way to use shapes to make a square? What kind of designs can you make?

I can ...
model with math to solve a problem that involves making a design with 2-D shapes.

© **Mathematical Practices** MP.4
Also MP.5, MP.6
Content Standards 1.G.A.2
Also 1.G.A.1, 1.G.A.3

Name _____

Solve & Share

Draw a line inside the blue circle to show 2 parts that are the same size.

Draw a line inside the yellow circle to show 2 parts that are **NOT** the same size.

How do you know the 2 parts you made in the blue circle are the same size?

I can ...
determine if shapes are divided into equal shares.

© **Content Standard** I.G.A.3
Mathematical Practices MP.4, MP.6, MP.7

Shapes can be divided into parts, or shares. Sometimes the shares are equal.

Sometimes the shares are not equal.

Which shows 2 **equal shares**?

___2___ equal shares

Which shows 4 equal shares?

___4___ equal shares

Convince Me! Is this shape divided into equal shares? Explain how you know.

Guided Practice Decide if each picture shows equal shares. Then circle **Yes** or **No**.

1.

(Yes)   No

2.

Yes   No

3.

Yes   No

4.

Yes   No

5.

Yes   No

6.

Yes   No

Name _____

Tools   Assessment

Independent Practice Write the number of equal shares in each shape.
If the shares are **NOT** equal, write 0.

7. _____ equal shares

8. _____ equal shares

9. _____ equal shares

10. _____ equal shares

11. _____ equal shares

12. _____ equal shares

13. _____ equal shares

14. _____ equal shares

15. **Higher Order Thinking** Draw a
square, a circle, or a rectangle.
Divide your shape into equal shares.
Then write the number of equal
shares in your shape.

_____ equal shares

16. **Be Precise** Matt makes a flag with
4 equal shares. Which flag did he make?
Circle the correct flag.

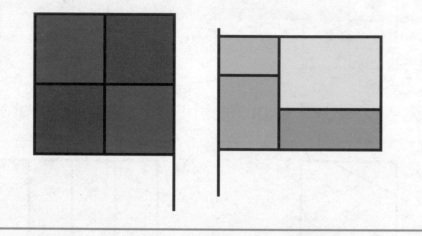

17. **Be Precise** Ruth picks a flag with
equal shares. Which flag did she pick?
Circle the correct flag.

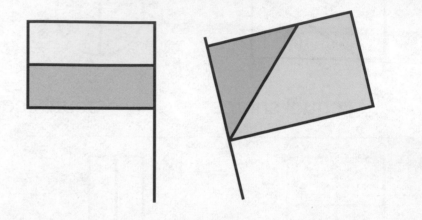

18. **Higher Order Thinking** Mr. Kelly
made 2 pizzas. He sliced each one into
4 slices. Each slice is the same size
piece. How many slices are there?
Draw a picture. Then write an equation.

_____ + _____ = _____ slices

19. ☑ **Assessment Practice** Which square
does **NOT** show 4 equal shares?

Ⓐ   Ⓑ

Ⓒ   Ⓓ

Topic 15 | Lesson 1

Name _____

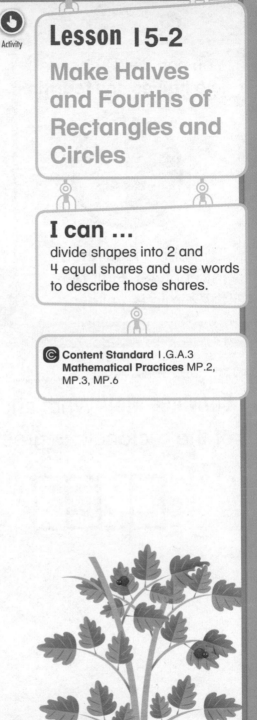

Solve & Share

Draw a line inside the circle to show 2 equal shares. Color 1 of the shares. Then write numbers to tell how many shares you colored.

Draw lines inside the rectangle to show 4 equal shares. Color 2 of the shares. Then write numbers to tell how many shares you colored.

I can …

divide shapes into 2 and 4 equal shares and use words to describe those shares.

© Content Standard 1.G.A.3
Mathematical Practices MP.2, MP.3, MP.6

I colored _____ out of _____ equal shares.

I colored _____ out of _____ equal shares.

You can divide shapes into **halves** and **fourths**.

The circle is divided into halves. Half of the circle is yellow.

This rectangle is divided into halves.

2 of the halves make 1 whole rectangle.

This circle is divided into fourths or **quarters**.

4 of the quarters make 1 whole circle.

One quarter of the circle is blue.

Half of the rectangle is green.
One fourth of the rectangle is yellow.
One quarter of the rectangle is orange.

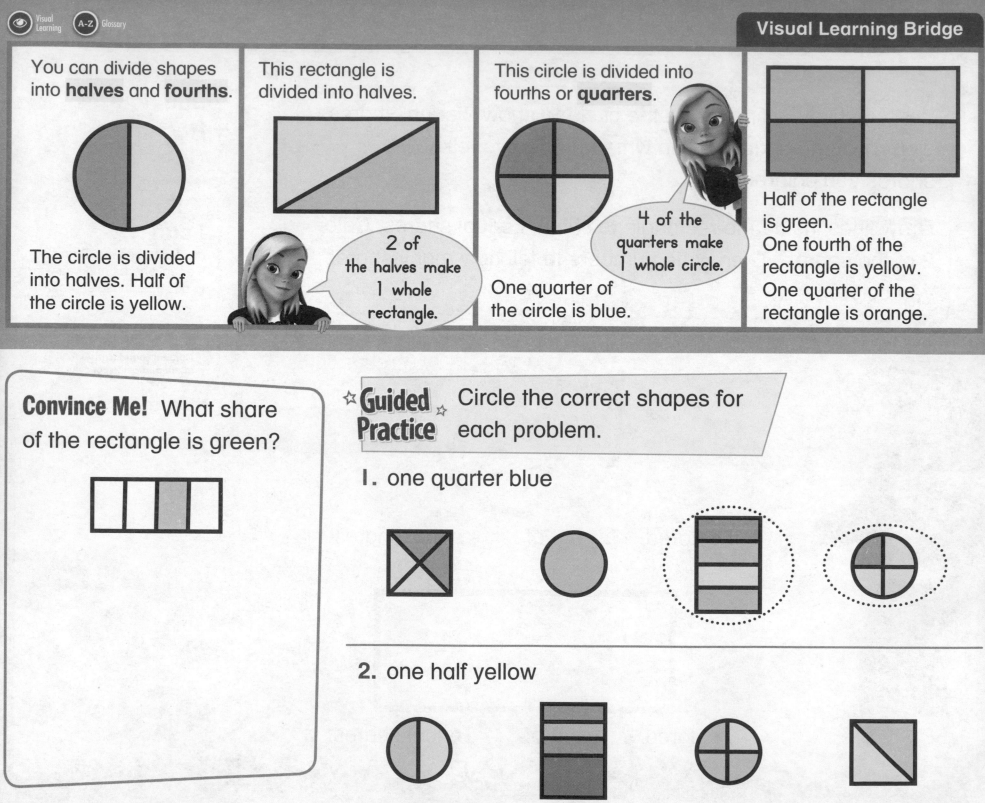

Convince Me! What share of the rectangle is green?

☆ **Guided Practice** ☆ Circle the correct shapes for each problem.

1. one quarter blue

2. one half yellow

Name _____

Independent Practice ☆ Color the shapes for each problem.

3. one half red

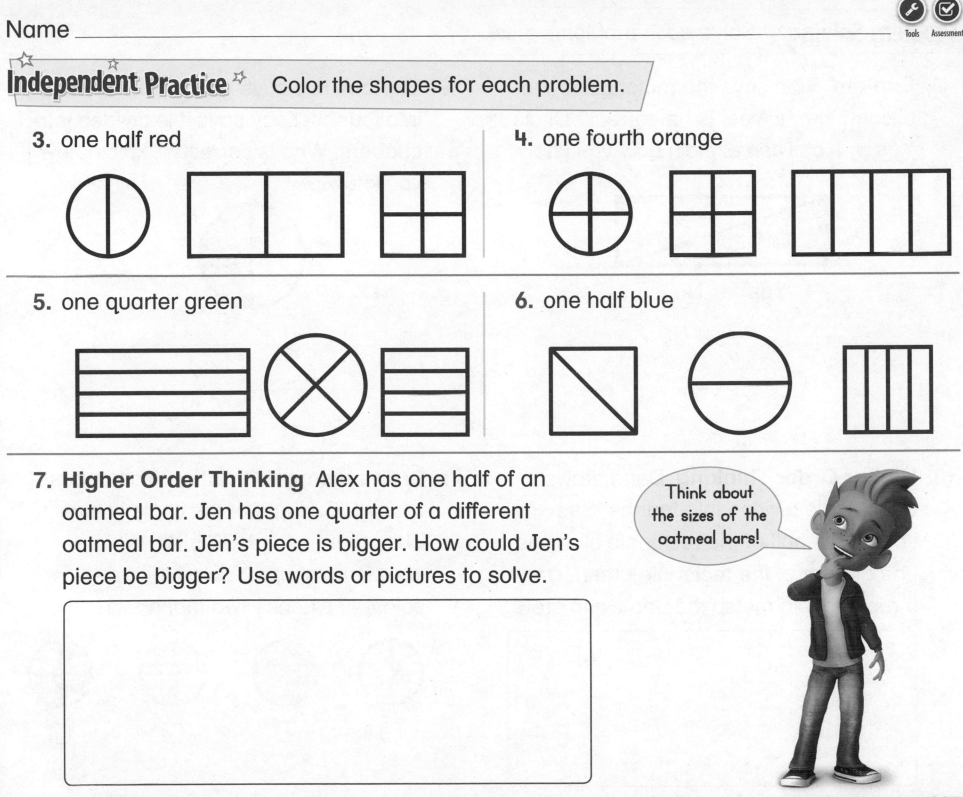

4. one fourth orange

5. one quarter green

6. one half blue

7. Higher Order Thinking Alex has one half of an oatmeal bar. Jen has one quarter of a different oatmeal bar. Jen's piece is bigger. How could Jen's piece be bigger? Use words or pictures to solve.

Think about the sizes of the oatmeal bars!

8. **Explain** Sam says the rectangle is divided into halves. Is he correct? Circle **Yes** or **No**. Then explain how you know.

Yes   No

_____

_____

_____

9. **Explain** Mia says the circle is divided into fourths. Lucy says it is divided into quarters. Who is correct? Explain how you know.

_____

_____

_____

10. **Higher Order Thinking** Dana draws a rectangle divided into fourths. She colors one half of the rectangle blue and one quarter of the rectangle green. Draw a rectangle to match the one Dana drew.

11. ☑ **Assessment Practice** Yao colors a circle. One half of the circle is blue. The other half is **NOT** blue. Which shows the shape Yao could have colored? Choose two that apply.

☐   ☐   ☐   ☐

Name _____

Solve & Share

Which is larger: one half or one fourth of the same sandwich?

Divide the sandwiches. Then circle the sandwich that has larger equal shares.

I can ...
tell that more equal shares of the same whole creates smaller shares.

© **Content Standard** 1.G.A.3
Mathematical Practices MP.2, MP.4

Divide into halves

Divide into fourths

Visual Learning Bridge

These pizzas are the same size.

This pizza is cut into 4 equal shares. Each share is one fourth of the whole.

This pizza is cut into 2 equal shares. Each share is one half of the whole.

The pizza with fourths has smaller shares.

The pizza with halves has fewer shares.

Convince Me! David has a sandwich. Is half of the sandwich more or less food than one fourth of the sandwich? Explain.

☆ **Guided Practice** ☆   Circle the shape that has more equal shares.
Put an **X** on the shape that has larger equal shares.

1. fourths   halves

2. halves   quarters

3. fourths   halves

4. quarters   halves

618 six hundred eighteen

Independent Practice ☆ Solve each problem.

5. Draw a line to divide this shape in half.

6. Shade one quarter of this shape.

7. Draw lines in the orange square to make smaller equal shares than are in the blue square.

8. Higher Order Thinking Joan cuts a rectangle into 2 equal shares. Then she cuts each share in half. How many equal shares are there now? What are these shares called? Use words or pictures to explain.

9. **Reasoning** Steve cuts one pan of cornbread into halves.
He cuts another pan of cornbread into fourths.
Each pan is the same size.

How many pieces did Steve cut in all? Which pieces
are larger, the halves or the fourths? Use the picture
to help you solve.

_____ pieces in all   The _____ are larger.

10. **Higher Order Thinking** Burke and
Alisha each have a sheet of paper.
Both sheets are the same size. Burke
uses one half of his sheet. Alisha uses
two fourths of her sheet. Alisha says
that they used equal amounts of paper.

Is she correct? Explain your answer.
You can draw a picture to help.

_____

_____

_____

11. ☑**Assessment Practice** Joey has two circles of the same size. He cuts one into halves
and the other into fourths. Which words describe how the halves compare to the fourths?

smaller, more   smaller, fewer   larger, more   larger, fewer

Ⓐ   Ⓑ   Ⓒ   Ⓓ

Name _____

Solve & Share

Mary's blanket is divided into 2 equal shares. One share of the blanket is yellow and the other is orange. How can you describe the share of the blanket that is yellow? Draw and color the blanket to show your work.

I can ...
make a drawing or diagram to show a problem about equal shares.

© **Mathematical Practices** MP.4
Also MP.2, MP.3
Content Standard 1.G.A.3

Thinking Habits

Can I use a drawing, diagram, table, graph, or objects to show the problem?

Miss Rose's curtain is divided into 4 equal shares. She dyes 2 shares red and 2 shares blue.

How can you describe the shares of the curtain that are red?

Can pictures and objects be used to show the problem?

I can draw a picture of the curtain with 4 equal shares.

I can color in the equal shares to match the problem.

You draw a picture to show how the quantities in the problem are related.

You can use words to describe the drawing.

The drawing shows 4 equal shares. 2 of 4 shares are red.

Convince Me! Amy buys a green and blue rug. It is divided into 4 equal shares. Half of the rug is green. The rest is blue. How many shares are blue? How do you know?

★ **Guided Practice** ★ Draw a picture to solve the problem. Then complete the sentence.

1. Pete makes a purple and yellow flag. The flag is divided into fourths. 2 shares are yellow. The rest of the flag is purple. How many of the shares are purple?

  2 out of 4 equal shares are purple.

Name _____

Tools   Assessment

Independent Practice ☆ Draw a picture to solve each problem. Then complete the sentence.

2. Tracy's pizza is cut into halves. She eats 1 of the shares. How many shares of the pizza does she eat?

Tracy eats _____ out of _____ equal shares.

3. Mia cut her sandwich into quarters. 2 of the shares have cheese. What share of the sandwich does **NOT** have cheese?

_____ out of _____ shares do **NOT** have cheese.

4. **Algebra** Color the correct number of shares to continue the pattern.

Problem Solving

Pizza Shares Kim cuts a pizza into 4 equal shares.
She gives half of the pizza to Stephen.

5. **Model** Draw a picture to show the shares of the pizza that Stephen has.

6. **Reasoning** How many shares of the pizza are left after Kim gives half to Stephen? Write the missing numbers.

_____ out of _____ shares are left.

7. **Explain** What if Kim gives Stephen only 1 share of the pizza? Explain how you can find the number of shares that Kim has left.

_____

_____

_____

Name _____

Find a Match

Find a partner. Point to a clue. Read the clue. Look below the clues to find a match. Write the clue letter in the box next to the match. Find a match for every clue.

I can ...
add and subtract within 10.

© Content Standard 1.OA.C.6
Mathematical Practices MP.3, MP.6, MP.7, MP.8

Clues

A $4 + 2 + 1$

B $4 - 1$

C $5 - 3$

D $2 + 2 + 2$

E $5 - 1$

F $1 + 3 + 1$

G $4 + 4$

H $1 + 3 + 6$

☐ $2 + 1$	☐ $3 + 1$	☐ $6 - 1$	☐ $4 + 2$
☐ $6 + 1$	☐ $1 + 1$	☐ $1 + 9$	☐ $9 - 1$

A-Z Glossary

Word List
- equal shares
- fourths
- halves
- quarters

Understand Vocabulary

1. Fill in the blank.

I can cut my sandwich into two equal parts called _____.

2. Fill in the blank.

When you share a sandwich equally with three other people, you cut it into _____.

3. Fill in the blank.

If you want everyone to get the same amount of a sandwich, you need to cut it into _____.

4. Fill in the blank.

Four people share one whole carton of juice and each person gets the same amount. The whole carton is divided into _____.

Use Vocabulary in Writing

5. Explain one way you could share a snack with one or more friends. Use at least one term from the Word List.

Name _____

Set A _____

You can divide a whole into shares.

4 equal shares

0 equal shares

Write the number of equal shares in each shape. If the shares are **NOT** equal, write 0.

1.

_____ equal shares

2.

_____ equal shares

Set B _____

You can divide shapes into equal shares. You can describe the shares using the words *half* or *fourth*.

Divide and color the shapes for each problem.

3. one half green

4. one fourth orange

one __fourth__ blue

You can compare shares of the same shape that are different sizes.

These circles are the same size, but they are divided differently.

The red circle has larger equal shares.

The yellow circle has more equal shares.

Divide the shapes. Then circle the words that complete the sentences.

quarters   halves

5. The blue square has **smaller / larger** equal shares than the green square.

6. The green square has **more / fewer** equal shares than the blue square.

Thinking Habits

Model with Math

How can I use math words I know to help solve the problem?

Can I use a drawing, diagram, table, graph, or objects to show the problem?

Draw a picture to solve the problem.

7. Maya's scarf is divided into 4 equal shares. 1 share is green. 2 shares are yellow. The rest is blue. What share of the scarf is blue?

_____ out of _____ equal shares is blue.

Name _____

1. A. Which shape shows 2 equal shares?

Ⓐ   Ⓑ   Ⓒ   Ⓓ

B. Describe the shares in your answer to **A**.

_____

2. A. Which shape does **NOT** show one fourth colored blue?

Ⓐ   Ⓑ   Ⓒ   Ⓓ

B. How do you know your answer to **A** is correct?

_____

3. Divide the rectangle into halves. Then color half of the rectangle.
Explain how you know that you colored the right amount.

_____

_____

4. Compare the two shapes. Circle two ways to describe the equal shares in each.

quarters   larger equal shares

halves   smaller equal shares

thirds

quarters   larger equal shares

halves   smaller equal shares

thirds

5. Ron draws a flag divided into 4 equal shares. 2 shares are purple and the rest are blue. How many shares of the flag are blue?

Draw a picture to solve the problem. Then complete the sentence.

_____ out of _____ equal shares are blue.

   Topic 15 | Assessment Practice

Name _____

Kerry's Kitchen

Kerry loves to cook!

She makes many different foods.

1. Kerry bakes a loaf of bread.
   She cuts it into equal shares.
   How many equal shares are there?

_____ equal shares

2. Kerry makes a pizza.
   She cuts it so that she and her sister each get an equal share.
   What are the shares called?

   _____

   Show two ways that Kerry could divide the pizza.

3. Kerry makes a sandwich.
   She eats one half of it.
   Color to show how much she ate.

How many halves make the whole sandwich?

_____ halves

Think about what "half" means.

4. Kerry makes a pan of oatmeal bars.
She cuts up the bars.
Kerry says that she divided the bars
into fourths.

Is she correct?   Circle **Yes** or **No**.

Explain your answer.

_____

_____

_____

5. Kerry makes a salad.
She cuts a tomato into four equal shares.
She puts 1 equal share of the tomato in
the salad.

Part A
Draw a picture to show the share of the
tomato that is in the salad.

Part B
The equal shares that Kerry cut are
called fourths.
What is another name for these shares?

_____

Part C
How many fourths are in the whole tomato?

There are _____ fourths in the whole tomato.

Photographs

Photo locators denoted as follows: Top (T), Center (C), Bottom (B), Left (L), Right (R), Background (Bkgd)

1 MattiaATH/Shutterstock; **3** (T) Shawn Hempel/Shutterstock, (C) Apiguide/Shutterstock, (B) Jennifer Photography Imaging/iStock/Getty Images; **4** (Bkgrd) ESB Professional/Shutterstock, Nancy Hixson/Shutterstock; **53** Karen Faljyan/Shutterstock; **55** (T) Images-USA/Alamy Stock Photo, (B) Scott Prokop/Shutterstock; **56** (T) NASA, (B) Blickwinkel/Alamy Stock Photo; **105** (L) Fotografie4you/Shutterstock, (R) Chris Sargent/Shutterstock; **107** (T) Blickwinkel/Alamy Stock Photo, (C) Alison Eckett/Alamy Stock Photo, (B) Racheal Grazias/Shutterstock; **108** (Bkgrd) Best Photo Studio/Shutterstock, Bay015/Shutterstock; **157** (L) FloridaStock/Shutterstock, (R) 611248/Shutterstock; **159** (T) Foodcollection/Getty Images, (B) DeymosHR/Shutterstock; **160** (T) Frank Romeo/Shutterstock, (B) Steve Heap/Shutterstock; **209** Willyam Bradberry/Shutterstock; **211** (T) Sanit Fuangnakhon/Shutterstock, (C) 123RF, (B) Art Vandalay/Digital Vision/Getty Images; **212** (Bkgrd) Wckiw/123RF, Valdis Torms/Shutterstock; **249** (L) Nick barounis/Fotolia, (C) Umberto Shtanzman/Shutterstock, (R) Gudellaphoto/Fotolia; **251** (T) PK-Photos/E+/Getty Images, (B) Kira Garmashova/Shutterstock; **252** (T) Rawpixel.com/Shutterstock, (B) Gary Corbett/Alamy Stock Photo; **281** John Foxx Collection/Imagestate/DK Images; **283** (T) PhotoAlto/Anne-Sophie Bost/Getty Images, (C) Lakov Filimonov/Shutterstock, (B) Melnikof/Shutterstock; **284** Rawpixel.com/Shutterstock, (B) Suwat Wongkham/Shutterstock; **321** (L) Chaoss/Fotolia, (R) Lipsett Photography Group/Shutterstock; **323** (T) Brent Hofacker/Shutterstock, (B) Prasit Rodphan/Shutterstock; **324** (T) Brent Hofacker/Shutterstock, (B) Kevin Schafer/Alamy Stock Photo; **361** Anton Petrus/Shutterstock; **363** (T) Anton Foltin/Shutterstock, (C) HD Cineman/iStock/Getty Images, (B) Markara/Shutterstock; **364** (Bkgrd) Nadya Eugene/Shutterstock, Mauro Rodrigues/Shutterstock; **397** (L) Baldas1950/Shutterstock, (R) Shooarts/Shutterstock; **399** (T) Brian J. Skerry/National Geographic/Getty Images, (B) Westend61/Getty Images; **400** (T) Lori Skelton/Shutterstock, (B) Andrea Izzotti/Shutterstock; **449** Yarek Gora/Shutterstock; **451** (T) Josh Cornish/Shutterstock, (C) Gregory Adams/Moment Open/Getty Images, (B) Shaun A Daley/Alamy Stock Photo; **452** (Bkgrd) I-m-a-g-e/Shutterstock, Yellow Cat/Shutterstock; **489** Studio 37/Shutterstock; **491** (T) Vojta Herout/Shutterstock, (B) Kohei Hara/Digital Vision/Getty Images; **492** (T) Light Field Studios/Shutterstock, (B) Studio 1One/Shutterstock; **517** Vereshchagin Dmitry/Shuhtterstock; **519** (T) George Rudy/Shutterstock, (C) People Image Studio/Shutterstock, (B) Sally and Richard Greenhill/Alamy Stock Photo; **520** (Bkgrd) 123RF, Maxop-Plus/Shutterstock; **553** Sergey Dzyuba/Shutterstock; **555** (T) Joyfull/Shutterstock, (B) R.Nagy/Shutterstock; **556** (T) Nattanan726/Shutterstock, (B) Roman Korotkov/Shutterstock; **605** (TL) Sumire8/Fotolia, (TR) Janifest/Fotolia, (BL) Isuaneye/Fotolia, (BR) Ftfoxfoto/Fotolia; **607** (T) Africa Studio/Shutterstock (C) Wollertz/Shutterstock, (B) Digitalpress/123RF; **612** (Bkgrd) Dmitry Melnikov/123RF, David Homen/Shutterstock, Melnikof/Shutterstock.

ADVANCE PRAISE FOR

Heal Your Heart with EECP

WATER DAMAGED

10/08

"As an invasive cardiologist and leading researcher in the field of EECP therapy, I am astounded by the benefits EECP has provided to my patients, without surgery and without risk. Even individuals who have exhausted all other options are brought back to life with EECP. Dr. Braverman is a visionary in the clinical use of EECP, and I admire her commitment to making one of the last decade's most revolutionary and exciting cardiac therapies available to each and every heart patient in the country."

—Rohit Arora, MD, FACC, FACP

Professor of Medicine in the Division of Cardiovascular Disease, University of Medicine and Dentistry of New Jersey

WITHDRAWN

"As a cardiologist, I welcome EECP as a core strategy to fight heart disease. Not everyone is a candidate for balloons, stents, or surgery. Imagine a therapy with no significant risks, only great benefits!

I cannot think of a better messenger to spread the word about EECP. I advise my patients to go to only the most experienced surgeons, and I advise my patients with active chest pain to see the most experienced clinician in EECP, Dr. Braverman, for treatment and have been truly amazed by the clinical results."

—Richard L. Weiss, MD, FACC, FACP

Clinical Associate Professor of Medicine at the University of Pennsylvania Health System

"After medications have been tried, EECP might be considered as an adjunctive to conventional surgery and invasive procedures instead of being used after these procedures are performed or have failed."

—David Holmes, MD, FACC, FACP

Professor of Medicine in the Cardiovascular Disease Division, Mayo Clinic and Foundation

"Dr. Debra Braverman has written this book to share her experiences as a physical medicine and rehabilitation physician who has chosen to pursue a unique physical treatment modality for those heart disease patients advised; 'there is nothing more that we can do for you.' Heart disease is the major cause of death in the United States today, but not as well-known is the fact that it is also responsible for disability in several million citizens because of recurrent chest pain and congestive heart failure. It is because of the significant results these disabled heart disease survivors receive from this remarkable treatment that Dr. Braverman is committed to her work with such energy and passion."

—Carl V. Granger, MD, FAAPMR

Professor and Chairman Emeritus in the Department of Rehabilitation Medicine, School of Medicine and Biomedical Sciences, University at Buffalo, State University of New York

"Given the increasing number of people with heart disease, new treatments are key in trying to improve symptoms and prognosis once symptomatic heart disease develops. For those patients who have persistent symptoms despite optimal drug treatment, the use of EECP has become increasingly popular as a noninvasive method to help patients with chest pain and other symptoms of heart disease. Given Dr. Braverman's commitment to, experience in, and knowledge of this new therapy, she is well-suited to enlighten patients and their families, as well as medical professionals, regarding this new treatment option."

—Susan C. Brozena, MD, FACC, FACP

Associate Director of the Heart Failure and Transplant Program; Director of the Heart Failure and Ambulatory Care Center; and Associate Professor of Medicine at the University of Pennsylvania Medical Center

"The desire is for EECP to be considered a treatment option when a patient does not respond to medication but before revascularization."

—William E. Lawson, MD, FACC

Professor of Medicine in the Division of Cardiology, State University of New York, Stony Brook

HEAL
Your Heart
with EECP

~

HEAL
Your Heart
with EECP

*The Only Noninvasive Way
to Overcome Heart Disease*

DEBRA BRAVERMAN, MD

Edited by Melissa Levy

Foreword by Julian Whitaker, MD

CELESTIAL ARTS
Berkeley | Toronto

Celestial Arts
P.O. Box 7123
Berkeley, California 94707
www.tenspeed.com

Distributed in Australia by Simon & Schuster Australia, in Canada by Ten Speed Press Canada, in New Zealand by Southern Publishers Group, in South Africa by Real Books, and in the United Kingdom and Europe by Airlift Book Company.

Cover and interior design by Toni Tajima
Production by Katy Brown

Library of Congress Cataloging-in-Publication Data
Braverman, Debra, 1966–
    Heal your heart with EECP : the only noninvasive way to overcome
heart disease / Debra Braverman ; foreword by Julian Whitaker.
        p. cm.
    Includes bibliographical references and index.
    ISBN-13: 978-1-58761-244-2
    ISBN-10: 1-58761-244-5
    1. Enhanced external counterpulsation—Popular works. 2. Heart—Diseases—Alternative treatment—Popular works. 3. Coronary heart disease—Alternative treatment—Popular works.   I. Title.
    RC684.E53B73 2005
    616.1'206—dc22

                                                            2005015553

First printing, 2005

Printed in the United States of America

1 2 3 4 5 6 7 8 9 10 — 09 08 07 06 05

~

This book is dedicated to Allen Braverman. His strength of mind, body, and character have been a constant source of inspiration for me. His unconditional love and support has fueled my journey. He is my father, my partner, and my friend.

Contents

Acknowledgments

FIRST AND FOREMOST, this book would not exist without the dedication and collaboration of my colleague, Melissa Levy. We have spent countless hours brainstorming, writing, and editing together. She has been a tireless sounding board and springboard for ideas. Her commitment to our mission—to educate, to inspire, and to change the status quo—is unshakable.

I thank my agent, Jeanne Fredericks, for sharing our vision and dedication to this project. I am grateful for her guidance and for her achievement in finding the right home for this book.

I thank our editor, Brie Mazurek, and publisher, JoAnn Deck, at Celestial Arts. Their enthusiasm for this book was evident from the start. Their energy and effort toward making the final product the best it could be have been deeply appreciated.

I thank my patients, who, despite their pain and suffering, demonstrate daily the triumph of the human spirit. The spark of hope in their eyes inspires me to continue my work each and every day.

I thank my valuable staff at Braverman EECP Heart Centers for providing consistently outstanding care to all of our patients with compassion and devotion. I especially thank Arvina Farooqi, my nurse practitioner and clinical associate, who has worked beside me from the beginning and has played an integral role in developing our standards of excellence in treating patients with EECP.

I thank my mother, Annette, who has offered unconditional encouragement, as always, during the writing of the book.

Lastly, I thank my family, Sharon and Ari. Their unbelievable patience, constant support, and keen editing skills have made this book possible.

—Debra Braverman, MD

I GRATEFULLY THANK: Debra Braverman, for inviting me on this journey, and for lots of laughter along the way. With her integrity, compassion, and clarity, she embodies the very best of what it means to be a physician. There is no one better suited to lead us on this adventure.

Allen Braverman, for his trust, wisdom, and guidance. For opening the door, and asking me to change direction when I least expected it.

My parents, Harriet and Steve, for giving me the tools to think critically, feel deeply, and remember what really matters.

Mike, for always challenging me to question.

Harper, for his unwavering encouragement, patience, kindness, and love.

—Melissa Levy

Foreword

Ten years ago Richard came to me in desperate straits. He had undergone two bypass surgeries and multiple angioplasties, but his symptoms of coronary artery disease had returned with a vengeance. Despite using a nitroglycerin patch, he had significant chest pain, and his exercise tolerance was so poor that he only lasted five minutes on an exercise stress test due to shortness of breath and chest tightness. Several cardiologists agreed that, thanks to extensive scar tissue from his previous procedures, repeat surgery was not an option. Richard was at the end of his rope.

This was about the same time I first heard about enhanced external counterpulsation (EECP). I was skeptical. Even though I had read glowing reports about this "new" therapy, in all my brilliance at the time I couldn't see how a simple mechanical treatment could do much for such an advanced case of cardiovascular disease. However, since I wasn't sure how much vigorous diet changes could help this very sick man, I suggested he give it a try.

I saw Richard after he completed his course of EECP, and the results were absolutely miraculous. His chest pain was gone, and his exercise tolerance was markedly improved. Furthermore, a repeat PET scan of his heart showed the growth of sufficient collaterals to relieve his chest pain. EECP had actually facilitated the growth of new blood vessels to bypass his blocked coronary arteries!

A few months later, I received a letter from Richard. He had moved to New Zealand, where he had bought a farm and was up to his elbows in manual labor. He wrote, "I must tell you the EECP certainly was a great success. There is no comparison in the way I feel now and then. No question about it, the 'big squeeze' was great."

This patient's experience convinced me of the value of EECP, and I have been utilizing it in my clinic ever since. This is a therapy that everyone—physicians and patients alike—needs to get to know, and I can think of no better place to start than *Heal Your Heart with EECP.*

In this book, Debra Braverman, MD, clearly describes the mechanics of this low-risk, noninvasive therapy and how it dramatically improves blood flow throughout the body. She explains its potential in the treatment of a wide variety of diseases and shows how its enduring benefits allow patients to maintain function and reduce hospitalizations to a greater extent than other therapies for cardiovascular disease.

Dr. Braverman also writes a very thoughtful chapter on why EECP has not been embraced by conventional medicine. The answer is simple: It will never generate the kind of money that high-tech surgical procedures and expensive drugs generate. Never. In most cases, a full course of EECP costs a small fraction of an angioplasty or stent, and less than the sales tax on bypass surgery, and it can be administered outside a hospital by a nurse. All the plusses of EECP for the patient are minuses for conventional medicine.

Heal Your Heart with EECP is also Dr. Braverman's story. Having achieved her lifelong ambition of attaining a prominent place in academic medicine, she describes the joy she felt as she sat in her new office. She had arrived. Then something happened. She discovered a valuable therapy that could help untold numbers of patients. Safe, relatively inexpensive, easily administered—it had everything going for it. Then she discovered conventional medicine's resistance.

Dr. Braverman eventually realized that she would have to leave academic medicine in order to become the physician she was meant to be. This book is a result of her subsequent experiences. It is not only a good read, easy to understand, and fascinating from beginning to end, but it also has an action plan that can dramatically improve and in many cases save patients' lives. For physicians, it is a clarion call to utilize a therapy that could replace most of the drugs and virtually all of the surgical procedures currently used to treat cardiovascular disease.

—Julian Whitaker, MD

Test Your Heart Disease Knowledge

True or False?

1. Many individuals with heart disease are not facing an urgent medical crisis and can safely delay surgery.

2. If you have smoked cigarettes for thirty years, it does not pay to quit because the damage has been done.

3. Both men and women should consume two alcoholic drinks per day to improve their blood pressure and cholesterol level.

4. The only type of exercise that provides cardiovascular benefit is thirty uninterrupted minutes of aerobic activity.

5. An LDL ("bad") cholesterol level of 75 mg/dL is desirable.

6. High blood pressure (hypertension) is commonly called the "silent killer" because it is often present without symptoms.

7. Bypass surgery is the best way to cure heart disease.

8. Those who exercise regularly not only feel better and look better, they are likely to live a lot longer than physically inactive people.

9. Angina may feel like indigestion or burning in the throat.

10. The movement to ban smoking in public places is driven by politics. There is no health data to support such bans.

11. If a severe blockage is identified on a cardiac catheterization, it must be corrected immediately with surgery, an angioplasty, or a stent.

12. Fatigue is the most common symptom of heart disease in women.

13. An angioplasty will remove a blockage from an artery.

14. Brushing and flossing your teeth daily and seeing the dentist every six months may lower your risk of many illnesses, including heart disease.

15. An HDL ("good") cholesterol level of 75 mg/dL is desirable.

16. A heart attack occurs when there is a complete, sudden blockage in a coronary artery, leaving an area of the heart without blood flow.

17. According to the American Heart Association, more than one-third of all Americans lead a sedentary life with no leisure-time activity and no regular exercise.

18. Smoking is the leading preventable cause of death and disease in the United States.

19. Obesity and physical inactivity are two major risk factors for diabetes.

20. The blood pressure of an average healthy person is approximately 150/90 mmHg.

For answers, see page 183.

Getting to the Heart of Heart Disease

IT IS TIME TO CHANGE our national discussion about heart disease. Our treatment approach is tragically outdated, which is why heart disease continues to be the most costly and deadly disease in the United States, claiming more lives each year—one every 45 seconds—than all forms of cancer *combined*. Currently, 13 million Americans (7.1 million men and 5.9 million women) live with heart disease. But we have the power—*today*—to strip this illness of its dubious distinction as our number-one killer and get heart disease sufferers back to living the lives so many have given up. It's not with a pill, a diet, an exercise program, or a hospital visit, but simply by aligning our treatment methods with our most current knowledge of the disease.

ON THE WRONG TRACK

For many years, scientists thought heart disease was a "plumbing" problem: they considered blockages in the heart arteries to be the source and definition of the disease. Therefore, heart disease treatments have historically focused on opening or bypassing one blockage at a time. But if heart disease is simply about blockages, and all of these procedures "correct" blockages, why does heart disease continue to be the leading cause of death and disability in the nation, despite millions of procedures performed each year at a cost of more than $65 billion? Why do heart attacks occur even after these blockages have been "fixed"? Why is it that many patients' symptoms and suffering—signals that the heart is not getting enough blood flow—persist or return soon after surgery? Why do 54 percent of angioplasty patients, 20 percent of stenting patients, and 8 percent of bypass surgery patients require repeat procedures within a few years?[1] And how can we explain cardiac syndrome X, or microvascular angina, which causes a patient to have all the symptoms of heart disease but doesn't show any visible blockages on a catheterization?[2] All of these questions suggest there is more to heart disease than we thought. It cannot be a simple matter of distinct blockages in the major coronary arteries.

A NEW DEFINITION EMERGES

An overwhelming volume of research in recent years has provided clear evidence that heart disease is *not* a plumbing problem, defined by blockages in the arteries that bring blood to the heart. Instead, we now recognize that heart disease is a *chronic, system-wide* illness in which poorly functioning blood vessels weaken circulation, particularly in and around the heart. These blood vessels—most likely damaged by inflammation and autoimmune conditions, genetic predisposition, chronic infections, and lifestyle habits—create an atmosphere where blockages can develop and flourish. At its core, then, heart disease is not defined by blockages, but by their *underlying cause*: damaged blood vessels that inhibit blood flow.

As knowledge of the true nature of heart disease has emerged, so has the growing recognition of inflammation's role in a wide variety of conditions. Inflammation is a basic biological defense mechanism, and it has been found to be a major contributing factor in numerous debilitating conditions, including cancer, Alzheimer's disease, and arthritis. Heart disease is no exception, and several clinical studies have identified inflammation as the primary suspect in the quest to unravel the origins of our most deadly disease. This epic moment in the history of heart disease shatters the conventional wisdom that blockages define the disease.

To illustrate this point, marking a monumental shift in our understanding of heart disease, the *New England Journal of Medicine* published a study in 2002 showing that the blood level of C-reactive protein (CRP), a substance that the liver releases in response to inflammation in the body, is a better heart attack predictor than cholesterol level.[3]

Even more recently, researchers identified a new inflammatory marker released specifically by blood vessel cells, called *placental growth factor* (PIGF). PIGF has also been linked to heart attack risk, again pointing to inflammation as a key factor in heart disease.[4]

There is increasing evidence that chronic infections, such as periodontal (gum) diseases, may play a role in the development of coronary artery disease. They are believed to do so by subjecting an individual to persistent, low-grade inflammation. There is also some evidence that the bacteria at the root of gum disease may interact directly with blood vessels, causing changes to cholesterol molecules and the rupture of atherosclerotic plaques.[5] Gum disease is 38 percent more common in people with heart disease than in people without it. And the worse their dental disease, the more likely they are to have coronary artery disease.[6]

Evidence of the role that inflammation and other autoimmune factors play in heart disease continues to grow. In one large review study published in the *Journal of the American Medical Association,* researchers found that elevated levels of antibodies to *Chlamydia pneumoniae* (the common bacteria for walking pneumonia, bronchitis, and sinus infections) indicating exposure to infection, increased the risk of developing coronary artery disease and having a heart attack.[7] (A variation of this microbe is also responsible for a sexually transmitted disease.) There is emerging evidence that other infections, such as cytomegalovirus and *Helicobacter pylori*, increase the risk of coronary artery disease as well.[8] Other studies conclude that some antibiotics may slow the progression of atherosclerosis, further strengthening the link between inflammation and heart disease.[9]

This is a dramatic departure from the theories that have driven heart disease treatment and management for decades, and it signals the need for a complete shift in the way we think about and address the disease. In particular, this new research calls into question the usefulness of procedures that target individual blockages, and it offers a reason why so many problems often persist even after patients have undergone such operations. Instead of treating the *disease*, the procedures only treat a *byproduct*.

DIAGNOSING HEART DISEASE

As a result of the historical focus on blockages, heart disease is commonly diagnosed by identifying and quantifying the specific blockages in coronary arteries. For many patients, the diagnosis seems to come without warning. Their experience might go something like this: They tell their doctor they have not been feeling quite right lately, prompting their doctor to recommend a battery of tests, including a stress test. (A stress test may also be recommended as a routine screening tool.) The test identifies an abnormality, indicating that an area of the heart is not getting enough blood. To further diagnose the cause of this abnormality, their doctor recommends a cardiac catheterization (also called an *angiography*). A catheterization is a diagnostic test during which a catheter (tube) is inserted into a peripheral artery (usually the femoral artery in the groin) and threaded first into the aorta and then into the major arteries feeding the heart. During the catheterization, dye is injected into the coronary arteries and X-ray pictures are taken to see whether any blockages are present. If blockages exist, their locations in specific arteries will be pinpointed, and their degree of obstruction quantified (e.g., 50 percent, 70 percent, or 90 percent). The patient is then handed their diagnosis. They have heart disease.

CARDIAC CATHETERIZATIONS

Cardiac catheterizations are widely performed in the United States, almost in epidemic proportions. In 2002, more than 1,463,000 cardiac catheterizations were performed at a cost of $23.3 billion. The test is not without risks, including bleeding, infection, and cardiac complications. There is also a 1 percent death rate from cardiac catheterizations gone wrong.[10] In addition, it has been estimated that as many as 50 percent of cardiac catheterizations may be unnecessary or could at least be postponed.[11]

However, new noninvasive technology that can diagnose heart disease may make catheterizations a thing of the past. Ultrafast CT (computed tomography) scans use X-rays to visualize the coronary arteries in such detail that they are comparable to invasive catheterizations and can substitute for angiography.[12] An ultrafast CT scan identifies plaque in vessel walls, often before it begins to interrupt blood flow. The scan is simple to perform: The patient lies down on an exam table while passing through the "donut" of the scanner. About fifteen minutes later, the test is complete.

TAKING ACTION

One day, you seem to be fine. The next, your physician informs you that you have serious blockages and urges you to immediately undergo a "corrective" procedure, such as a coronary artery bypass graft operation (CABG, or bypass, for short), angioplasty (a procedure in which a balloon is inserted into a blockage and inflated to push the blockage out to the perimeter of the artery and allow blood to flow through the vessel), and/or placement of a stent (a scaffold-like device inserted into a blockage in an artery to allow blood flow). According to the American Heart Association, more than 1.7 million invasive procedures are performed annually.[13] Specifically, 515,000 bypass operations (cost: $31.3 billion) and 1,204,000 angioplasties and stent placements (cost: $34.3 billion) are performed each year, and these numbers continue to rise.[14]

This diagnosis and turn of events is alarming to most people. The idea that there are blockages in the arteries bringing blood to your heart is scary, and many people want to believe that a "routine" procedure will "take care of" the blockages so they will not have to worry about them anymore. Patients often do not realize that blockages typically take years to develop, and in most cases, the situation is not an emergency. You are the same person you were thirty minutes earlier, before the catheterization took place. The only difference is that now you *know* about your blockages. Still, with seemingly little time to think, many patients heed the advice of their doctors and undergo one of these recommended invasive procedures, often expecting they will be as good as new afterward.

But bypassing or opening specific blockages is like directing traffic at one intersection when the whole city is in gridlock: it may get some people moving, but it only offers a short-term fix that fails to address the fundamental problem. Just as it is only a matter of time before another traffic jam develops, if an individual blockage—rather than the core illness—is your target, it is only a matter of time before a new blockage will arise and cause difficulty. What about the rest of the diseased artery, which offered an environment for the blockage to develop and will likely do so again? What about the other blood vessels in the heart, which may house blockages soon, if not already? With this knowledge, it is easy to understand why so many heart disease patients become repeat cardiac customers and find themselves in a revolving door of procedure after procedure.

Your challenge and responsibility is to learn as much as you can about your disease and about all of the treatment options available to you. Only then will you be able to make an educated decision about how to proceed to achieve heart health. This book aims to be a source of information for you and your loved ones, with the hope that it will empower you to make truly informed decisions in your best interest.

SHATTERING THE MYTHS
OF HEART DISEASE

Despite the tremendous volume of research that has redefined heart disease in recent years, patients and their loved ones are still walking around with a great deal of misinformation regarding the true nature of heart disease and the treatments available to address the core problem. This misinformation prevents people from making educated decisions about how to manage their disease. Four widely held myths must be dispelled if we are to treat heart disease successfully.

Myth #1: Heart disease is about blockages. Heart disease is a systemic, or system-wide, illness. Above all else, it is about impaired blood flow. It is not about blockages, and it is most likely not even confined to the heart arteries.

Myth #2: Procedures such as bypass surgery, stents, and angioplasties are essential treatments and help eliminate heart disease. These procedures target individual blockages only, *not* the underlying disease. Though they temporarily improve blood flow to the heart, they simply place a Band-Aid on a symptom. The logical goal in treating heart disease is not just to bypass or open a particular blockage, but to maximize and normalize blood flow throughout the heart muscle and the entire body, on a systemic level. If blood can find alternate routes—around, in spite of, and beyond the blockages—to reach the areas of the heart that are not getting the necessary blood, the blockages become irrelevant, and so do the procedures aimed at opening or bypassing them.

Let me be clear: I am not suggesting there is never a need for invasive procedures. They are certainly necessary at times, and I openly embrace all forms of medical care that are supported by scientific research. Bypass surgery in particular is a groundbreaking procedure that has made an extraordinary contribution to the evolution of medicine. It has saved, and continues to save, thousands of lives around the globe. However, there are only two specific circumstances in which bypass surgery has been shown in clinical studies to prolong life. The first is when the left main coronary artery is significantly blocked (greater than 70 percent). The second is when each of the three major coronary arteries has significant blockages and the heart muscle is weak. If the state of the disease does not fit either of these descriptions, there is no data to show that bypass surgery will offer long-term benefit, enhance survival, or prevent a heart attack.

The data for angioplasties and stents is even scarcer. There are *no* long-term outcome studies on either of these procedures; there is no evidence that they prolong life or will prevent a heart attack; and there are no head-to-head comparisons of angioplasties, plain stents, drug-coated stents, and bypass surgery to see which procedure is the best option in particular types of patients. There are also *no* long-term assessments of the impact on overall quality of life among patients who undergo these procedures.[15]

Some physicians recognize that many of these procedures are performed unnecessarily. "We are very aggressive when we think a patient needs angioplasty or bypass surgery," said Thomas Graboys, MD, associate clinical professor of medicine at Harvard Medical School. "But the vast majority of folks undergoing interventional procedures in the United States don't really need them."[16]

Despite the lack of scientific evidence to support their use, increasing numbers of these procedures are performed each year, and many heart disease sufferers continue to incorrectly believe their heart disease will be "taken care of" once they undergo one of these "quick, routine" surgeries. With this misconception as the basis of their decision-making process, they will inevitably be disappointed.

Myth #3: As soon as your heart disease is diagnosed, you must undergo an invasive procedure or operation immediately. If you don't, you might die. Heart disease progresses slowly, and blockages take many years to develop. Just because a diagnosis has been made and blockages have been identified does not mean operating on them is a dire emergency. In most cases, you have time to take a breath, educate yourself, weigh your options, and make a careful decision. One study, conducted at Harvard, provided a powerful illustration of this lack of urgency. Of eighty-eight patients who had been advised to undergo bypass surgery, seventy-four (84 percent) received a second opinion contradicting that recommendation. Of them, sixty (68 percent of the total) chose to indefinitely delay the operation. None of the patients who opted against bypass died during the nearly two and a half years of follow-up. The study concluded that the number of surgical interventions could be reduced by as much as 50 percent among patients who receive a second opinion that removes the sense of urgency from their decision-making process.[17]

Myth #4: You'll be as good as new, with no need to worry about your heart disease, after a routine invasive procedure or operation. This is actually two myths in one. First, there is no such thing as a "routine" invasive procedure or operation. The risks of any operation are numerous, potentially serious, or even deadly.

Second, it is important to understand that heart disease is a chronic illness for which there is no cure. Nothing you do will make you "good as new." Heart disease is something you have to live with for the rest of your life. But you can live a rich, active life *with* the disease. You can keep symptoms at bay and slow the disease's progression by making careful, educated treatment and lifestyle decisions.

If this information contradicts much of what you thought you knew about heart disease, rest assured you are not alone. But while it is challenging to dispel these widely held myths, doing so is critical to our success in battling the number-one killer.

REALIGNING PRACTICE WITH KNOWLEDGE

Our understanding of heart disease has completely transformed in recent years, so it is logical to expect that our treatment methods have transformed as well. Unfortunately, however, this has not been the case. While new scientific knowledge calls for a fundamental shift in medical practice, the same tragically outmoded techniques we have used for decades continue as the norm, and we have lost valuable time in our quest to rein in the number-one killer in our country.

Some doctors simply do not accept the irrefutable science that has redefined heart disease. Although they know the old "heart disease is about blockages" model no longer holds, they still base their practice on it and continue to open blocked arteries anyway.[18] In a candid exposé in the March 21, 2004, *New York Times,* Dr. Eric Topol, an interventional cardiologist at the Cleveland Clinic, stated bluntly: "There is just this embedded belief that fixing an artery is a good thing."

In the same article, Dr. David Hillis, an interventional cardiologist at the University of Texas Southwestern Medical Center, offered a possible explanation for this mentality, suggesting business plays a significant role. "If you're an invasive cardiologist and Joe Smith, the local internist, is sending you patients, and . . . you tell them they don't need the procedure, pretty soon Joe Smith doesn't send patients anymore," he explained. "Sometimes you can talk yourself into doing it even though in your heart of hearts you don't think it's right."[19]

Dr. Hillis cited another possible explanation for the continued prevalence of artery-opening procedures: "I think it is ingrained in the American psyche that the worth of medical care is directly related to how aggressive it is." According to Dr. Hillis, a patient may come in to the doctor's office convinced that an invasive procedure is the right course of action. "Americans want a full-court press," Dr. Hillis said, "I think they have talked to someone along the line who convinced them that this procedure will save their life. They are told, 'If you don't have it done, you are . . . a walking time bomb.'"

But whether it is a force of habit, a fear of losing patient referrals, or a patient's desire for aggressive techniques, the bottom line is that very little, if any, scientific evidence supports the widespread use of shotgun, site-specific, artery-opening procedures. Instead, Prediman K. Shah, MD, director of cardiology and director of the Atherosclerosis Research Center at Cedars-Sinai Medical Center in Los Angeles, has estimated that heart attack risk could be reduced by as much as 80 percent by using a comprehensive, noninvasive approach to treatment.[20] The *Times* article included this summation from Dr. David Waters of the University of California: "[Coronary artery disease] is a systemic disease. It occurs throughout all the coronary arteries. If you fix one segment, a year later it will be another segment that pops and gives you a heart attack, so systemic therapy . . . has the potential to do a lot more." But, he added, "There is a tradition in cardiology that doesn't want to hear that."[21]

Not only does traditional cardiology not want to hear it, but since most patients rely on their doctors to educate them about their disease, many heart disease sufferers do not get the information they need to make appropriate treatment decisions. The exciting findings about EECP—which could and should save patients the time, risk, and expense of invasive procedures—have not trickled down to the average heart disease sufferer. If they had, many patients would refuse to undergo surgeries that are essentially unnecessary and unhelpful, and the number of these procedures performed each year would drop, not rise as they currently do.

ENVISIONING THE PERFECT TREATMENT

Let us remember for a moment the overriding goal in treating heart disease. It is not to cure it—there is no cure. It is not to clear blockages—they are only manifestations of the disease. The goal is to help patients *live* with heart disease, as long and as well as possible. This means alleviating their symptoms, preventing complications such as heart attacks, and maximizing their quality of life.

As we have seen, the latest research proves unequivocally that the most sound, effective heart disease treatment would take a systemic, rather than a localized, approach. It would counteract inflammation, strengthen the vascular system, and improve circulation throughout the body and, in particular, to the heart—*beyond the blockages*. It would enable the heart to receive and pump as much blood as it needs, and do so more effectively.

We have such a treatment at our fingertips, one that accomplishes all of these goals noninvasively, safely, and comfortably. It has been the best-kept secret in medicine. Until now.

Enhanced external counterpulsation (EECP) is a groundbreaking treatment that offers patients a ticket out of heart disease's all-too-common downward spiral. It is a noninvasive treatment that is accepted by mainstream medicine, FDA approved, Medicare approved, covered by insurance, and available throughout the United States and around the world.

My mission with *Heal Your Heart with EECP* is to help patients and their loved ones understand the true nature of their disease and empower them to make informed health-care decisions knowing all of their treatment options.

Heal Your Heart with EECP is not critical of conventional medicine. On the contrary, it relies on both historical perspective and a review of the latest scientific research to explain why the procedures traditionally used to address heart disease are often misguided, and to argue that medical practice at its best should allow science, not habit, to guide the way. With this new understanding, *Heal Your Heart with EECP* offers and celebrates a welcome solution. EECP is a revolutionary, proven, lifesaving treatment that makes it possible for patients to stop living with the pain of heart disease, stands to curtail billions of dollars in health-care costs, and truly "does no harm," in the words of the Hippocratic oath. For these exciting reasons, its rightful place is at the forefront of heart disease management.

I am the founder of Braverman EECP Heart Centers, the largest EECP practice in the United States and the only medical practice solely dedicated to the treatment. I have treated more than two thousand patients with EECP, and I am continually amazed by the monumental impact this simple, little-known treatment has on the health and quality of life of those who receive it. For five years, I have worked to educate both physicians and patients throughout the Philadelphia area and around the world about EECP. I lecture extensively, appear regularly on television and radio, and provide interviews in newspapers and magazines. Still, the vast majority of heart disease sufferers and their families have never heard of EECP. That is why I have chosen to write this book.

Stories about some of my patients' remarkable experiences with EECP are sprinkled throughout this book. Their lives move and inspire me every day, and I am confident they will do the same for you.

Enjoy your journey as you learn about EECP, one of the most exciting medical innovations of the last fifty years. When you have finished, please pass this information on. For the sake of the millions of heart disease sufferers and all those who love them, join me in my effort to make EECP the household name it ought to be.

1
~

There Is No Cutting on the Cutting Edge

IMAGINE TREATING HEART DISEASE without surgery, drugs, pain, or risk. And imagine that the treatment was not only clinically proven and covered by Medicare and private insurers, but that it made patients less likely to require hospitalization and actually saved money in the long run. Next, imagine the treatment was comfortable and provided on an outpatient basis, so people could receive it during their lunch break, before work, on the way to the mall, or any time that was convenient for them. Then imagine the treatment was so safe and adaptable to so many body types and medical problems that it suited virtually every heart disease sufferer.

There is no need to keep imagining. The treatment exists. It is available right now, all over the country and around the world. It is enhanced external counterpulsation (EECP), and it is changing the way people *live* with heart disease every day.

The news about EECP gets better and better. As the only treatment that works on a systemic level, it is the most logical treatment for heart disease. It is simple and noninvasive. Clinical research has proven—dozens of times over—that it is tremendously effective.

I am a physician because I want to make a real difference in the lives of individuals who are sick. When I first learned about EECP, it seemed too good to be true, and I insisted on doing extensive research before I would believe it. But everywhere I looked, I found only encouraging news—no skeletons in the closet whatsoever.

With EECP, I help people live better, fuller lives, without risk. I am constantly astounded by the benefits my patients receive from the treatment. The results sometimes border on miraculous, and they bring me enormous personal and professional satisfaction.

There is no catch, no fine print. In this chapter, I will explain what makes EECP a no-brainer and show you why it represents all that I love about being a physician.

MY JOURNEY TO EECP

My lifelong dream was to be a physician at an Ivy League medical center. Everything I did was with that goal in mind. I graduated from Cornell University Medical College (now known as the Weill Medical College of Cornell University), and I went on to become a resident at the New York Hospital–Cornell Medical Center (now known as the New York Presbyterian Hospital). I wrote and published several articles and was appointed chief resident, all the while keeping my sights on an academic career. When I completed my residency, I was appointed to a full-time position at the University of Pennsylvania School of Medicine as an assistant professor in the Department of Rehabilitation Medicine. My dream had come true.

I remember sitting in my new office on my first day, looking out the window at the campus's incredible architecture. I felt tremendous pride, and I felt at home. I loved teaching, caring for patients, writing articles, and conducting clinical research. I thought I was there to stay.

But three years later, I learned about EECP. I had never heard the acronym, let alone knew what it stood for. I assumed it was a fad or gimmick, and with a skeptical eye, I began to do some research. The more I learned and read about EECP, the more enthralled I became. A treatment that has scores of clinical studies to back it up, carries no risk, and brings suffering, end-stage cardiac patients back to life? It seemed impossible. I had to see it for myself.

I flew to the West Coast to visit an EECP clinic. The treatment certainly got my attention; it was unlike anything I'd ever seen before. During EECP, blood pressure cuffs are wrapped around the patient's legs. The cuffs squeeze and release in sync with the patient's heartbeat, promoting blood flow throughout the body, particularly to the heart. The effects of this blood flow, I would soon learn, are astounding.

I met a ninety-seven-year-old man whose activities were so limited prior to starting EECP that he could barely care for himself. But only halfway through his EECP treatment program, he had thrown away his cane, and he was now walking without difficulty and enjoying life again. His transformation took my breath away. I also met a fifty-four-year-old woman with diabetes who had already undergone bypass surgery and several stent placements, but was still unable to climb a flight of steps without taking nitroglycerin to ease her chest pain. In her last week of EECP, she was walking two miles a day with no pain. With tears in her eyes, she told me, "EECP saved my life."

I met numerous patients that day, each with their own incredible story, and I was blown away. While I had read the studies on EECP, I did not understand the profound impact the treatment had on patients' lives before I spoke to them myself. EECP, I could clearly see, embodied the reason I became a physician in the first place: to enable the sick to live the life they desire.

As I flew back to Philadelphia, I made a decision I never had imagined for myself. I decided to leave my coveted position at the University of Pennsylvania and open my own practice, solely dedicated to EECP. Heart disease sufferers deserved to know this incredible treatment was available to them, and I was determined to do everything in my power to see that they did.

Word spread on campus, and my colleagues were convinced I was crazy. They warned me that most doctors who go into private practice fail. But my mind was made up.

I started out with one small office. Five years later, I have five offices—the largest EECP practice in the country, and it's still growing. Each day, another patient tells me how EECP has changed their life, and I am reminded that I made the correct decision.

THE MARVEL OF EECP

Here is a look at what makes EECP such a remarkable and exciting treatment.

EECP Is Safe

Consider the magnitude of this statement. There are no exceptions, no caveats, no ifs or buts. Of the thousands of patients who have been treated with EECP, *not one* has died, suffered complications, or experienced any negative side effect as a result. With EECP, there is *no* risk to your heart, lungs, brain, or any other organ. The treatment cannot cause a heart attack—in fact, the FDA approves EECP as a treatment for use *during* a heart attack. It cannot cause a stroke, infection, cognitive impairment, or bleeding complication, all of which are common side effects of surgical and invasive heart disease treatments.

EECP's safety is an accepted and undisputed medical fact. In this way, EECP may very well be in a class by itself. Can you think of any other medical treatment, procedure, or drug that has *no* risks or side effects?

EECP Requires No Recovery Time

Because EECP is completely noninvasive and is provided as an outpatient treatment, patients schedule it like any other doctor's office visit. There is no pretreatment preparation, no period of convalescence or recovery time afterward, and no interruption of daily life. Many people come in for their treatment before work, on their lunch break, or at some other convenient time. When they are done with a session, they simply get off the EECP bed, put on their coat, and go on their way. Most patients go to work, go shopping, or participate in volunteer or other activities when they leave my office.

EECP Works

As we will review in more detail in chapter 3, more than a hundred articles and studies on EECP have been published in major medical journals. *All* of them document the treatment's staggeringly high rate of effectiveness in reducing or eliminating angina (chest pain, shortness of breath, fatigue, and other symptoms) and nitroglycerin use. EECP enhances the ability to exercise and engage in physical activity, and it improves blood flow to the heart, stress test perform-ance, psychological and emotional outlook, and overall quality of life. EECP can even transform the lives of patients whose heart disease is so advanced that they cannot eat or dress without severe symptoms, allowing them to return to activities they thought they had given up forever.

EECP's Benefits Last

Clinical studies have shown repeatedly that EECP's positive effects last for years. EECP establishes improved blood flow patterns to the heart, which allows patients to be more active, and their increased activity level sets them on an upward spiral. Perhaps even more exciting are EECP's preventative effects. Patients are less likely to have a heart attack or require hospitalization in the years following EECP than those who had surgery or no treatment at all.

The importance of these beneficial effects cannot be overstated. Once heart disease sufferers undergo their first bypass, stent, or angioplasty, many brace themselves for a seemingly endless stream of additional invasive procedures. They are often told that it comes with the territory of having heart disease. But since these invasive proce-dures do not get to the heart of heart disease, it is understandable that they must constantly be repeated. EECP, on the other hand, provides lasting improvement to a person's circulation and strengthens the blood vessels throughout their body. In doing so, it places them on a healthier course for the future. EECP proves it is possible for a heart disease sufferer to break out of the vicious symptom-surgery-recovery-symptom-surgery cycle, and it gets them back to doing the things they love.

EECP Is Truly Noninvasive

I'm sure you have heard advertisements and read articles about new, cutting-edge treatments for heart disease that are "minimally" or "partially" invasive. But consider this: if something penetrates the body, whether it is a drug, a needle, a knife, or any other foreign object, it is invasive. And when a treatment is invasive, the chances that complications will arise skyrocket. EECP is the only truly non-invasive treatment for heart disease. It involves absolutely no drugs, no needles, no intravenous infusions, no tubes, and no knives. Nothing violates the body. The entire procedure is external, which is partly why EECP is so utterly safe.

EECP Is Painless

When people visit my office and get their first look at an EECP treatment, they often laugh and tell me it looks unusual. Since patients lie on blood pressure cuffs that inflate and deflate in time to their heartbeat, they do appear to be bouncing up and down on the bed, even though they are not. Despite its appearance, the treatment actually feels as if you were lying on a balloon that lifts and lowers your body in a very controlled motion.

EECP is so comfortable that many of my patients fall asleep during the treatment, snoring and all. There are no pinching or painful sensations. They feel nothing in their heart or chest. One patient remarked that it felt as if six massage therapists were simultaneously providing a deep muscle massage to their legs. If they don't fall asleep, many patients read, listen to music, or chat during the treatment. Afterward, they typically feel invigorated, even euphoric, as if they had just completed a stimulating workout while resting at the same time.

I know from experience how EECP feels. I personally train all of the therapists who work in my practice, so while I do not have heart disease, I have received many treatments. By periodically hopping on the bed at each of my offices and being treated by my staff members, I can continually ensure that they are doing a great job. At the same time, I get the added benefit of all of that blood flow!

EECP Is Covered by Medicare and Private Insurers

EECP is accessible to the people who need it. Based on the enormous body of clinical evidence demonstrating that EECP is effective, Medicare began paying for the treatment in July 1999. In the months following Medicare's announcement, private insurers across the country established their own policies making EECP available to their members.

EECP Is Inexpensive and Saves Money in the Long Run

Since EECP is covered by Medicare and private insurance carriers, there are no out-of-pocket expenses for insured patients who receive the treatment. But since heart disease sufferers are keenly aware of how expensive their medical treatments can be, it is interesting to compare the cost of EECP to that of invasive heart procedures.

EECP is dramatically less expensive than bypass surgery, angioplasty, and stents. In addition, by making patients less likely to have a heart attack or be hospitalized, EECP actually saves insurers money over time. It creates a win-win situation for patients and insurers alike.

Up-front costs. A full course of EECP costs insurers approximately $6,000. This is in sharp contrast to bypass surgery, angioplasties, and stents, which can cost anywhere from $20,000 to $100,000 or even more.

For example, if you went to an emergency room complaining of chest discomfort or difficulty breathing, it would be necessary to determine the source of the problem. Multiple physicians would evaluate you, give you medications, run tests, do blood work, and perform procedures. Even if they concluded you were simply having indigestion and sent you home, your visit to the emergency room, without being admitted to the hospital, would cost about the same as an entire course of EECP.

Figure 1. Long-term health-care costs for patients who receive EECP, angioplasty, and bypass.

Long-term savings. Being noninvasive and performed in an outpatient setting, it is no surprise that EECP is by far the least expensive clinically proven treatment for heart disease. What continues to shock the medical community, however, is the long-term cost savings for patients treated with EECP compared to those who undergo bypass surgery or angioplasty. If you tally all of the costs associated with caring for heart disease sufferers (hospital visits, procedures, tests, medications, and so on) for the five years after they received EECP treatments and compare it with the cost of care during the same time period for patients who underwent bypass surgery or angioplasty, you will find that the EECP patients are far less costly to treat. During the five years following their treatment, EECP patients typically generate approximately $26,000 in heart-related health-care expenses, while bypass and angioplasty patients have closer to $65,000 to $70,000 in expenses.[1] More than $66 billion is currently spent each year on heart disease treatments.[2] That cost could be reduced by as much as two-thirds if EECP was used on a wider scale.

The most important point, of course, is that EECP patients feel better, which creates immeasurable economic ripple effects. They are more likely to stay away from the doctor and live an enriched quality of life. And the effects extend far beyond the health-care system. The better patients feel, the more they enjoy life and remain productive. They are more willing and able to work, shop, vacation, and partici-pate in everything life has to offer, without the symptoms, limitations, and fears that often dominate the lives of heart disease sufferers and their loved ones. Imagine returning to the economy even a percentage of the $71.4 billion lost annually due to reduced productivity caused by heart disease.[3]

EECP Is Right for Almost Anyone

My practice has treated more than two thousand patients with EECP, and our vast, diverse experience leads to our high success rate. Our patients have ranged in age from thirty-six to ninety-seven. They have weighed as little as 82 pounds and as much as 489 pounds. While the treatment is relatively simple, each person is different, with a unique size, shape, and list of medical issues. Some medical conditions require special attention while a patient undergoes EECP. For these reasons, the treatment must be individualized. Before treating any patient, I review their medical records, speak with them at length, and perform a thorough physical exam to identify any spe-cial circumstances or precautions that must be taken during their treatment. I have successfully treated amputees; cancer survivors; oxygen-dependent and dialysis patients; heart and kidney transplant recipients; patients with osteoporosis, colostomies, hernias, hip and/or knee replacements, insulin pumps, and severe cognitive deficits; patients who have had neck or spine surgery; and more. I even treated a patient with a cast on her leg, and she experienced amazing results. By being creative, personalizing the program, and recognizing that a patient's comfort is critical to their success, we can make the treatment work for just about anyone.

CASE STUDY

In the last year, Pamela S., age forty-seven, suffered three heart attacks. Despite having two stents placed, she continued to have angina daily with most activities. She also had a nonhealing ulcer on the bottom of her right foot (a complication of poor leg circulation and insulin-dependent diabetes). Finally, her cardiologist sent her for EECP. After six EECP treatments, a cast was placed on her leg to aid in healing the wound—a process she had been through many times over the years for various ulcers. We were able to work around the cast and continue her EECP treatments uninterrupted. After her twenty-sixth treatment, the cast was removed. Her podiatrist was stunned at how quickly and thoroughly the ulcer had healed this time, saying, "The blood flow from EECP made all the difference!" By the end of her course of EECP, Pamela was having angina only once a week and could engage in more physical activities without limitations.

EECP Is Good for the Soul

When you feel better physically, you feel better emotionally and psychologically. Several clinical studies have documented the quality of life and emotional improvements that result from EECP's physical benefits. I often marvel at the way many of my patients become giddy as they begin to feel the treatment's effects. With the boost in blood flow to their heart and throughout their body, they are simply overjoyed to be reminded how feeling good feels!

EECP Does the Seemingly Impossible

With EECP, patients can sleep and exercise at the same time. It sounds silly, but that is precisely what is happening. EECP is passive exercise. As the blood pressure cuffs squeeze and release in time to a patient's heartbeat, they stimulate the patient's circulation for them. By enhancing blood flow, EECP provides the same benefits as endurance training, stimulating blood vessels throughout the body so they grow, become stronger, and become better able to deliver more blood, oxygen, and nutrients to the body's cells and organs. This is especially good news for heart disease sufferers who are often so limited by their symptoms that they cannot perform even the most basic tasks—walking, climbing steps, carrying groceries—let alone exercise vigorously enough to achieve long-term benefit. EECP gives them the benefit of exercise despite their limitations; it is exercise for those who cannot exercise. And not only does a patient get the circulatory benefits of exercise while resting, they are able to do so comfortably, noninvasively, and without checking in to the hospital.

There Is No Downside to EECP

You may be thinking, as I once did, that EECP sounds too good to be true. But it is that good. There is no significant downside to the treatment. The most common complaint my patients have is not finding a good parking space at our office buildings! Some patients anticipate a problem with the time commitment that a daily treatment regimen will require. However, once they begin their program—and start to feel the incredible, sometimes immediate, benefits—they find it isn't hard at all to keep to the schedule. Most even look forward to it: fewer than 5 percent of my patients drop out of the program.

Some patients may occasionally experience skin irritation on their legs from the cuffs' squeezing action. In my practice, we help patients avoid this by providing tight-fitting Lycra exercise pants for them to wear during their treatment. The pants do not buckle or

CASE STUDY

Madeline G., age seventy-four, suffered from congestive heart failure, hypertension, and diabetes. She had suffered a silent heart attack and a series of ministrokes. She was diagnosed with heart disease twenty-five years ago and refused to have bypass surgery, angioplasties, or stents, relying only on medication to manage her illness. She had been doing well until she reached age seventy, when she realized she was having more and more angina with less and less activity. She suffered almost daily chest pain, shortness of breath, and fatigue, especially when she walked, talked on the telephone, or exerted herself. "I wasn't able to do much of anything," she said. She had become dependent on friends and neighbors to do her household chores and run her errands. She heard about EECP on the radio and thought, "This is exactly what I have been waiting for." After EECP, Madeline's energy increased dramatically, her angina disappeared, and she stopped using nitroglycerin for the first time in twenty-five years. She was independent again, could do things for herself, and was able to be more social. She returned to using public transportation to visit her friends and family. "I feel like a new person! I have no chest pains," Madeline said. "I thank God I came!"

bunch up under the cuffs, so they eliminate friction on a person's legs. If a patient has particularly sensitive skin or a high risk of skin irritation (for example, from diabetes, neuropathy, or peripheral vascular disease), I recommend that they moisturize daily and wear nylon pantyhose beneath their exercise pants to provide another layer of protection. A well-trained EECP therapist helps patients avoid skin problems by assessing their needs daily, wrapping the cuffs properly, and using extra padding (such as foam, sheepskin, or rubber) where needed.

While some patients with a history of low back pain may experience a flare-up at the start of their treatment, many see their back pain actually improve as a result of EECP. The improved blood flow to the spine and surrounding tissue provides nutrients and oxygen and washes away the metabolic waste products and chemicals that stimulate nerves to transmit pain signals. Again, a skilled EECP therapist is trained to prevent any difficulties and will address them immediately if they should arise.

COMMON QUESTIONS

Many heart disease sufferers have special concerns about whether they would be good candidates for EECP. Individuals who have pacemakers or irregular heartbeats, for example, often ask whether they can still receive the treatment. Likewise, patients who have recently undergone invasive cardiac procedures, who have had blood clots in their legs, who take Coumadin, or who suffer from peripheral vascular disease routinely inquire about whether their particular situation is suited to EECP. In all of these circumstances, there is good news. Because EECP is safe and noninvasive, it is appropriate for nearly all heart disease sufferers. In this section, we will review what makes EECP a successful treatment approach in each of these special cases.

Pacemakers, Internal Defibrillators, and Irregular Heartbeats

I have treated hundreds of patients with these devices and rhythm disturbances without any difficulty and with excellent clinical results. There is no risk that a pacemaker or defibrillator will malfunction due to EECP, and the treatment cannot cause abnormalities in someone's heart rhythm. Patients with cardiac pacemakers and defibrillators can expect to enjoy the same reduction in symptoms and improvement in quality of life as those without pacemakers.[4] Similarly, an irregular heartbeat does not interfere with EECP. For example, the treatment is just as effective with patients who have a rate-controlled atrial fibrillation (50 to 100 beats per minute) as it is

CASE STUDY

Mary S., age sixty-six, had congestive heart failure and a pace-maker, and she had suffered several heart attacks. She never had surgery because her blockages were inaccessible. Before EECP, Mary was oxygen dependent, and she was on a heart transplant waiting list. Most activities, particularly walking and climbing steps, triggered angina. She could not walk half a block without having to stop and rest. After EECP, she was taken off the heart transplant list, was no longer oxygen dependent, and could walk eleven blocks and climb steps with ease!

with patients who have a regular beat.[5] Each person's unique heart-beat makes the machine operate and triggers the cuffs to squeeze and release. So the blood pressure cuffs will squeeze a patient's legs in an irregular fashion if they have an irregular heartbeat, in direct response to their heartbeat. In every other way they get the same treatment and the same excellent results as those with a regular heartbeat.

Invasive Heart Procedures

A recent cardiac catheterization, angioplasty, and/or stent place-ment does not preclude having EECP, and these procedures do not create any additional risk. Patients can start EECP as quickly as one week after undergoing one of these groin procedures. The only rea-son to delay EECP treatment is if there is any tenderness or swelling in the groin. The cuff that we wrap around the upper thigh goes all the way to the groin, so if the area is still very sensi-tive, the wrap will be uncomfortable.

The decision about how quickly to proceed with EECP after bypass surgery is based on the patient's overall recovery from the operation and their general medical condition. At a minimum, if a vein was taken from a leg to use as a bypass graft, the incision must heal before the EECP cuffs can be wrapped comfortably. I have treated patients as soon as two months following bypass surgery without difficulty.

Leg Blood Clots

Patients with extensive blood clot histories (deep vein thrombosis, or DVT) may receive EECP without difficulty, pain, or complication. I have even treated patients with a Greenfield filter (a filter placed in the aorta of an individual who has a history of significant blood clots in their legs to prevent any future clots from traveling to the lungs) successfully and without complication. EECP cannot *cause* a blood clot. It actually has the opposite effect. When blood does not flow, when it is stagnant, it may begin to coagulate and clot. But EECP creates more blood flow in the legs than a patient may have had in years. It makes blood clots less likely to form.

If a patient has a history of blood clots, if they are unsure, or if they are concerned for any reason, I send them for an ultrasound of their legs prior to starting EECP to confirm that everything is clear. However, if a patient *currently* has a blood clot in one of the deep veins in their leg, I delay starting EECP until the clot resolves.

Coumadin or Other Blood Thinners

There is no trauma involved in EECP, and individuals on Coumadin, Plavix, aspirin, or any other blood thinner may undergo EECP safely and successfully, without risk of bleeding or bruising. The cuffs apply equal pressure around the circumference of the legs, so it would be more traumatic if someone poked you really hard with their finger than if you received EECP. We monitor Coumadin blood levels carefully, and we try to keep patients' international normalized ratio (INR) level to a maximum of 3.0 to 3.5. Even patients on Heparin who are fully anticoagulated (that is, the drug prevents their blood from clotting) have been treated at EECP centers around the country without any difficulty. I have also successfully treated patients with chronically low platelet counts (as low as 20,000, placing them at high risk of bleeding and bruising) without complication.

Peripheral Vascular Disease

Patients with peripheral vascular disease (PVD) resulting in poor leg circulation do quite well with EECP, although it may take them a bit longer to see a result. Poor leg circulation means that there is less blood in the legs for the EECP cuffs to pump back up toward the heart. To address this problem, patients with significant PVD often require more than the standard thirty-five EECP treatments to achieve a benefit. We routinely offer at least fifty treatments to these individuals to achieve optimal clinical results. The initial treatments improve blood flow in the legs, while subsequent treatments provide

CASE STUDY

William A., age seventy-five, had a quintuple bypass at age sixty-five, followed by two different angioplasty/stent procedures (at age seventy-one and age seventy-four). He had also suffered a stroke and had hypertension and diabetes. William suffered from severe peripheral vascular disease, had had multiple bypass surgeries on his legs, and had undergone a partial amputation of his left foot. Before EECP, William experienced "crushing" chest pain and shortness of breath with basic activities and walking. His cardiologist referred him for EECP. After two weeks of EECP treatments, he went for a routine checkup with his podiatrist, who said: "I feel pulses in your feet for the first time in years! Am I crazy?" William answered, "No; it's just EECP." By the end of his treatments, the severity and frequency of his angina had dramatically decreased. His energy level increased substantially, to the point that he was able to walk with his wife for twenty-five minutes daily without having to rest. He was back on the social scene—going shopping, dining out, and playing cards with his friends. "I didn't know I could feel this good," William reported.

an opportunity for the increased volume of blood in the legs to improve blood flow to the heart and the rest of the body. In my practice, even amputees and patients who have had bypass procedures on their legs have seen excellent results from EECP. Not only do their heart disease symptoms improve, the symptoms associated with poor blood flow in their legs—coldness, numbness, tingling, cramping, and fatigue—improve significantly as well, which often has an even greater impact on their quality of life.

However, patients who have leg pain at rest (while sitting or lying down) or gangrene will not likely improve with EECP. Circulation in these individuals is so compromised that it is probably too late for EECP. But receiving EECP before the disease advances to that point will likely help the patient.

Clinical trials are currently underway to study the effect of EECP on patients with PVD and to formally document the benefits that I, and many other leading EECP providers around the country, observe every day. I am confident the research findings will eventually lead to insurance coverage for EECP as a treatment specifically for PVD.

WHO SHOULD NOT HAVE EECP

Very few conditions preclude a patient from receiving EECP, and many of these conditions are temporary or can be addressed to allow for EECP at a later date. Here is the brief list.

Fever. A fever is an indication that the patient's body is fighting an active infection, and it is very likely that they have bacteria or viral particles circulating in their bloodstream. The increased blood flow that results from exercise and from EECP could promote "seeding" of the infection in the heart, causing damage. So, just as someone should not exercise if they have a fever, they should not receive EECP until their temperature returns to normal.

Open wound. If a patient has an open wound on one of their legs (where the EECP cuffs are applied), we would delay the treatment until the skin heals. However, nonhealing ulcers on the feet, as often experienced by diabetic patients or those who have severe peripheral vascular disease, do *not* interfere with EECP. The treatment improves blood flow in the legs, which helps to stimulate the wound-healing process.

Severe aortic insufficiency. This condition is rare and can be diagnosed using an echocardiogram, a noninvasive ultrasound of the heart. Patients with a leaky aortic valve so severe that it requires surgical repair should not have EECP, as increasing blood flow back to the heart during its resting phase (between beats, or diastole) may worsen this condition. However, after the valve is surgically repaired or replaced, a patient may receive EECP without difficulty. Patients with other valve disorders (for example, mitral valve prolapse, tight or stenotic valve, or leaky mitral, tricuspid, or pulmonic valve) are routinely treated, safely and effectively, with EECP. While the valve condition itself will not improve, blood flow to the heart muscle will alleviate symptoms related to poor circulation.

Abdominal aortic aneurysm. Individuals with large (5.0 cm or greater) abdominal aortic aneurysms who have been encouraged to undergo surgical repair should delay EECP treatment until after surgery. Again, this is a rare condition, and an abdominal ultrasound can determine whether or not a patient has an abdominal aortic aneurysm. For those who have already undergone abdominal aortic aneurysm repair, I often recommend that a diagnostic test such as a CT angiogram be performed prior to starting EECP to ensure that the repair is intact and that there are no microscopic leaks. I have treated many patients with abdominal aortic aneurysms smaller than 5.0 cm in diameter, as well as many patients after surgical repair, all with excellent results and no complications.

Superficial phlebitis. Superficial phlebitis is inflammation of the veins in the legs. EECP will be more comfortable if patients with active phlebitis delay treatment until the inflammation resolves.

Uncontrolled high blood pressure. Individuals with uncontrolled hypertension (greater than 180/110 mmHg) may not receive EECP treatment until their blood pressure is normalized.

Hemophilia. Individuals with rare severe bleeding disorders such as hemophilia should not receive EECP.

Pregnancy. A pregnant woman should not receive EECP, since scientists are not sure what the effect of increasing blood flow to the fetus via the placenta would be.

IT'S A NO-BRAINER

When heart disease sufferers learn about EECP's incredible advantages (and realize there is absolutely no downside), they all say the same thing: "It's a no-brainer!" Most wish they had heard about it sooner. As one of my patients recently said, "You have nothing to lose, but everything to gain."

As the *only* safe, noninvasive, proven treatment for heart disease, EECP is truly in a class by itself. Since it is appropriate for nearly every heart disease sufferer—regardless of their age, size, or other medical conditions—and is covered by insurance, EECP is changing lives for the better every day, and it is doing so painlessly and inexpensively. In the next chapter, we will discuss exactly how EECP strengthens the most fundamental element of good health.

2

It All Comes Down to Blood Flow

As we now know, heart disease comes down to an issue of poor blood flow. Rather than being defined by blockages, heart disease is a system-wide illness that impairs blood flow throughout the body—particularly to the heart. This was a seemingly inevitable discovery, because when we pinpoint the most fundamental element of health, we find agreement among all cultures, across the globe and throughout time. It is blood flow. In this chapter we will look at the common thread that connects nearly all schools of medical thought, and we will gain an appreciation for what makes blood flow so basic to a healthy body. Then we will examine how EECP supports the body's essential function and how it works—inside and out.

FLOW: A CONCEPT FOR THE AGES

For thousands of years, the idea of "flow" has been revered and recognized as central to life. It is a common denominator of most medical philosophies, treatments, and doctrines around the world. This is not a coincidence, but rather an affirmation of its importance.

Virtually every student of medicine, regardless of the language they spoke, the era in which they lived, or the approach they took to healing, has recognized that flow *is* health.

Traditional Chinese medicine. A central tenet of traditional Chinese medicine is the flow of a life force known as chi (pronounced "chee"). The belief is that chi is present in all living things and circulates throughout the body. Blood is essentially the tangible form of chi; the two concepts are inseparable. Traditional Chinese medicine teaches that illness, pain, and organ dysfunction result from stagnation of energy, blood, and body fluid. Health, on the other hand, results from free and unobstructed flow. In Western medicine, the principle is the same. Blood cannot be separated from life. Healthy blood flow is essential to healthy life.

Ayurvedic medicine. India's five-thousand-year-old system of traditional medicine is another example of a medical paradigm centering on flow. According to Ayurvedic thought, every person's health and well-being is determined by a delicate balance of energy. Yoga, probably the best-known component of Ayurvedic medicine, combines carefully timed breath and movement to drive the flow of prana (life energy, similar to chi), and enables it to flow freely throughout the body. When pranic flow is strong, the body functions more effectively—from the digestion of food to the prevention of disease, and from the healing of ailments to increased clarity of mind. Yoga's movements are also rooted in the idea of flow, where the breath leads the body in moving fluidly from one pose to another. And while many people think of yoga simply as gentle movement or stretching, each sequence of poses is carefully crafted to raise the heart rate, thus stimulating blood flow. Once again, we see that blood flow, energy flow, and life force are inextricable concepts.

Ancient Egyptian medicine. Ancient Egyptian anatomy and physiology texts illustrated the job of the heart and blood vessels. The heart was revered as the center of the body's functions, and it was believed to be the meeting point of the important vessels that carried all of the body's fluids, including blood, tears, urine, and sperm. The free flow of all fluids was recognized as essential for health and well-being.

Ancient Greek medicine. Hippocrates (ca 460–ca 377 BCE), considered the father of Western medicine, saw the body as governed by four corresponding "humors" (blood, phlegm, yellow bile, and black bile), just as the Greek universe was ordered according to the principles of four dynamic elements (fire, water, air, and earth). Blood was considered to be the dominant humor. According to Hippocrates's paradigm, all health and disease states were explained by humoral balance, imbalance, and flow or lack thereof. His *Theory of the Four Humors* provided the basis for medical thought for more than two millennia, until the time of the American Revolution. Galen, who lived five centuries after Hippocrates, crystallized the best work of Greek medicine. According to Galenic physiology, *pneuma* (air or breath, similar to chi or prana) was the fundamental life force. *Pneuma* was responsible, among other things, for regulating blood flow and body temperature.

Blood flow is the most fundamental element of good health. It is the source of life. Cells are the building blocks in our bodies. A group of cells makes an organ, organs make a system, and systems combine to make the body: a complex machine, driven by the most powerful known pump—the heart. In a lifetime, the heart never stops to rest because its job—to keep blood flowing—is too important.

There is no replacement for blood flow. It is essential for the entire body to function. Blood, the body's most abundant fluid aside from water, has the vital job of carrying oxygen and nutrients to each and every cell in your body, giving them what they need to be healthy, and then carrying away waste products. If blood does not bring oxygen and nutrients to cells, and therefore fails to carry away cells' toxic waste products, disease will result.

It is not a coincidence that so many cultures, philosophies, and medical practices have historically recognized the fundamental importance of blood flow. It is also not a coincidence that people feel alive and alert when their blood is pumping. The more active you are, the more your heart pumps, the more blood flows, and the better you feel. Conversely, the less active you are, the less your heart pumps, the less blood flows, and the worse you feel. It is literally that basic. We now know that the underlying cause of the most common diseases and conditions—heart disease; stroke; pain, arthritis, and joint disease; peripheral vascular disease; and premature aging, just to name a few—is lack of blood flow. Poor blood flow leads to the death of cells, tissues, organs, systems, and ultimately, the body. While this process naturally occurs throughout a lifetime, there is no need to despair. By improving blood flow and strengthening the body's ability to pump blood on its own, we maximize health and wellness, help the body heal itself, and prolong life. The more you do every day, the more you *can* do every day. And the less you do, the less you are able to do. This is a fact we all must accept, particularly as we age.

THE ANATOMY
OF HEART DISEASE

The heart beats continuously, an average of eighty times per minute. It adjusts and responds, shifting the quantity of blood flow to the areas of the body that need it most: to a runner's legs, to an engineer's brain, or to your stomach after a meal. The heart also varies the number of times per minute that it beats since you certainly need more oxygen to run up two flights of stairs than to watch TV!

In coronary artery disease, a number of factors can impair blood flow to the heart. Arteries are blood vessels that carry oxygen-rich blood to all of the tissues in the body, including the heart. Healthy arteries—including coronary arteries (those that feed the heart)—are clean, smooth, and slick. The artery walls are dynamic, flexible, and able to expand to let more or less blood through when necessary. Heart disease is thought to begin with damage, such as cracks, to the linings of the artery walls. This injury makes arteries stiffer and more susceptible to the slow, progressive buildup of plaque deposits. These fatty deposits on the arteries' inner walls, called *atherosclerosis*, develop from cholesterol, cellular waste products, calcium, and other substances in the blood. Plaque buildup often progresses very slowly over many years, causing blood vessels to narrow (stenosis), harden, and develop blockages. When this buildup affects the coronary arteries, it is called *coronary artery disease* (CAD). When coronary artery disease affects the heart muscle, it is called *coronary heart disease* (CHD). Here, we use the term "heart disease" to refer to both coronary artery disease and coronary heart disease.

The stenosis may be at a specific site, or it may spread out along the length of the blood vessel. In either case, the stenosis can reduce coronary blood flow. Diseased coronary vessels are more susceptible to periodic constriction (vasospasm), which can lead to temporary, stress-induced restriction of coronary blood flow both at rest and during activity. Finally, the formation of a blood clot (thrombus), particularly at the site of a ruptured blockage (atherosclerotic plaque), can partially or completely block a coronary vessel, causing unstable angina or a heart attack (myocardial infarction).

In short, in patients who have heart disease, the blood vessels that feed the heart are narrowed and may eventually become blocked, allowing less and less blood to reach the heart. If the heart does not get the blood and oxygen it needs, it cannot perform its job properly, and it cries out to the body: "I need more oxygen! I am not getting enough blood!" This cry comes in the form of angina. Or it may be more devastating: a heart attack.

Angina: More Than Just Chest Pain

The heart's persistent cry for help is called *angina*, and while many people think the term is interchangeable with crushing chest pain, it can take many forms. Signals that the heart needs more blood are different in everyone.

THE SYMPTOMS OF POOR BLOOD FLOW

The heart has many—including some quite unexpected and seemingly illogical—ways to communicate that it is not getting the blood and oxygen it needs. Angina is actually a collection of symptoms. Any or all of them may occur in a heart disease sufferer, depending on their particular body. A patient, for example, might experience shortness of breath, fatigue, a feeling similar to indigestion, or discomfort in the throat, jaw, teeth, ears, neck, upper back, shoulder blades, or arms. They might perspire, feel nauseous, or vomit. Any of these symptoms may signal inadequate blood flow to the heart.

An estimated 6.8 million people in the United States suffer from angina.[1] This is likely a gross underestimation because oftentimes patients and their doctors miss the diagnosis. Since so many patients think severe chest pain is the only sign of heart disease, they don't get the message when their heart cries out in a different way and do not realize there is trouble to report to their physician. Doctors, on the other hand, often fail to ask their patients the few key questions that would allow them to properly diagnose angina.

Instead of crushing chest pain, millions of people experience their angina as a vague "sensation," pressure, or tightness in the chest. It might even be fairly mild in severity. They often tell me: "It's not *pain*. It really doesn't feel that bad." But chest pain does not have to be severe to be serious. And many people with heart disease never experience chest pain at all.

The diagnosis of angina—and therefore of heart disease—is frequently overlooked in women. Fewer than 30 percent of women with heart disease experience chest pain, the symptom most physicians look for in making an initial diagnosis. The most common heart disease symptom among women is fatigue (71 percent), followed by sleep disturbance (48 percent), shortness of breath (42 percent), indigestion (39 percent), and anxiety (35 percent).[2]

All these symptoms come under the broad category of angina. They all result from the lack of blood flow, and subsequent lack of oxygen, to the heart, which is the hallmark of heart disease.

Patients who experience their angina as fatigue or shortness of breath may get to know which activities will tire them out too much, and either completely refrain from doing them or carefully pace themselves during the day to avoid difficulty. They may not even realize they are making adjustments to their daily schedules, much less connect it to their heart disease. I often meet people who tell me they rest for an hour or two after dinner in order to digest their food. Only after enough time has passed do they go ahead and take out the trash or clean up the kitchen. They know they might get angina if they try to do an activity right after eating, and with good reason. Remember, heart disease sufferers already have impaired blood flow to the heart. When blood is stolen to fuel the digestive process, even less blood is available to feed the heart.

You might lead a sedentary life and have no symptoms. But once you get off the sofa to do something, you have difficulty. Or you might take a nitroglycerin tablet before engaging in an activity to avoid getting into trouble, using the nitro as a preemptive strike against angina. These adjustments are important to recognize. They are signs that you are changing your habits to accommodate your heart disease. But modifying or curbing what you do in order to prevent angina *is* how angina may manifest for you.

IT'S NOT JUST ABOUT AGE

Many people attribute the pain or discomfort of heart disease to something else. I often hear: "I'm just getting old," "I'm just worn-out," or "I'm out of shape." While these statements may be true, it is more often the case that these individuals become easily tired or winded because their heart is not getting the blood and oxygen it needs. In other words, it is their heart disease—not their age or fitness level—talking.

Learning to recognize how angina presents itself in your body is the critical first step in managing your heart disease. Doing so can help you gauge the progression of your disease, give you a chance to seek treatment early on, improve your quality of life in terms of your ability to do the activities you enjoy without limitation, and possibly even prevent a heart attack.

Heart Attack: Sudden, Complete Blockage

Remember, blood flow is the body's fundamental source of health and life. When there is a sudden, complete blockage of an artery that supplies blood to an organ or tissue and there is no alternate route for blood flow, that organ or tissue is in danger and will often die. It occurs in the brain as a stroke, in the intestine as severe abdominal pain and possible bleeding, in the eye as sudden blindness, in the kidney as pain and the inability to create urine, in the foot as gangrene, and anywhere else in the body where blood vessels are affected.

A heart attack, or myocardial infarction, occurs when there is a sudden, complete blockage of a coronary artery. If blood cannot use an alternate route to reach the portion of the heart that the blocked artery feeds, that piece of the heart is cut off from its blood supply and may become injured or die. If blood flow is restored within minutes, heart function may be impaired for twenty-four to forty-eight hours, but recovery would be expected. However, a total blockage that persists for more than twenty minutes makes it likely that the heart will be permanently damaged and its function as the body's circulatory pump will be permanently impaired. The ramifications of such an event are serious and may even be deadly, as the heart does not have the ability to regenerate. If a piece of the heart dies, it cannot be replaced.

For decades, our understanding of the natural progression of coronary artery disease was that atherosclerotic plaques grew larger and larger until they eventually blocked an artery completely and caused a heart attack. As a result of this perception, coronary arteries that are more than 70 percent blocked are the ones typically targeted for bypass surgery, angioplasty, or stent placements. However, the last decade has brought a radically different understanding of how heart attacks occur. We now know that gradual plaque buildup is not the culprit. Instead, heart attacks are usually caused when a piece of inflamed, fatty plaque suddenly erupts from within the blood vessel wall, much like a volcano, and bleeds. The bleeding creates a blood clot that becomes lodged in the artery.[3] So it is not plaque, but a sudden blood clot that blocks the blood vessel and causes a heart attack. In addition, the plaques at the greatest risk of rupturing in this way are the smaller ones, which create artery blockages of less than 50 percent, not the larger ones targeted by surgical methods.

For a variety of reasons, it is not possible to surgically bypass, stent, or perform angioplasty on all of the smaller blockages. First, many of these vulnerable obstructions are too small to be identified on cardiac catheterizations. Second, when an artery is less than 70 percent blocked, ample blood may still flow through that vessel. Therefore, if such a blockage was located and surgically bypassed, the bypass graft would not be utilized and would eventually scar and close. This enormous shift in our understanding of how heart attacks occur reinforces the dire need for a system-wide approach to treating heart disease.

In the last thirty years, public awareness of certain warning signs of a heart attack has grown considerably. But we still have a long way to go. You probably know that if you have severe chest pain, perhaps accompanied by pain that travels down your left arm, it is a serious matter and might indicate that you are having a heart attack. But as we saw earlier, many people with heart disease never experience chest pain. Just as angina takes many forms, ranging from subtle to debilitating, the signs of a heart attack vary tremendously from patient to patient. Some individuals may feel dizzy, nauseous, or particularly tired, or they may experience a variety of other symptoms during a heart attack. Other people may feel nothing at all. These are the patients who find out later, much to their surprise, that they had suffered a "silent" heart attack sometime in the past.

GOING BEYOND THE BLOCKAGE

As an individual with heart disease experiences symptoms that indicate their heart is not getting enough blood, they often find themselves in a brutal downward spiral. It begins when their doctor recommends a "routine" procedure to open or bypass a blockage (which may bring undesirable or even more serious side effects), and then instructs them to remain sedentary during a prescribed recovery period. This inactivity weakens their circulation even more, allowing other blockages to grow. In the process, blood flow to the heart may be further impaired and additional symptoms may develop. The patient finds that they must limit their activities, their quality of life has decreased, and their frustration and depression reaches new depths. Seeking a way out, they go back to their doctor, who recommends additional invasive procedures, and the downward spiral continues. The less they are able to do, the more likely they will need (or think they need) additional surgeries, and the more they will be required to remain sedentary during a recovery period, and so on. Before they know it, they barely recognize their lifestyle; they have become a shadow of who they used to be.

Given what we know now about heart disease, it is obvious that a patient will only break out of the vicious symptom-surgery-symptom cycle when their overall blood flow is improved. If the heart gets enough healthy blood flowing to it, the blockages become irrelevant.

There is no doubt that strong blood flow is absolutely critical to overall health and that we must do everything we can to keep our blood pumping. Heart disease sufferers are prime examples of the devastating effects that lack of blood flow to the heart can have on one's ability to live life to its fullest. Many do the best they can to modify their lifestyle choices and maximize blood flow. Many attempt to exercise, but are too limited by their heart disease to achieve enough blood flow to significantly improve their condition. If there were a way for heart patients to get a jump start, they would certainly seize the opportunity to get back on track.

What we need is a way for doctors to improve patients' blood flow for them—a passive form of exercise. It would curb the debilitating symptoms that signal the heart's cries for more blood and allow the heart to function normally, which would help the body function normally. Such an aid would improve the patient's circulation, let them emerge from the rut of inactivity, and set them on an upward spiral where they can exercise on their own. With an outside aid to blood flow, patients could finally regain the active lifestyle they thought was lost forever.

A LOW-TECH SOLUTION FOR A HIGH-TECH PROBLEM

Historically, all attempts to restore normal blood flow to the heart in patients with coronary artery disease have addressed specific blockages, one at a time. Physicians would locate a blockage, and then attempt to surgically bypass it, push it out of the way using procedures such as balloon angioplasty and/or stent, scrape it away (atherectomy), or radiate it (brachytherapy). But while patients may experience immediate relief from these focused efforts to restore blood flow beyond a particular blockage, these procedures miss the underlying problem, are likely to offer only temporary benefit, and do nothing to stop the progression of the illness. Remember, heart disease is a system-wide illness, not a local one, and as such requires a system-wide treatment. This exciting discovery signals the opportunity to shift away from the localized treatment approaches we have used for decades. Even more exciting is that a system-wide treatment already exists. It is EECP.

To understand EECP, we will examine it on three levels. First, what does it look and feel like? Second, what does it do to your blood flow? And third, what does it do to your blood vessels? Let's answer each question individually.

CASE STUDY

Before EECP, Russell W., age eighty, had angina regularly after eating, while walking, or when breathing cold air. He had suffered five heart attacks, had undergone bypass surgery, and had had multiple stents implanted. He also had a pacemaker. In March 2004, more than a year after completing his EECP treatment, I received a letter along with three pictures of him parasailing four hundred feet in the air while on a cruise with his wife to celebrate his eightieth birthday. He wrote: "My cardiologist says I am in better health now than I was two years ago. I am a poster boy for EECP. And I owe it all to you." A year later, he reported that he regularly walked a four-mile circuit in the park near his home and said, "My cardiologist is amazed I'm still walking around. I can do anything. As far as I'm concerned, EECP is the best thing you can do."

What Does EECP Look and Feel Like?

EECP is a beautifully simple treatment (see figure 2). You lie down on a comfortable, specially designed bed, and a therapist wraps a set of oversized blood pressure cuffs tightly around your calves, thighs, and buttocks. An air hose connects each cuff to an air compressor inside the bed. The blood pressure cuffs fill with air sequentially—first the calves, then the thighs, then the buttocks, with a fifty-millisecond delay between each—and then release simultaneously (see figure 3). The trigger for the cuffs to inflate and deflate—what makes the machine operate—is your own heartbeat. With three stick-on electrodes on your chest, the computer reads your EKG continuously throughout the treatment and uses it to synchronize the inflation and deflation of the cuffs to your body's rhythms. When your heart beats, the cuffs relax. And when your heart rests, between beats, the cuffs squeeze around your legs, promoting blood flow back up to your heart and throughout your body. So the cuffs' squeeze-and-release rhythm—a "pumping" action—mirrors your heartbeat.

**Figure 2.
Dr. Braverman
treating an
EECP patient.**

Feeling the cuffs inflate (squeeze) and deflate (release) around your legs is painless. It feels like a deep, rhythmic massage to your legs. You feel nothing above the waist and nothing in the heart or chest. And the synchronization to your heartbeat adds to the comfort and sense of relaxation during the treatment. It creates biofeedback, where hearing and feeling your own heartbeat encourages you to quiet your mind and enjoy the full benefit of the treatment. EECP is actually so comfortable that most patients listen to music, read, or even fall asleep during their treatment.

What Does EECP Do to Your Blood Flow?

The second layer in understanding how EECP works relates to what is actually going on with your blood flow and physiology, also known as *hemodynamics*, during the treatment. First, let's review a bit about the human circulatory system. The heart muscle is the body's pump. Every time it beats (the phase of the cardiac cycle known as *systole*), the heart contracts, sending blood throughout

Figure 3. Schematic of EECP cuffs.

the entire body by way of the aorta, the largest artery in the body, and then the rest of the arterial system. After each contraction, the heart rests for a moment (the phase of the cardiac cycle known as *diastole*). During this resting phase, blood returns from the body to the heart by way of the venous system, first passing through the lungs to pick up oxygen. The oxygenated blood enters the heart's chambers, so when your heart beats again, it sends that oxygen-rich blood back out to the body. During diastole (the resting phase), blood also enters the heart's own circulation (called *myocardial perfusion*) by way of the coronary arteries and provides the heart muscle itself with nutrients and oxygen. The two earliest branches of the aorta (nearest to the heart) are the right coronary artery, which supplies the right heart, and the left main coronary artery, which divides into the left circumflex artery and the left anterior descending artery, and supplies the left heart (see figure 4). This process continues, over and over, approximately eighty times per minute, every minute of every hour, every hour of every day, every day of every year, for your entire life.

It is precisely during diastole—while the heart is resting—that the EECP blood pressure cuffs squeeze your legs, enhancing the natural return of blood to the heart. As the cuffs squeeze your legs with a circumferential pressure of 260 mmHg, blood flows retrograde

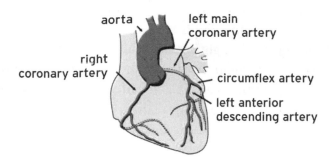

Figure 4. The heart.

through the arteries—that is, back up to the heart—and into the coronary circulation. The treatment has been shown to increase, or augment, diastolic blood pressure—a measure of the blood flow to the heart while the heart is resting, between beats—by 93 percent, and to increase overall blood flow to the heart by 28 percent.[4] These improvements are linearly related to the pressure of the EECP cuffs, meaning that the tighter the cuffs squeeze your legs, the more blood will flow into your heart muscle.

We measure this blood flow back to the heart during EECP by placing a clip on your finger. The clip uses an infrared light to measure blood flow in the tiny arteries in your finger. This measurement, called a *finger plethysmographic waveform,* accurately reflects what is going on in your coronary arteries and all the arteries throughout your body.[5] We monitor and record this data several times during each treatment.

Just before the heart contracts again, the blood pressure cuffs rapidly deflate, thereby decreasing resistance to blood flow throughout the body (systolic pressure). Doing so "unloads" the heart, making it easier for your heart to pump blood with greater force. As the heart is able to do its job more efficiently and with greater ease, it demands less blood and oxygen. Very simply, EECP assists the heart, feeding it extra oxygen and nutrients and decreasing its workload.

You may ask, "What is the point of all this blood flow, and how does it help people who have blockages in their coronary arteries?" The answer to this question is the key to what makes EECP such a remarkable tool in the fight against heart disease. Mother Nature, in all her wisdom, recognizes that the heart is the most important organ in the body and is essential for life. Accordingly, she has provided the heart with a backup plan to obtain blood if the main arteries are blocked or dysfunctional, as is the case in people with heart disease. This backup plan is the vast network of collateral, or extra, microscopic blood vessels in and around the heart. These collateral vessels are really "potential" blood vessels, and they are lazy by nature. If all of the major arteries in and around the heart are able to bring enough blood to the heart muscle, the collateral vessels are not needed and remain inactive. However, if blockages in the main arteries prevent the heart from receiving adequate blood, the heart cries out to the body in the form of angina. Ideally, the body will respond by waking up those microscopic vessels and/or creating new ones to allow more blood to reach the heart. But in many individuals with heart disease, the body is not strong enough to develop collateral blood vessels on its own, and chronic angina persists. This is where EECP comes in.

As we all know, fluids travel the path of least resistance, and blood is no exception. In other words, it is easier for blood to flow through unblocked arteries than through blocked arteries. EECP sends more blood back up to the heart during its resting phase than blocked coronary arteries are used to accommodating, and so other blood vessels must step in. This is when Mother Nature's backup system swings into action. The increased blood flow created by EECP causes the tiny, lazy collateral blood vessels to wake up and begin doing their job. Once recruited in and around the heart, they enlarge and strengthen, creating new, lasting pathways for the blood to reach the parts of the heart that need it most, naturally bypassing the blockages. These collateral blood vessels set off a positive chain reaction: the overall blood and oxygen supply to the heart is improved, allowing the heart to function normally again. In turn, angina is reduced or eliminated, enabling the patient to return to the activities they thought they had given up forever.

So, in a nutshell, EECP is an external heart and circulatory assistant that helps the body heal itself. It strengthens the heart's oxygen and nutrient supply, creates new pathways for this increased supply to reach the heart, and decreases the heart's oxygen demand and workload, making its fundamental job easier. In fact, the heart works less strenuously when you are receiving an EECP treatment than when you are asleep! And nurturing and supporting the heart while it rests allows it to work more efficiently when you are active.

Is there such a thing as too much blood flow? No. The body is smart. It has an inherent regulatory control that protects against excessive blood flow. A good example is the eye. A German study found that patients with circulatory problems in the eye who were treated with EECP enjoyed an increase in ophthalmic artery blood flow, while individuals with normal ophthalmic arteries who received EECP treatments had no increase in blood flow to the eye. The study concluded that EECP may increase blood flow to the eye in people who need it, but not in people who do not.[6] Similarly, the body prevents any changes in blood pressure and blood flow from adversely affecting the brain, a process called *autoregulation*. So in both healthy people and heart disease sufferers, the increased blood flow in the body stimulated by EECP does not translate to adverse levels of blood flow to the brain.[7] As we will see in chapter 5, the treatment *does* enhance blood flow to the brain in people who need it, such as those suffering from a stroke or dementia. In these individuals, just as in those described above with impaired blood flow to the eye, the body recognizes the need for additional blood flow to the affected area and responds accordingly.

Can all of this blood flow cause a piece of plaque to break off and become lodged, causing a heart attack or stroke? No. Plaque in blood vessels is not soft or delicate. In fact, it is quite the opposite. Plaque is largely made up of calcium; therefore, it is hard and strong like bone, creating tremendous resistance to blood flow. The body, like everything else, obeys the laws of physics. One of these laws, as we have discussed, is that fluid travels the path of least resistance. It is easier for blood to travel through nondiseased vessels where there are no plaque obstructions than to fight its way through blocked arteries. This is precisely the process that naturally produces collateral blood vessels, and it explains why blood flow does not cause pieces of plaque to dislodge.

What Does EECP Do to Your Blood Vessels?

Blood vessels are not tubes or pipes like the ones under your sink. They are not fixed, inanimate structures. They are organs—alive, dynamic, and growing—that carry blood throughout your body. They need to be exercised in order to stay healthy, and the only way to exercise them is to give them adequate blood to transport. The more blood that flows through your blood vessels, the better they perform. Therefore, by increasing blood flow, EECP makes blood vessels healthier. I'll explain.

The friction, or shear stress, of blood moving along the endothelial cells (cells that line the blood vessels) releases natural chemicals. These chemicals, called *angiogenic growth factors*, stimulate blood vessels to grow and mature. In humans, the very powerful vascular endothelial growth factor (VEGF) increases by as much as 21 percent in response to just one hour of EECP.[8] This dramatic increase in VEGF levels persists for at least one month, which in biochemistry is a staggering length of time.[9]

The shear stress that EECP creates also has an anti-inflammatory effect. Researchers at the University of Pennsylvania's Institute for Medicine and Engineering found that increased shear stress of blood flow on blood vessels—as achieved during exercise—can mimic the anti-inflammatory actions of powerful medications used to fight chronic inflammatory diseases.[10] The study provides the first direct evidence that the mechanics of blood flow are themselves anti-inflammatory. Increased blood flow—whether achieved during exercise or EECP—is a natural way to protect blood vessels and counteract inflammation, a key underlying cause of heart disease.

EECP improves blood vessels' ability to expand and contract (vascular reactivity), another of the many ways in which the treatment recreates the beneficial effects of exercise and improves circulatory health. It does this by improving endothelial cell function throughout the body. Specifically, EECP affects two important substances that endothelial cells produce and release: nitric oxide (NO) and endothelin (ET-1).[11] These two substances are largely responsible for endothelial cell health and function. We will discuss each of them in turn.

Nitric oxide (also called *endothelial-derived relaxing factor*) promotes blood flow by dilating blood vessels. It also strengthens the arterial lining, making it resistant to clotting, cracking, and spasm, thereby helping arteries to function normally and protecting them from disease. There is considerable evidence that numerous conditions—including hypertension, obesity, high cholesterol, diabetes, heart failure, atherosclerosis, aging, and vascular injury—are associated with endothelial dysfunction and reduced nitric oxide levels. Anything that increases nitric oxide will have a long-term beneficial effect on heart disease and angina, and will improve the circulation in your entire body. EECP does just that. It increases nitric oxide by nearly 60 percent during treatment and by 20 percent one month after treatment.[12]

Endothelin has several damaging effects on the body. It impairs blood flow by prompting blood vessels to constrict, forcing the heart to work harder against the increased resistance. It also causes the body to retain salt and water by increasing the levels of two hormones, aldosterone and atrial natriuretic peptide, thus contributing to the development of hypertension and congestive heart failure (CHF).[13] To illustrate endothelin's potency, studies involving heart failure patients have shown that blocking its activity prolongs life. EECP reduces endothelin levels in the body by nearly 40 percent during treatment and by 20 percent one month after treatment.[14] EECP also markedly decreases levels of another vasoconstrictor, angiotensin II.[15]

These positive effects of EECP emerge almost instantly. In fact, typically, nitric oxide levels rise and endothelin levels fall following the very first EECP session, and these biochemical changes persist throughout the course of treatment and over subsequent months. This partly explains why some patients feel better within the first week of starting their EECP program. While it takes several weeks for collateral blood vessels to grow and develop, changes in cellular biochemistry occur almost immediately.[16]

A JUMP START

As passive exercise, EECP offers the jump start that heart disease sufferers need to get their blood flowing again and to set them on the path to better health and fuller lives. In the next chapter, we will look at the tremendous volume of evidence that makes EECP such an exciting alternative to surgery.

3

~

Clinical Proof That EECP Works

THE MOST EXCITING NEWS ABOUT EECP IS YET TO COME. Not only is it the most logical treatment for heart disease, which we now know to be a systemic condition. And not only is it simple, noninvasive, and painless. But we also have an enormous body of scientific evidence that unequivocally affirms that it works. EECP has been the focus of clinical research for more than thirty years. Leading medical journals, including the *Journal of the American College of Cardiology*, *Circulation*, and *Cardiology*, have published more than one hundred articles documenting EECP's safety and effectiveness. In this chapter, we will look at how the treatment has evolved over the years and at the proof that it is a powerful tool in the fight against heart disease.

IN THE BEGINNING

While EECP is a newer medical innovation, the technology at the heart of the treatment has existed for more than fifty years. In the early 1950s, two Harvard researchers—brothers by the name of Kantrowitz—first experimented with the concept of counterpulsation as a technique to assist patients with what they termed "coronary inadequacies."[1] A decade later, that research was used to develop an internal counterpulsation device called the *intra-aortic balloon pump* (IABP). The IABP consists of a catheter with a small balloon attached to the tip, which is inserted through an artery in the groin (the femoral artery) and threaded into the body's main artery (the aorta). The IABP supports circulation in critically ill cardiac patients by inflating during diastole, the heart's resting phase, to help increase oxygen and blood flow to the heart muscle through the coronary arteries. The balloon rapidly deflates just before the heart beats, decreasing the heart's workload. The IABP is a lifesaving device and is still used every day to help sustain critically ill patients in circulatory crisis by providing immediate relief to the parts of the heart that are starving for blood. The increased blood flow stimulates collateral vessels to grow and develop, creating new, sustainable pathways for blood and oxygen delivery throughout the heart. If this description sounds familiar, there is good reason. EECP works via exactly the same mechanism. The only difference is that the IABP works internally, while EECP works external to the body.

In the early 1960s, Birtwell, Soroff, and others developed the external counterpulsation device.[2] This first-generation apparatus was a hydraulic system that pumped water in and out of cuffs placed on the patient's legs. Along with promoting arterial blood flow back to the heart, like the IABP, this external unit offered the added circulatory advantage of stimulating flow from the veins and lymphatic vessels in the legs. Researchers were intrigued and eager to work with external counterpulsation because it was easy to use, it was safe, and it could duplicate the physical effects of the IABP while also promoting venous and lymphatic flow.

THE FIRST SIGNS OF SUCCESS

The Canadian Cardiovascular Society developed a classification system that gauges how angina symptoms affect an individual's quality of life and ability to function. The system consists of four classes, with class I angina being the mildest and class IV angina being the most severe. The scientific research on EECP has focused on individuals who have class III or class IV angina. Class III describes a patient who has marked limitations on their ordinary physical activities, such as walking one or two blocks or climbing one flight of stairs. Patients with class IV angina are unable to engage in almost any physical activity without discomfort, and they may even have angina at rest.[3]

In the early 1970s, external counterpulsation was found to increase survival among patients treated during a heart attack and during cardiogenic shock (complete circulatory system failure), and it was also found to relieve angina. One of the first studies of external counterpulsation was conducted in 1973 by Banas, Brilla, and Levine. In it, twenty-one patients suffering from angina (seven with class III and fourteen with class IV) received a one-hour treatment daily for five days. Immediately after receiving the five treatments, seventeen of the patients were completely angina free. After one month, some of the patients had experienced a mild recurrence of angina, but all remained significantly improved: ten had class I angina (defined as angina that may occur with strenuous activity or exercise only, not with ordinary daily activities), and eight had class II (which poses a slight limitation on ordinary activities such as walking or climbing stairs, but only when done rapidly or under emotional stress). This study was the first to demonstrate that external counterpulsation, by providing more blood and oxygen to the heart, reduce or eliminate angina. In addition to being reflected in the participants' everyday improvements, the results were documented objectively. When angiographies were performed on eleven patients after the treatment, five showed increases in the network of blood vessels (vascularity) around the heart.[4]

In another study, 129 patients experiencing a heart attack in an emergency room were treated with three hours of EECP during the first day, in addition to receiving the usual treatments of oxygen and medications. Researchers compared the outcomes of these patients to another group of 129 heart attack sufferers who were treated only with oxygen and medications. Those patients who were treated with EECP not only had a lower death (mortality) rate than the other group (8.3 percent versus 17.5 percent), they experienced fewer complications as well.[5] One study found that the standard death rate of 85 percent among patients in cardiogenic shock can be drastically reduced to 45 percent by treating them in the first day with three to five hours of EECP.[6]

Sign of the Times

Despite these striking documented benefits, EECP technology did not receive significant widespread attention in the United States during the 1970s. Instead, our focus during this time period was on emerging high-tech, invasive approaches, such as coronary artery bypass surgery (CABG) and angioplasty.

Dr. John Gibbon (1903–1973) invented the heart-lung machine, also known as the *cardiopulmonary bypass machine*, and it was first used successfully on a patient in 1953. It marked a dramatic advance in medicine. With this device, a surgeon was literally able to bypass both the heart and lungs and allow the machine to take over the pumping and oxygenation of blood, so the patient would remain alive while the surgeon operated on their heart. The machine's first use was to repair a birth defect in a woman by opening her heart muscle.

The first diagnostic coronary angiography was performed in 1958, enabling physicians to pinpoint blockages in coronary arteries and develop strategies to operate on them. In an angiography (also known as *cardiac catheterization*), a catheter is inserted into an artery in the arm or leg and guided to the heart, contrast dye is injected, and X-rays of the coronary arteries are taken to identify any blockages. This new diagnostic technique, coupled with added years of experience performing cardiac surgery, led physicians to assert in 1960 that it was safe to use the cardiopulmonary bypass machine to perform coronary artery bypass surgery. The first such operations were performed in the mid-1960s, and they continued to be refined for approximately a decade. By the time the first studies on EECP were published in the United States in the early 1970s, bypass had gained widespread popularity, with surgeons and hospitals moving quickly to incorporate it into their services. The popularity of bypass grew steadily—it was for many years the most widely performed operation worldwide—until 1995, when the number of procedures performed annually began to plateau. Still, more than 515,000 such operations are now performed each year in the United States at a cost of $31.3 billion.[7]

Bypass was not the only technologically advanced procedure that quickly gained credibility and large-scale adoption during this time. The first human coronary balloon angioplasty was performed in 1977, and the first use of a coronary stent in a human was reported in 1987. A variety of other cardiac interventional devices were also invented and perfected in the years from 1987 to 1993, including lasers, rotational atherectomy devices (Rotablator), and various types of stents. The use of angioplasty and stents has grown steadily since then; in 2000, the number performed annually in the United States surpassed that of bypass. The number of angioplasties, for example, skyrocketed by 324 percent between 1987 and 2002. Presently, 1,204,000 angioplasties and stent implantations are performed annually at a cost of $34.3 billion.[8]

Use in China

While the American medical establishment turned its attention in the 1970s to high-tech surgical procedures to treat heart disease, EECP was far from forgotten. Tremendous interest in the treatment was growing in China, where physicians were captivated by its non-invasiveness and cost-effectiveness. EECP is consistent with Eastern philosophy, which teaches that medical treatments should help the body heal itself, enhancing and aiding its natural tendencies rather than interfering with them. China has begun to adopt more Western approaches in recent years. But at the time, surgery and other invasive techniques were used only as an absolute last resort.

In the 1970s, Dr. Zeng Sheng Zheng and his colleagues at the Sun Yat-sen University of Medical Sciences in the People's Republic of

China refined the technology behind EECP, developing the more comfortable and easier to use sequential pneumatic (air) cuff mechanism. This is the design used today, in which the blood pressure cuffs inflate from the calves to the thighs to the buttocks, promoting the flow of blood back up toward the heart. Chinese scientists also added arm cuffs to the treatment, calling it SECP (sequential ECP).

By 1990, 1,800 EECP centers were operating in China. A large study of more than six thousand patients was published there, and it concluded that the treatment offered improvement to more than 90 percent of participants. Another long-term study there found that 74 percent of EECP patients maintained improvement in their heart disease symptoms seven years after completing their treatment, and they were four times less likely to suffer a cardiac death in the eight years after receiving EECP than heart patients treated with medication alone.[9]

Between the mid-1970s and the mid-1990s, EECP became the first and most trusted treatment for heart disease in many parts of China. A number of factors explain why. As mentioned, the Chinese tended to perform surgery only as a last resort. Therefore, invasive procedures such as bypass and angioplasty, which proliferated in the United States, were nearly unheard of in China. In addition to the prevailing preference for noninvasive treatments, EECP was attractive because of its proven effectiveness and safety.

The structure of China's health-care system at that time holds another key to understanding EECP's tremendous popularity there. Until several years ago, physicians in China were not paid per procedure or office visit. Instead, they received a salary based on their success in keeping their pool of patients out of the hospital. (The structure, of course, is just the opposite in the United States. Here, doctors are compensated when patients require consultations, undergo tests and procedures, or are hospitalized.) Therefore, the overall goal of physicians in China was to help patients avoid unnecessary procedures and complications and to stay healthy. It is no wonder that more than one million individuals there have received

EECP! And in China, EECP is not just a once-in-a-lifetime treatment. On the contrary, most individuals who receive EECP do so periodically, with regular maintenance programs being the norm.

Today, China's health-care industry is in a state of flux, and like many aspects of the country's culture, seems to be taking Western cues. The medical system appears to be heading toward a structure more like the one in the United States, and invasive procedures are being used more widely. However, many advocates of EECP are currently working to ensure that the treatment is considered to be in line with modern cardiac therapy, and to reestablish it as the heart disease treatment of choice.

China has found enormous success improving lives with EECP, not only in cardiac patients, but in individuals with a wide variety of circulatory conditions, including strokes, Parkinson's disease, and visual impairments. China is decidedly ahead of the curve in discovering and implementing EECP's varied applications, and it offers us an exciting glimpse of things to come. We will look at the long list of documented noncardiac benefits of EECP in chapter 5.

A FOOTHOLD IN THE UNITED STATES

Cardiologists in the United States began to show renewed interest in EECP upon the publication of a scientific paper in 1992. Authored by researchers at the State University of New York, Stony Brook, the article documented the results when EECP was provided to eighteen desperate heart patients who had debilitating angina despite all surgical treatments and medications and who were considered inoperable. All patients had nuclear stress tests before starting their EECP treatments, and all their tests were abnormal, indicating inadequate blood flow to areas of the heart. All eighteen patients received thirty-five one-hour EECP treatments over a seven-week period (one hour per day, five days per week). When the treatment course was complete, all patients' angina improved and no side effects were reported. Sixteen (89 percent) of them were symptom free during their usual daily activities. Twelve (66 percent) had completely normal nuclear stress tests at the end of the program, indicating that normal blood flow had been restored throughout the heart, while two patients (11 percent) had significantly improved (but still abnormal) stress tests. The fourteen patients (77 percent) with improved nuclear scans were able to exercise 22 percent longer on a treadmill after receiving EECP. In four patients (22 percent), stress test results did not change.[10]

These remarkable results shocked the cardiology community. But the real question was, would the benefits last? The answer came when the original team of researchers published a three-year follow-up study on the same eighteen patients. Some patients' medications had been adjusted in the time since their EECP treatment, and eight patients had received additional EECP treatments—but no other interventions—during the three years since their initial course. Of the original fourteen patients whose stress tests improved, eleven (79 percent) had sustained improvement over the three-year follow-up period, remaining symptom free. One had suffered a heart attack, one had undergone bypass surgery, and one was lost to follow-up. Of the four patients who had unchanged nuclear stress tests but improved angina, two remained without significant angina, one had had bypass surgery, and one had undergone angioplasty. These patients came into the original study with severe, disabling heart disease symptoms that had failed to respond to all medications and treatments prior to EECP. But three years after receiving EECP, fourteen (78 percent) of them remained free of disabling symptoms and none had died.[11]

A Longer Life Span
Can Mean More Heart Disease

The renewed interest in EECP was largely due to the changing face of the American cardiac patient. Advances in health care in recent decades have increased our life span, making Americans more likely to live long enough to develop heart disease. This trend extends to existing cardiac patients; new medications and treatments have extended their life expectancy as well, increasing the need for suitable treatments for older, frail heart disease sufferers who have advanced conditions. For example, the millions of individuals who underwent bypass surgeries and angioplasties in the 1970s through the early 1990s are surviving longer. As they age, symptoms of this chronic disease will continue to reappear, prompting them to return to their doctor each time. However, older cardiac patients are likely to develop additional medical problems, making it much more dangerous to perform repeat surgical or other invasive procedures. Given the growing population of aging, frail, and complicated heart disease sufferers, it is easy to see why cardiologists took note of these early, encouraging findings on EECP—a safe, noninvasive treatment option—and why researchers embarked on many additional studies to further evaluate EECP's efficacy.

The FDA Gives Its Stamp of Approval

In the ensuing years, numerous studies were published, and all reinforced EECP's safety and effectiveness. In response, the FDA approved EECP in 1995 as a treatment for chronic stable angina and cardiogenic shock, as well as for use during a heart attack. These are the same FDA-approved indications for the intra-aortic balloon pump (IABP). In a study from Dokkyo University School of Medicine, Tochigi, Japan, comparing the IABP to EECP in patients who underwent urgent angioplasty after a heart attack, the two devices were found to be equally effective in restoring lifesaving blood flow throughout the heart. In fact, EECP was slightly more successful in increasing blood pressure in collateral vessels and improving the strength of the heart's contraction.[12] After these studies were published, EECP was affirmed as a noninvasive IABP, and it joined the ranks of lifesaving devices. Most recently, in June 2002, the FDA expanded the list of EECP's approved uses to include the treatment of congestive heart failure. We will discuss this promising development in detail in chapter 4.

Published Studies Proliferate

As EECP was slowly introduced to patients across the country and abroad in the 1990s, the body of scientific literature on the treatment steadily grew. One of the most important areas of study focused on EECP's lasting benefits, which have since been confirmed time and again. One investigation by Dr. William Lawson, a leading researcher in the field of EECP, looked at thirty-three patients with the most advanced form of heart disease. These patients still suffered considerably despite having undergone multiple surgeries and invasive procedures and taking numerous medications. They each received thirty-five hours of EECP and were then followed for a period of five years. Initially after completing the course of EECP treatments, all thirty-three patients saw an improvement in their angina. Nuclear stress tests revealed that twenty-six (79 percent) of the subjects had improved blood flow in their hearts, and eleven (33 percent) of them were able to cut back on their cardiac medications. Over the following five years, thirteen (40 percent) of the patients received additional EECP treatments; twenty-nine (88 percent) were still alive. Of the twenty-six patients whose stress tests improved immediately after EECP, twenty-four required no surgery or procedures during the five years following their treatment, nor did they suffer a heart attack. Only one of the original group went on to have a heart attack, and two underwent surgery, an extraordinary statistic when you consider that these were classified as end-stage heart patients, being inoperable with symptoms that do not respond to other treatments or medications (refractory angina). Remarkably, these outcomes were similar to those of elective bypass surgery performed on low-risk, first-time cardiac patients.[13]

Multiple studies have documented the improved blood flow to the heart, or myocardial perfusion, that EECP creates. Positron emission tomography (PET) scan images, our most accurate measure of cardiac blood flow and oxygen delivery, captured before and after EECP, illustrate this phenomenon (see figure 5).[14] The body responds to this increased blood flow by developing and enlarging collateral coronary arteries—additional pathways for blood to reach the heart.

EECP not only improves angina and myocardial perfusion, it has also been shown to offer long-term preventative and protective benefits in heart disease patients. Another long-term follow-up study compared 117 patients who received EECP to 198 patients treated only with medications over a seven-year period. The researchers found that the patients treated with medications alone were 2.3 times more likely to have a heart attack or cardiac-related death than those who underwent EECP.[15]

Before EECP   **After EECP**

Figure 5. Positron emission tomography scans demonstrating improved blood flow to the heart after EECP.

Weighing the Alternatives

Let's compare some of this outcome data to bypass surgery and angioplasty data (see figure 6). The Bypass Angioplasty Revascularization Investigation, or BARI study, the largest randomized clinical trial to compare bypass surgery and angioplasty, found that 21 percent of bypass patients and 22 percent of angioplasty patients had heart attacks or died during the first five years after surgery. In addition, 8 percent of bypass patients and 54 percent of angioplasty patients required repeat surgery or other invasive procedures within

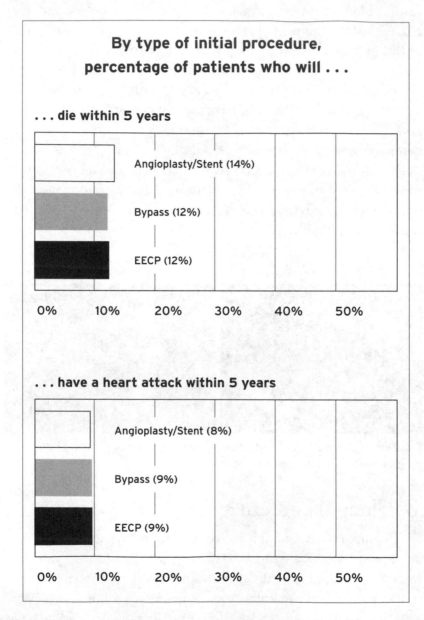

Figure 6. Risk of death or heart attack for angioplasty/stent, bypass, and EECP patients. Note that angioplasty/stent and bypass recipients were uncomplicated, first-time patients, while EECP recipients were end-stage patients who had failed surgery and/or invasive procedures.[16]

the five-year period.[17] During the first year of follow-up in the German Angioplasty Bypass Surgery Investigation, 18 percent of the patients who had bypass surgery died, had a subsequent heart attack, or required additional surgery.[18] The Randomized Intervention Treatment of Angina (RITA) study found that 16 percent of bypass patients and 17 percent of angioplasty patients had heart attacks or died during the first 6.5 years after surgery. In addition, 13 percent of bypass patients and 45 percent of angioplasty patients underwent repeat surgery or invasive procedures within the same time frame.[19]

A comparison of 323 refractory angina patients (who experience persistent symptoms despite trying all possible medications and invasive or surgical procedures) treated with EECP to 448 patients earlier in the progression of their heart disease who underwent elective, nonemergency angioplasty is also quite interesting. First, the EECP patients had much more complicated medical histories, including previous angioplasty (53.0 percent versus 33.3 percent), previous bypass surgery (42.1 percent versus 18.6 percent), previous heart attack (56.4 percent versus 27.8 percent), history of congestive

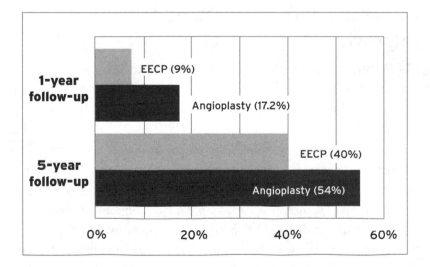

Figure 7. Repeat treatment rates for EECP and angioplasty patients.[20]

heart failure (16.8 percent versus 9.2 percent), and history of diabetes (37.9 percent versus 23.5 percent). In following up one year after the two groups of patients received their respective treatments, researchers at the University of Pittsburgh (Pennsylvania) found that the survival rate was the same in both groups, over 96 percent. The percentage of patients who underwent bypass surgery in the year since the initial treatment was also the same in both groups, about 5 percent. Repeat angioplasty rates were higher than repeat EECP rates during the first year. Remember, the EECP patients were much sicker at the outset, had more complicated medical histories, and had fewer repeat treatments, yet they achieved the same outcome with EECP as the less-ill patients did with angioplasty (see figure 7).[21]

WIDE-RANGING BENEFITS

From reducing patients' time in the hospital to helping them become active again to improving their emotional outlook and enjoyment of life, EECP's benefits are wide-ranging and dramatic. Here, we will review them in detail.

Increasing Activity Levels and Improving Quality of Life

EECP enhances a patient's ability to exercise and engage in physical activity. The increase is measured in terms of treadmill time and myocardial perfusion during an exercise stress test. In one study, investigators at New York Medical College, Valhalla, looked at patients' maximum exercise ability before and after receiving EECP. Twenty-five patients with angina exercised as much as they could until they had to stop, whether due to chest pain, shortness of breath, fatigue, or other symptoms (called a *maximal symptom-limited exercise tolerance test*). At the end of their thirty-five-hour EECP program, twenty-three of the twenty-five patients (93 percent) had reduced or eliminated symptoms and improved their ability to perform daily routine and leisure activities without limitation. During the stress

PREDICTING SUCCESS

Is there a way to forecast which patients will achieve the best results with EECP? This is always an important question in medicine. We try to select the patients we expect will do well with a particular treatment in order to help as many patients as possible. With EECP, the anatomy of the heart's circulation seems to play a role in predicting success. Three major arteries feed the heart. Of course, they later branch and divide numerous times, so there are many important arteries in and around the heart, but at the beginning of the heart's circulation, there are three major arteries. Patients are classified based on how many of these three arteries are diseased or narrowed, and they are referred to as having one-, two-, or three-vessel disease. In one clinical study, fifty patients underwent a cardiac catheterization to classify the severity of their heart disease by determining how many of their major arteries were blocked. After completing a full course of thirty-five EECP treatments, all patients reported decreased angina, and each underwent a nuclear stress test to quantify their success. Of those with one, two, and three major blockages, 95 percent (eighteen out of nineteen), 90 percent (seventeen out of nineteen), and 42 percent (five out of twelve), respectively, had improvement in cardiac blood flow. The overall average rate of effectiveness was 80 percent (forty out of fifty), EECP's often-quoted success rate.[22]

In trying to predict which patients will do best with EECP, it is believed that if a patient has at least one good vessel, whether it is one of their three original vessels or an open vessel from a previous bypass surgery or other procedure, that vessel will allow blood to flow deeper into the heart muscle before branching into the collateral network. This open artery improves blood pressure and volume in the farthest reaches of the heart's circulation, which paves the way for lasting results. More extensive heart disease responds more slowly because there are fewer available collateral vessels to bring blood to the heart, but these patients also respond well in time. Therefore, patients with extensive disease routinely receive extended courses of treatment (fifty treatments or more) in order to achieve the desired results.

test following their treatment, these patients were able to walk longer and faster on the treadmill before experiencing symptoms. Their EKGs and cardiac blood flow improved, even though they were exercising more vigorously than before. These results illustrate that when the heart gets more blood flow, it is able to work harder, longer, and more efficiently.[23]

Another study, involving 175 angina patients, was performed at seven centers in the United States, Europe, and Asia. Three-quarters of the participants had previously undergone angioplasty or stent placement, and 41 percent had undergone bypass surgery. About half (51 percent) had suffered at least one heart attack, and 21 percent had diabetes. All subjects underwent a maximal symptom-limited exercise tolerance test before receiving EECP to measure their baseline ability to exercise. After receiving a full course of thirty-five EECP treatments, angina improved in 85 percent of the patients, and none of the patients' conditions worsened. Ninety-seven of the patients underwent stress tests during which they exercised at the same level as they did during the test prior to treatment, meaning the test was terminated when the patient reached

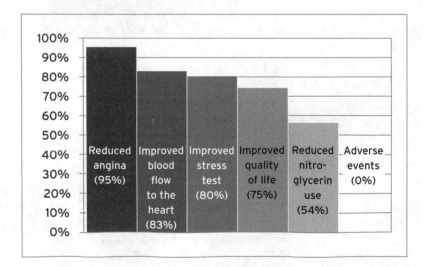

Figure 8. The benefits of EECP that last three or more years.

their pre-EECP maximal exercise level. Compared to the baseline test, 83 percent of the patients had improved blood flow to their heart. The remainder of the patients underwent a maximal stress test, similar to the one before receiving EECP, and all were able to exercise significantly longer before they had to stop. In addition, 54 percent of those patients whose maximal exercise capacity improved after EECP had corresponding improvement in blood flow to their heart. When an individual exercises to the maximum, their heart requires much more blood. Since EECP does not open blocked arteries, this study demonstrates that the treatment created *natural* bypasses, improving blood flow to the heart *around* the blockages, in 54 percent of participants. Follow-up six months later found that patients retained these benefits.[24]

Reducing Hospital Stays

EECP has also been shown to reduce the frequency and length of hospital stays for the sickest heart patients. A study in Ireland involved forty inoperable patients whose angina did not respond to medications. At the end of thirty-five EECP treatments, 87 percent of participants responded with dramatically improved angina, ability to exercise, and blood flow to the heart. The average number of days they spent in the hospital dropped from 14.5 in the year prior to receiving EECP to 7.8 in the year following treatment. EECP had a significant impact on these patients' quality of life. They experienced improvement in physical functioning, general health, energy, emotional health, and social functioning.[25]

Improving Emotional Health

Patients' sense of well-being—their general perception of their health and quality of life—also improves with EECP. One study from the State University of New York, Stony Brook, looked at both the treatment's quantifiable physical outcomes and its psychosocial effects. After completing their course of EECP, nuclear stress tests revealed that 75 percent of participants had improved blood flow to the heart. The average frequency of all participants' angina decreased by 85 percent, and their average nitroglycerin use dropped 96 percent. No patients reported psychological or emotional stress as a result of the treatment. In the formal psychosocial evaluation after treatment was complete, all patients reported improvement in their energy level, sense of well-being, overall health condition, and ability to work. Two-thirds reported improvement in their family life and social life, and one-third reported improvement in sexual activity.[26]

Another study, conducted at Massachusetts General Hospital in Boston, demonstrated that EECP significantly reduces depression, anxiety, and physical manifestations of emotional stress (somatization). Given the fact that depression significantly increases the risk of cardiac-related death, EECP's ability to alleviate depression is a critically important finding.[27]

A NEW SET OF RULES

Numerous other studies conducted throughout the 1990s confirmed that EECP improves exercise capacity, blood flow to the heart, and quality of life and that it reduces angina, heart attacks, surgery rates, nitroglycerin use, and the frequency and length of hospital stays in even the sickest heart patients. Despite this data, however, most physicians in the United States were unwilling to change the way they treated their heart patients. By and large, they would not consider offering EECP even to their end-stage cardiac patients—those who were unable to undergo additional surgeries or procedures and were still suffering despite being on maximum medications. Most physicians refused to accept that EECP worked. They discounted the research, suggesting the documented improvements were due to the placebo effect (because patients believed they would get better from the treatment). But how could patients change their EKGs, stress tests, and nuclear scans by just thinking positively? Clearly, ample scientific evidence existed to rule out the placebo effect.

THE SCIENTIFIC GOLD STANDARD

The gold standard of clinical research is the randomized, placebo-controlled trial, in which subjects are randomly divided into two groups: one that will receive the real treatment and one that will get a fake, or sham, treatment. The group that receives the sham treatment is called the *control group*. None of the subjects know which group is which; they all have an experience that looks and feels like the real thing. Only the physicians conducting the research know who is receiving an actual medical therapy and who is not. Those who evaluate the study's results are also unaware of which group is which until their calculations are complete, thus ensuring the data is interpreted with complete objectivity.

Many doctors who discounted the research on EECP criticized the fact that none of the studies included a control group. They wanted a gold-standard study.

Keep in mind, though, that comparative studies (which compare outcomes in two different treatment groups without a control group) and outcome studies (which follow one treatment group over time) such as the ones conducted to evaluate the effectiveness of EECP up to that point are well-accepted and widely used to shape medical practices. Bypass surgery, angioplasty, and stents are cases in point. There has never been, nor will there ever be, a randomized, placebo-controlled study of real versions of these invasive procedures versus sham versions. Medical ethics prohibit them, because sham procedures would expose patients to risks of bleeding, infection, heart attack, stroke, or even death while offering them no potential benefit whatsoever. In the case of bypass surgery, performing a sham procedure would require a surgeon to remove a vein from the subject's leg, cut open their chest, and then discard the vein and close the chest without performing the operation. A sham angioplasty or stent procedure would require a cardiologist to insert a needle into the patient's groin, thread a catheter into a blocked coronary artery, and then pull the catheter out without performing a procedure. Then researchers would have to follow, over months or years, the control group patients and compare their outcomes to those who underwent real procedures. Obviously, these invasive procedures could never be held to the gold standard of scientific research.

Instead, physicians have concluded that bypass surgery, angioplasty, and stent placements are useful in treating coronary artery disease by comparing data on those who underwent these procedures with those who were treated with medications only. In the case of bypass surgery, these comparative studies showed that only patients with very specific conditions benefit more from bypass surgery than from medication. The specific disease states that have been shown to benefit from bypass surgery are significant left main coronary artery blockage, triple-vessel disease with an ejection fraction of less than 50 percent, or an equivalent anatomic state. No studies support bypass surgery in other, more common clinical circumstances, such as those that would be treated with single or double bypass procedures, or triple-vessel disease with normal ejection fraction.[28]

So even without studies involving a control group, these invasive procedures became the norm in treating heart disease. Today, these procedures are performed at a rate of more than 1.7 million per year. Despite the widespread use of invasive procedures with only comparative and outcome studies to support them, the medical community held EECP to a higher standard.

Earning the Gold

The medical community's skepticism about EECP was finally quieted in 1999, when leading cardiologists from Columbia, Yale, Harvard, and other universities published the results of their Multicenter Study of Enhanced External Counterpulsation, or MUST-EECP. In the study, half of the 139 participating angina patients received thirty-five real EECP treatments, while the other half received thirty-five sham (placebo) treatments. Patients receiving a placebo treatment got on the EECP bed, were connected to an EKG, and had the cuffs wrapped around their legs. However, the cuffs would squeeze only minimally, and therefore did not promote blood flow to the heart. These control group patients did not know they were getting a sham treatment, since they had never received a real treatment to compare against.

Treadmill stress tests were performed on both groups before and after treatment. During the test following treatment, those who had received genuine EECP were able to exercise significantly longer without symptoms or EKG changes than they could prior to the treatment. There was no difference in the sham group's ability to exercise without such abnormalities. These results mean that the real EECP group had more blood and oxygen flowing to their hearts after treatment, and they were therefore able to exercise longer before the EKG indicated their heart's demand for blood was exceeding its supply. They also had less angina and used less nitroglycerin than before EECP. There were no adverse events, side effects, or treatment complications in either group.[29] At the end of the thirty-five-hour treatment course, and again one year later, patients who received actual EECP reported sustained improvement in their ability to perform daily living activities, ability to work, pain level, energy level, confidence in their health, ability to socialize, anxiety level, depression, and angina.[30]

The MUST-EECP study prompted Medicare to begin paying for EECP in 1999. Since then, most private health insurance companies have followed suit, and dozens of additional studies have demonstrated that EECP is an effective treatment for nearly all patients with coronary artery disease, including high-risk, complicated patients such as those who have already undergone multiple cardiac procedures, those who have diabetes or congestive heart failure, the elderly, and the frail.

Applying EECP in Diverse Settings

The MUST-EECP study was conducted in the ivory towers of institutions such as Yale, Columbia, and Harvard. Its results were impressive, and they prompted Medicare to formally recognize the treatment. But another group was looking at whether EECP was more widely applicable. The EECP Clinical Consortium, organized in 1995, included diverse practice settings (university hospitals, community hospitals, physicians' offices, and rehabilitation facilities) with varying degrees of experience in treating patients with EECP. Its goal: to assess whether the treatment was more successful when offered in certain clinical settings than in others.

One consortium study looked at 2,991 patients who had received EECP at eighty-four different sites across the country. All patients tolerated the treatment without difficulty, and angina improved by at least one class in 73.4 percent of participants. Women and men did equally well, and patients treated in a small private practice did just as well as those treated in a university hospital. At the end of their treatment, none of the patients had experienced a decline in their cardiac health or any negative effects from the treatment.[31]

The International EECP Patient Registry (IEPR) is another large-scale initiative to document EECP's safety, effectiveness, and patterns of use. Established in 1998, the IEPR is an independent, anonymous, volunteer patient registry housed at the University of Pittsburgh's Epidemiology Data Center. During the IEPR's first phase, more than five thousand angina patients treated in 140 centers around the globe (121 in the United States and 19 abroad) were enrolled, and their progress was followed for three years. Here are some fast facts about the participants:

- The average age was 66.8 years (in all, 59.7 percent of the patients were over sixty-five).
- The majority, 75.5 percent, were male.
- The average time since they had been diagnosed with heart disease was 10.8 years.

- The majority, 78 percent, had multivessel disease.

- Most, 85.8 percent, had undergone at least one bypass surgery and/or angioplasty or stent placement before receiving EECP.

- Two-thirds, 67.6 percent, had suffered at least one heart attack before receiving EECP.

- Nearly one-third, 31.7 percent, had congestive heart failure.

- Many, 41.3 percent, had diabetes.

- The vast majority, 84 percent, were deemed inoperable.

After following these patients for three years, IEPR researchers published impressive data. The lasting improvement in angina was staggering. Figure 9 presents a summary of their progress. Before receiving EECP, 68.8 percent of the patients regularly used nitroglycerin. Three years later, that number had decreased to 44.4 percent (see figure 10).[32]

Looking ahead, the IEPR's second phase will involve treating patients with EECP until a preset goal of reduced symptoms is achieved, rather than stopping after the standard thirty-five-hour course. Several substudies will examine how EECP improves particular issues related to diabetes, peripheral vascular disease, and erectile dysfunction.

Angina Class	Class IV	Class III	Class II	Class I	No Angina
Before EECP	23%	58%	15%	4%	0%
Three Years after EECP	5%	16%	25%	19%	35%

Figure 9. Angina classification before and after EECP.

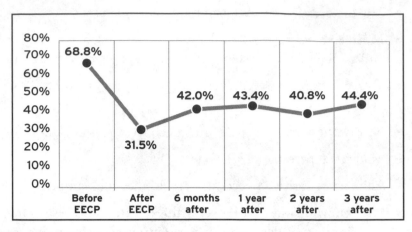

Figure 10. Nitroglycerin use before and after EECP.

Using EECP Sooner Rather Than Later

The decision to reserve EECP until all other options have failed is a purely American construct, a result of our preference for invasive procedures. To illustrate this point, consider that while only 5 percent of the world's population resides in the United States, almost half of the world's angioplasties, stents, and bypass operations are performed here. These procedures are typically the first step in treating an American's heart disease, but they are more often reserved as last resorts in other parts of the world such as Canada and Europe.[33] And as we saw earlier, in China EECP achieves equally impressive results when it is used sooner rather than later in the progression of a patient's illness.

Turkey is another country that usually offers noninvasive treatment earlier than the United States. The average EECP patient in Turkey is younger than their American counterpart (57.8 years versus 67 years) and receives the treatment for milder symptoms (only 67 percent of Turkish EECP patients have class III or class IV angina versus 84 percent of those in the United States). EECP recipients in Turkey are also less likely to have undergone a prior angioplasty, stent, or bypass operation (54 percent versus 86 percent), and they are less likely to be considered inoperable (55 percent versus 81 percent). A study comparing Turkish EECP patients with Americans who received the treatment found that both groups had the same success rate, measured in terms of reduced angina, reduced nitroglycerin use, and improved quality of life.[34]

Using EECP to Treat Unstable Angina

Most patients in the United States who are treated with EECP have stable (predictable), chronic angina, and the treatment's benefits begin to emerge within a few weeks. But what about patients with unstable angina, the type that comes on suddenly and quickly becomes more severe? In one study, researchers examined how both types of angina patients responded to EECP. Both groups enjoyed substantial reduction in their angina; 74 percent of the stable patients and 80 percent of the unstable patients improved to the same degree. And both groups experienced the same rates of reduction in nitroglycerin use along with improved mood and ability to enjoy physical activities without limitation. While the medical community has not come to a consensus on where EECP belongs in the scope of treatments offered to patients with unstable angina, these findings indicate that it does have a place and should be further investigated.[35]

UNHEARD-OF SUCCESS RATES

The large body of clinical research on EECP offers consistent evidence that the treatment is suitable and safe for nearly every heart patient. Whether your heart disease is newly diagnosed or you have been living with it for years, whether you have no other notable ailments or have numerous complex medical conditions, EECP achieves practically unheard-of success rates of 80 to 90 percent. In the next chapter, we will look at exactly what you should expect during treatment, how patients who have undergone other cardiac procedures in the past respond to EECP, and what makes it an appropriate treatment for so many different groups of heart disease sufferers.

4

Logistics, Specifics, and Special Cases

WITH A FULL, CURRENT UNDERSTANDING of heart disease as a system-wide illness and the highly effective, system-wide treatment approach that EECP offers, most patients want to know how the treatment might apply to their particular situation. How will it fit into your daily life? What is the typical treatment schedule? What if you have undergone other cardiac procedures in the past? Is EECP just as effective in women as in men? What if you have other ailments, such as diabetes or congestive heart failure? In this chapter, we will answer all of these questions and more.

LOGISTICS AND SPECIFICS

EECP is like passive exercise: it gets your blood pumping the same way a vigorous, sustained cardiovascular workout does, but it does so while you're lying down! While EECP does not offer *all* the benefits of exercise, such as increasing your metabolic rate or burning calories, it does recreate the circulatory benefits of exercise while you are relaxing on the treatment bed. The repetitive blood flow stimulates your blood vessels to grow, develop, and function at their highest level.

CASE STUDY

Patricia C., age forty-six, was relatively healthy, until one day, while attending her son's high school graduation, she had a sudden heart attack—right on the football field. From that moment, she had persistent angina without relief. She underwent an angioplasty and a stent placement, but her condition did not change. Four months later, she had a repeat angioplasty followed by radiation (brachytherapy), again with little improvement. Finally, she had a triple bypass. But within one month, her angina returned, just as severe as before. A repeat catheterization found that two of the three bypasses had already closed. Patricia's angina occurred daily with most activities, at rest and even during sleep. Her husband, sons, and parents would not let her do much of anything for fear she would have another heart attack. Her quality of life was extremely poor. Out of desperation, her cardiologist referred her for EECP. After completing her EECP treatment, her angina was very rare and quite mild, and she went from taking approximately twelve nitroglycerin tablets per day to taking two, one, or none at all. She was able to walk, sleep, cook, shop, and do just about anything without symptoms. "I am so much better," she said. "I am ready to start exercising again. I feel so good that I'm planning a trip to Italy!"

Just as with exercise, it takes time for EECP's positive effects to emerge, and repetition is the key. The body must recognize that a physiologic change needs to happen, then it must make the change, and then it must incorporate the change into its regular functioning so the benefits will persist. You may know this from your own experience. If you begin to lift weights because you want to strengthen your arms, but you only do so once, what will happen? You will likely be sore and tired the next day, but not stronger. You must lift weights day after day for your muscles to understand that a change is to occur and to respond accordingly. The same rule applies if you want to improve your cardiovascular fitness. If you begin a walking program and walk ten miles, but only once, what will happen? You will likely be sore and tired the next day, but you will not have more stamina or pep. You must engage in aerobic activity *regularly and frequently* for the body to understand that a physiologic change needs to occur and to respond by increasing your stamina. The need for frequent repetition also applies to EECP, the passive form of exercise.

Treatment Schedule

Since the body requires repetition to be trained to function differently, the typical EECP treatment course consists of thirty-five one-hour sessions. This magic number was not chosen randomly; it is based on the clinical research of the last fifteen years and grew out of China's experience with EECP. The Chinese began by providing patients with thirty-six treatments and performing stress tests after every twelve treatments to monitor their progress. Some patients improved after twelve treatments, even more did so after twenty-four treatments, and by the thirty-sixth treatment, EECP's effect had reached a plateau in the majority of patients. Follow-up six months later found that the benefits were sustained and even improved somewhat.[1] Of course, unlike the Chinese, who typically work six days per week, Americans are accustomed to a five-day workweek. To accommodate this schedule when EECP was reintroduced to the United States, the treatment regimen was adapted to one treatment per day, five days per week, for seven weeks. All of the Western clinical studies have been conducted based on this thirty-five-hour schedule, and it has become the standard of care among EECP providers in the Western world.

Doubling up. If you prefer, you may condense the overall length of your EECP program and achieve the same clinical results by taking two treatments per day. If you do opt for a second treatment on any given day, you must take a break of at least one hour between the two sessions. Regardless of the schedule you choose, regularity is the key to success with EECP, so doubling up one day does not mean you may skip your treatment the next day. The more regular you are with your treatments, the better your long-term results will be.

Seeing results. Many patients ask when they can expect to start feeling the treatment's benefits. This is a good question, and it is important for patients to begin their treatment program with realistic expectations. Most patients begin to experience beneficial results from EECP between their fifteenth and twenty-fifth treatments. These benefits include increased stamina, improved sleeping patterns, decreased angina, and less reliance on nitroglycerin and other medications. There is variation, certainly, and some patients start to feel better as soon as their first week of treatment.

Additional treatments. Although all the clinical studies confirm that thirty-five treatments are essential to achieve benefit with EECP, we must recognize that these studies, like most medical research, were performed in a "perfect world." By this I mean that only patients with narrowly defined coronary artery disease and angina were included. Patients with additional medical problems, scheduling conflicts, and other issues that would inhibit their response to the treatment were excluded. Therefore, while the typical course of treatment is thirty-five sessions, EECP providers around the country agree that, in some circumstances, additional treatments are medically necessary. Additional treatments are most often recommended when an individual's lifestyle is still limited after completing the initial thirty-five treatments and they continue to suffer with chest pain, shortness of breath, fatigue, or other symptoms. I have found that the most common reasons for extending treatment are as follows:

1. While EECP is painless and comfortable, some individuals take more time than others to adjust to the treatment. This prolonged period of adjustment may be due to anxiety or fear of the unknown, other medical problems, frailty, or low tolerance to the pressure from the cuffs. When this is the case, the patient will require a gradual increase in the length of each treatment and the amount of pressure used until the target sixty-minute treatment time at full pressure (260 mmHg) is achieved. This may take from several days to two weeks, in some cases, and would prolong the overall treatment regimen since the full

benefit of the program is obtained from thirty-five one-hour sessions at full pressure. In all the clinical research on EECP, each subject was treated at full pressure for a period of sixty minutes during each of thirty-five treatments, beginning with the first session.

2. Patients with poor leg circulation (peripheral vascular disease) are slower to respond to EECP. Since they have less blood in their legs to begin with, less blood is being pumped back up to their heart with each squeeze of the cuffs. All of the clinical research on EECP has excluded subjects with peripheral vascular disease to ensure that all participants, beginning with the very first treatment, have optimal blood flow to their heart. Patients with poor peripheral circulation do achieve great results with EECP, but in most cases, they require more than thirty-five treatments. I have found that such individuals need at least fifty treatments to achieve clinical benefit. The first two to three weeks of their program is typically spent improving their leg circulation, and improved cardiac circulation follows.

3. Some patients may complete thirty-five treatments but continue to experience symptoms and limitations due to the advanced stage of their heart disease or their particular physiology. In the clinical research, these individuals were considered "nonresponders" to EECP and were not offered additional treatments. However, in day-to-day clinical practice, our goal is to make *every* patient a "responder." Giving these individuals ten to fifteen additional treatments typically allows them to enjoy EECP's full benefits.

4. Some patients may have a gap in their EECP treatment regimen. Whether due to illness, unexpected travel, or various other circumstances, this interruption is not recommended because it delays the patient's clinical response. As a result, additional treatments are required to make up for lost time.

A recent study formally documented the benefits of additional EECP treatments beyond the initial thirty-five sessions. It reviewed data on 4,733 patients who were treated at 106 practice sites across the country. Researchers found that 17 percent of the patients received more than thirty-five successive hours of treatment as part of their initial course. Seventeen of the busiest sites reported that more than 30 percent of their patients received more than thirty-five consecutive treatment hours. (This figure is consistent with my practice as well.) In general, the investigators found that patients' results were proportional to the number of EECP treatments they received. They concluded that, while a minimum of thirty-five hours is needed to achieve optimal benefit, even further benefit can be achieved when a patient goes on to have more than thirty-five treatments.[2]

Repeat Procedures

As you know, heart disease is a chronic, progressive illness. Therefore, once patients receive treatment for it, it is possible—even likely—that their symptoms will resurface at some point in the future and require further treatment. Patients and their families are periodically faced with complex decisions about whether and when to undergo repeat treatments, and which treatments are likely to offer the best results. They must weigh potential risks against quality of life concerns and factor in other medical issues that may complicate the situation. They may also be unwilling to undergo additional invasive procedures. All of these considerations make EECP the only treatment option in some cases, and the preferable one in others.

EECP after bypass surgery. Bypass grafts tend to close over time, impairing blood flow to the heart and typically leading to the return of a patient's symptoms. When this occurs, changes in their coronary artery anatomy sometimes make a second operation too technically difficult. Or, patients may have developed other health problems that would preclude them from undergoing a bypass operation again. Individuals who are physically able to tolerate surgery, but undecided about whether to undergo another bypass, grapple with the reality that the procedure brings twice the risk the second time around. Others, despite being physically able, may simply refuse to have surgery again. Many of my patients have said, "Having open-heart surgery once is more than enough!"

Countless bypass patients fall into one of the above categories, and they may want to consider the alternatives. So the question arises: how does EECP affect patients who have undergone bypass surgery but now have closed bypass grafts? One study, conducted at the State University of New York, Stony Brook, set out to answer this question. It compared twenty-five patients who received EECP after their bypass grafts had closed with thirty-five EECP patients who had never undergone bypass surgery. Catheterizations were performed on all patients prior to starting EECP, and patients were classified by the number of blockages in either their original arteries or their bypass grafts. Patients with one or two narrowed bypass grafts did just as well with EECP as those with one or two blockages in their native arteries (80 to 88 percent success rate). The surprise from this study was that former bypass patients with three narrowed bypass grafts received as much benefit from EECP as all patients with single- and double-vessel disease, and they enjoyed much greater benefit than those with triple-vessel disease in their native arteries. The bottom line: post-bypass patients usually respond extremely well to EECP, and they can expect the same results as those who have not undergone surgery in the past.[3]

EECP after angioplasty or stent placement. Approximately 30 percent of patients who undergo angioplasty or stent placements find that the targeted blood vessels close again (a process called *restenosis*) within the first six months. As a result, repeat interventions are frequently performed to reopen these narrowed vessels. Sometimes, however, repeat procedures may be prohibited due to scar tissue buildup or certain anatomical changes in the coronary arteries. Or, as is often the case with bypass patients, individuals may refuse to undergo another angioplasty or stent procedure after the first has failed. For this reason, many patients who receive EECP have undergone angioplasty and stent placements at some point in the past. Significant research has examined how these patients respond to EECP, as compared to those EECP recipients who have not been through such procedures.

In one study from the International EECP Patient Registry at the University of Pittsburgh (Pennsylvania), 3,179 patients who had already undergone and failed to benefit from an angioplasty or stent procedure and turned to EECP as a last resort were compared to 215 patients who were candidates for invasive procedures but instead chose EECP first. The study found that the patients who underwent angioplasty and stent placement first responded to EECP with decreased angina and nitroglycerin use, and their angina improved at a rate similar to the EECP-first patients. Treatment with EECP resulted in sustained, and often progressive, reduction in angina in both groups over the following six months. The authors went one step further, concluding that EECP should be offered as a first-line treatment for heart disease.[4]

Incidentally, when EECP is provided immediately after an angioplasty or stent placement, it reduces the rate of restenosis (blood vessels reclosing) by as much as 30 percent. Therefore, EECP could help improve the success rates and long-term benefit of these invasive techniques if it was offered to patients immediately following their recovery from the procedure.[5]

EECP after EECP. Patients who receive EECP, just like any other treatment, may need to return for additional courses to address recurrent symptoms. Clinical experience and medical literature widely support the fact that some patients require and respond favorably to repeat courses of EECP. The University of California San Francisco Medical Center recently studied 1,192 patients who underwent a standard thirty-five-hour treatment regimen and found that 18 percent returned for additional treatment within two years. The average length of time before patients returned was just over one year. Reasons for repeating EECP were persistent and/or increasing

CASE STUDY

Herb S. had suffered a heart attack and underwent bypass surgery at age thirty-nine, and again at age fifty-one. He was an elite amateur tennis player all of his life, and he was able to return to singles tennis after each of his surgeries with the help of aggressive rehabilitation. At age sixty-three, his angina, which severely limited his activity level, slowly and progressively returned. He was unable to climb one flight of stairs without chest pain, let alone pick up a tennis racket. His cardiologist told him he was not a candidate for additional operations and referred him for EECP instead. Herb did exceptionally well with the treatment. His angina disappeared, and he was able to return to the tennis court for a few volleys. Several months later, he had a mild recurrence of angina and received another round of EECP treatments, which enabled him to play doubles. A few months after that, Herb again experienced some angina and he went through the program once more. By the time he finished his third round of treatments, he was playing singles tennis again without any problem.

angina. The repeat regimen was effective: 70 percent experienced a significant decrease in angina and had a corresponding decrease in nitroglycerin use.[6] Other studies echo these findings, confirming that initial and second courses of EECP are similarly effective.[7] Researchers have found that approximately 40 percent of patients treated successfully with EECP will require repeat courses of treatment within the first three to five years.[8] Medicare and most private insurers pay for additional rounds of EECP.

For most patients who return for additional rounds of EECP, the decision is easy. Unlike invasive procedures, there are no concerns about risks or complications. And since the treatment is comfortable and noninvasive, patients do not feel emotional stress or apprehension at the prospect of returning, as they often do with surgery. On the contrary, many look forward to it!

SPECIAL CASES: SUBPOPULATIONS

Not all heart disease sufferers are created alike. Some, such as the elderly and frail, are particularly high risk. Others, such as women, have anatomical considerations that often make them poor candidates for the invasive cardiac procedures commonly offered to men. Here, we will examine how EECP provides a safe, effective, and welcome treatment option for these groups.

Elderly and Frail Patients

As we saw earlier, the elderly and frail comprise a high-risk and growing population of heart disease sufferers. These individuals respond extremely well to EECP. In one study, I reported on twenty-four of my patients over the age of eighty (their average age was 84.75 years). After EECP, twenty-three (96 percent) experienced reduced symptoms, increased activity level, and improved physical mobility and emotional outlook as a result of the treatment. EECP was found to be a safe treatment for this population; no adverse events were reported.[9] In another study, from the International EECP Patient Registry at the University of Pittsburgh, 249 patients over eighty years of age were assessed immediately after receiving EECP, and again one year later. Immediately following treatment, 76 percent of the participants reported improved ability to perform physical activities and reduced symptoms, and 81 percent of these responders maintained their benefit at the one-year follow-up.[10] These studies are important because they demonstrate that EECP is both effective and harmless in this population, which is at an increased risk of complication (such as heart attack, death, bleeding, infection, or stroke) from invasive procedures and is more likely to prefer a noninvasive treatment option.

Women versus Men

We know by now that heart disease is not a man's disease. In fact, not only is it the number-one killer of both men and women in the United States, but almost as many women are disabled by the symptoms and limitations arising from heart disease as are men (1.9 million versus 2 million).[11] The numbers are staggering. Of female heart disease sufferers aged fifty-five to sixty-four, 36 percent are disabled by the condition. That number rises to 55 percent among women with heart disease over the age of seventy-five.[12]

CASE STUDY

Irene D., age sixty, underwent a triple bypass operation after suffering a heart attack, but her symptoms returned soon after. "I started feeling so tired. I'd fall asleep on my husband's shoulder in a restaurant. I could pitch a baseball to my grandchildren, but I couldn't run the bases. My former cardiologist said, 'You're almost sixty. You don't need to run the bases.' But I can't be the sick grandma. That's not who I am." After EECP, Irene said, "I'm doing terrific. I'm no longer yawning in my clients' faces. My thinking is so much clearer. People say, 'What are you doing? You look so much better. You're glowing.' The treatment lasted me a year and a half the first time, and then I went back. I decided, if I have to repeat it every two or three years, then I'm going to repeat it every two or three years. I'll tell you what—it beats crackin' my chest."

Treating female heart disease sufferers poses serious challenges for physicians who rely on invasive procedures. First, since women tend to have small arteries, they are often physically unable to undergo angioplasty, stent placement, or bypass surgery. Those who can receive these treatments must reconcile with the facts: women find it much more difficult than men to recover from invasive cardiac procedures, and their risk of complication is significantly higher.

Procedural complications account for half of all deaths resulting from angioplasty and stent placements, and they are a particular problem for women.[13] The disparity between men and women in response to bypass surgery is of equal concern. In addition to having a higher risk of death from bypass surgery than men, women have substantially more challenging and prolonged recovery periods, both physically and mentally. Women are also twice as likely as men to be readmitted to the hospital during their recovery period. And in addition to these risks and difficulties, researchers have found that women's physical and mental functioning is likely to decline, rather than improve, after a bypass.[14]

EECP offers tremendous hope to this population. Women respond to the treatment just as well as men, if not better.[15] In a study by Soran, Kennard, and Feldman, the investigators found that women responded to EECP with the same significant reduction in angina as men, and had even greater improvement in self-assessed health status, quality of life, and lifestyle satisfaction.[16] EECP is an overwhelmingly effective treatment for women, who may have few other acceptable options to address their heart disease.

SPECIAL CASES: OTHER MEDICAL CONDITIONS

Many heart disease sufferers have other medical concerns that make invasive cardiac procedures too risky or even impossible. For these patients, EECP offers an effective method for treating their heart disease without risk of complication.

Diabetes

Individuals with diabetes are at high risk of developing coronary artery disease. Their blockages are often widespread, located in their smaller arteries, and in remote areas that are technically difficult or even impossible to reach with invasive techniques. Therefore, people with diabetes are often poor candidates for bypass surgery, angioplasty, or stent placement. The good news is that patients with diabetes respond just as well to EECP as patients who do not have diabetes. EECP stimulates healthy, nondiseased vessels throughout the coronary circulation to take over the job of transporting blood to the heart, so the size and location of blockages do not matter. In one study, 658 patients with diabetes and symptomatic heart disease were treated with EECP and followed over the subsequent year to chart their response. Of these patients, 87 percent had undergone an invasive cardiac procedure prior to receiving EECP and were not candidates for additional surgery. At the completion of their EECP treatment, 69 percent responded favorably, and 72 percent of these individuals had sustained benefit one year later. None of the patients' conditions worsened. In fact, patients enjoyed significant improvement in quality of life as a result of EECP. Despite the fact that individuals with diabetes are considered high-risk patients, the one-year mortality rate among those treated with EECP was equal to that among diabetics who undergo surgery.[17]

These exciting results have enormous implications. Nearly 20 million Americans—9.5 percent of the population—have diabetes. A recent study found that men born in the United States in 2000 have a 32.8 percent probability of being diagnosed with diabetes at some point in their lives. For women, the likelihood is even higher: 38.5 percent.[18] Accordingly, the number of cardiac patients with diabetes is growing dramatically, and the need for an effective treatment such as EECP for this subpopulation is dire.

Congestive Heart Failure

Physicians are extremely interested in how EECP may be used with patients who have congestive heart failure (CHF). In these individuals, the heart's ability to pump is impaired. The condition can be caused by a severe heart attack, a series of small heart attacks, a virus, toxins such as excessive alcohol in the body, long-standing hypertension, or untreated valve disease. Heart failure is measured by ejection fraction: the ratio of blood that is pumped out with each beat of the heart to the volume of blood that fills the heart between beats. A normal ejection fraction is 50 percent or more, meaning that a healthy heart pumps at least half of the blood that enters during its resting phase back out to the body when it contracts. A heart that is unable to produce an ejection fraction of 50 percent is impaired. The lower the ejection fraction, the weaker the heart muscle, and the less blood it can pump out to the body. The less blood the heart is able to pump, the more blood will accumulate in the lungs and the rest of the body, and the more severe the related symptoms of shortness of breath, swelling in the legs, and fatigue will be. In most cases, patients who develop heart failure symptoms have ejection fractions below 35 percent.

EECP is standard therapy for heart failure in China, and the body of evidence in the United States to support this practice continues to grow. When we look at end-stage, refractory (unable to have surgery and on maximum medications) angina patients who are treated with EECP, those with ejection fractions below 35 percent are sicker to begin with than those with higher ejection fractions. Several studies—most originating from the University of Pittsburgh's groundbreaking work—have shown that EECP is safe, improves quality of life, decreases symptoms, and improves exercise tolerance in even the sickest congestive heart failure patients. Those with congestive heart failure not only show immediate improvement with EECP, but two-thirds remain event free (that is, no heart attacks, hospitalizations, or procedures) and continue to have decreased angina six months after the program.[19]

Patients with congestive heart failure only, and no angina symptoms, also respond favorably to EECP. The treatment does not aggravate the condition; in fact, just the opposite is true. In one study, five congestive heart failure patients underwent a standard course of EECP—thirty-five treatment hours over seven weeks. At the end, their heart's working capacity improved by an average of 19 percent. The length of time they were able to exercise increased by 34 percent, and their quality of life and ability to function also significantly improved.[20]

Another study, with twenty-six congestive heart failure patients, found similar results. Patients saw a 21 percent improvement in exercise duration after their treatment, and they maintained a 16 percent increase six months later. Their overall cardiovascular fitness improved by 7 percent at the end of the program, and they showed an even further improvement of 27 percent six months later. Quality of life also improved throughout the follow-up period. Again, EECP did not cause any adverse events during the program or during the six months that followed.[21]

In addition to improving exercise capacity and quality of life in congestive heart failure patients, EECP strengthens the heart muscle itself. Since congestive heart failure is a condition where the heart muscle is weak and unable to pump all of the needed blood out to the body with each beat, the heart must beat faster to compensate. Achieving a slower heart rate in these individuals would indicate that their heart has grown strong enough to get its job done in fewer beats per minute. The lower the heart rate, the lower the heart's workload and stress level. EECP reduces the heart rate in congestive heart failure sufferers. In one study, EECP improved ejection fraction by 16 percent, increased overall heart muscle power by 28 percent, and decreased patients' heart rate by 11 percent.[22] These results—which lasted for at least six months after the treatment was completed—powerfully demonstrate that EECP not only enhances circulation, as in people with coronary artery disease, but also directly improves the condition of heart failure by making the heart muscle itself stronger and better able to function.

EECP has been shown to improve congestive heart failure in another way. Because the heart muscle is weak in these patients, blood does not circulate as it should. As a result, fluid often accumulates in the body, and it manifests as swelling in the legs and shortness of breath. The heart detects this excess fluid, and then tries to get rid of it by producing diuretic hormones, such as plasma brain natriuretic peptide (BNP), to stimulate the kidneys. EECP reduces BNP levels by as much as 14 percent, indicating that it improves fluid balance and heart muscle performance, and ultimately reduces swelling in the legs and shortness of breath.[23]

The FDA responded to the above studies, which proved EECP's safety and ability specifically to treat congestive heart failure, by approving EECP as a treatment for heart failure in July 2002. This landmark event promises to open a whole new world to the nearly five million Americans living with heart failure. Before the FDA's move, heart failure patients could only manage their condition by carefully balancing their medications, modifying their diet, curbing salt intake, and regulating their beverage consumption. Now, however, a physical treatment exists that can help congestive heart failure patients reduce their difficult symptoms. Because no invasive or surgical treatments exist for this condition, the medical community is expected to embrace the use of EECP as a treatment for heart failure much more rapidly than it has for angina.

Microvascular Angina and Cardiac Syndrome X

Approximately one-third of patients with angina have normal coronary angiograms, meaning none of their major coronary arteries are more than 70 percent blocked.[24] However, the fact that these individuals have symptoms indicates that blood flow to their heart must be impaired. It is assumed, therefore, that their blockages are located in microscopic vessels—too small to be visible on a catheterization—and they are given the diagnosis of *microvascular angina*. When an abnormal stress test confirms that blood flow to the heart is impaired, the condition is called *cardiac syndrome X*. Often, the two terms are used interchangeably.

Historically, patients with microvascular angina or cardiac syndrome X were not considered to be at significant risk of heart attacks or other dangerous outcomes, so the condition has not received tremendous attention. More recently, though, researchers have found evidence to contradict conventional thought. A large study found that 10 percent of women and 6 percent of men who go to the hospital during a heart attack have no significant blockages. The study confirmed that individuals with microvascular angina are, in fact, at significant risk of major cardiac events and that the condition is a serious one, which must be treated effectively.[25] However, because microvascular angina patients have no substantial, accessible blockages, surgical or invasive procedures are not suitable treatment approaches for them. Instead, physicians rely heavily on medications to treat this condition, achieving only marginal results.

EECP offers hope to such patients, who often feel hopeless. One study examined the benefits of EECP in twenty-one microvascular angina patients (fourteen women and seven men). After completing their course of EECP, all of the patients had a marked reduction in angina, and twenty (95 percent) maintained that improvement during the following year. Five months after their treatment, sixteen out of seventeen patients (94 percent) who underwent a stress test found that blood flow to their heart was completely normal.[26] This study provides encouraging evidence that EECP is an effective tool for another class of heart disease patients that has very few treatment options.

HIV and AIDS

It is common for individuals living with HIV and AIDS to have high cholesterol and elevated blood sugar levels (a signal of early onset of diabetes). Both are well-known risk factors for heart disease. As a result, a large study recently examined the risk of heart attack among these patients. The investigation revealed that the longer HIV-infected men are treated with anti-AIDS drugs (specifically protease inhibitors such as Crixivan or Viracept), the more likely they are to have a heart attack. Among patients who had been taking a protease inhibitor for fewer than eighteen months, the rate was 8.2 heart attacks per ten thousand people annually. The rate nearly doubled to 15.9 per ten thousand among those treated for eighteen to twenty-nine months, and more than doubled again to 33.8 among patients who had been on the drugs for thirty months or more. By comparison, the expected annual heart attack rate in the general population of similarly aged men is 10.8 per ten thousand people. HIV-positive men who have been treated with protease inhibitors for eighteen to twenty-nine months, then, have a 50 percent higher risk of suffering a heart attack than their healthy counterparts, and their increased risk jumps to more than 300 percent if they are treated for thirty months or more.[27] In short, these individuals face an unavoidable double-edged sword: their lifesaving medications enable them to live longer, but the drugs also put them at much higher risk for developing heart disease. Obviously, a noninvasive and effective treatment is ideal for this high-risk population. That treatment is EECP.

Lupus

Systemic lupus erythematosus (commonly referred to as lupus or SLE) is a chronic inflammatory autoimmune disease that primarily targets young women, a group largely unaffected by heart disease. Treatments for lupus have improved in recent years, and long-term survival rates have increased. However, many people with lupus develop heart disease at a comparatively young age and have substantially increased rates of death and disability from cardiovascular disease relative to the general population.[28] Individuals with lupus are five times more likely to have a heart attack than healthy people of the same age. In young women, that rate increases by a factor of as much as fifty.[29]

The reasons for this population's higher susceptibility to heart disease are poorly understood. Traditional risk factors for coronary artery disease such as high cholesterol, smoking, and high blood pressure are not likely to blame. It is possible that the chronic inflammation that characterizes the condition, or even the drugs used to control it, plays a role. Once again, we find evidence of inflammation's function in causing disease. In this case, it may form the link between lupus and heart disease.

How does EECP fit in here? Several considerations indicate that a noninvasive method would be preferable in treating heart disease among lupus sufferers. First, patients with lupus are at high risk for developing kidney dysfunction. As such, what might normally be considered a "routine" cardiac catheterization, which involves injecting dye into the patient to locate blockages, could easily result in complete kidney failure in a patient with lupus, necessitating dialysis. Second, lupus patients have a higher risk of suffering a stroke, making any invasive cardiac procedure more dangerous. Third, since many individuals with lupus are women, they are likely to have small blood vessels and have lower success rates after bypass surgery than men. And fourth, healing from any invasive procedure when you have a chronic illness and are taking immunosuppressive medications is much more difficult and prolonged than it would be otherwise. Immunosuppressive drugs slow the healing process in general, so even a catheterization poses significant risk. These drugs also greatly increase patients' risk of developing potentially deadly postprocedure or postoperative infections. In this population, therefore, it is particularly illogical and risky to use localized, invasive techniques like bypass surgery and angioplasty that target individual blockages. With all of these factors in mind, it becomes clear that EECP, a noninvasive and remarkably effective treatment, is the best method to treat heart disease in this complicated, high-risk group.

Rheumatoid Arthritis

Rheumatoid arthritis (RA) is a chronic inflammatory autoimmune condition that affects approximately 1 percent of the United States population. About 75 percent of rheumatoid arthritis sufferers are women. Patients typically experience pain, swelling, limits on their mobility, and deformity in multiple joints, especially the hands, wrists, knees, and feet. Individuals with rheumatoid arthritis have disproportionately high rates of heart disease, and their increased risk often exists long before they are diagnosed with rheumatoid arthritis. A recent study found that during the two years before their rheumatoid arthritis diagnosis, patients were three times more likely to have been hospitalized for a heart attack and five times more likely to have had an unrecognized ("silent") heart attack. After their diagnosis, patients with rheumatoid arthritis are twice as likely to experience silent heart attacks and sudden cardiac death. The link between rheumatoid arthritis and heart disease suggests that the two illnesses likely have the same origin; scientists suspect that they are both traced to inflammation.[30] Individuals with rheumatoid arthritis also have twice the risk of developing congestive heart failure over their lifetime than those who do not have rheumatoid arthritis.[31]

The key to understanding why individuals with rheumatoid arthritis have a relatively high rate of silent heart attacks and delayed heart disease diagnosis may lie in the fact that most are women. Women, as we have discussed, tend not to experience chest pain—the primary symptom most people associate with heart disease. Therefore, they may not recognize the warning signs as such, increasing the likelihood that a heart attack will unexpectedly occur or go unrecognized. The increased rates may also have to do with the painkilling medications that many rheumatoid arthritis patients take to manage their condition, which may mask painful heart disease symptoms.

EECP is an excellent treatment option for cardiac patients with rheumatoid arthritis, for a variety of reasons. First, as many rheumatoid arthritis patients are women, their blood vessels tend to be small, often making invasive procedures difficult or impossible. Second, rheumatoid arthritis may affect not just the joints, but the lungs, kidneys, skin, nerves, and other organs as well. As a result, individuals with the condition tend to be medically complex, placing them at significantly higher risk of surgical complications than the average patient. And since these patients are often on immunosuppressive drugs, just like lupus patients, they are at substantially higher risk for developing devastating infections from invasive procedures of any kind. Third, patients with chronic illnesses such as rheumatoid arthritis tend to be frail. Therefore, they are likely to be much weaker after surgery and experience significantly longer and more complicated recovery periods than average patients. Each of these factors makes a noninvasive treatment preferable for this population.

In addition to it being the most appropriate treatment for a host of reasons, EECP offers patients with rheumatoid arthritis a remarkable side benefit. By improving the flow of much-needed blood to affected joints, EECP not only aids mobility, it reduces joint pain as well.

BOOSTING BLOOD FLOW

EECP is effective in treating heart disease and the many subpopulations of patients with special needs and considerations because it strengthens circulation, noninvasively and without risk. As a result, patients are able to effortlessly integrate the treatment into their lives and begin to enjoy its benefits almost immediately. However, heart disease is only one of many conditions marked by poor blood flow. Since EECP boosts blood flow not only to the heart but throughout the body, it can be a valuable tool in treating, managing, and even preventing numerous ailments rooted in poor circulation. In the next chapter, we will review some of the noncardiac diseases and conditions that can be addressed more safely, more easily, and less expensively with EECP, and we will examine the treatment's ability to enhance athletic performance in healthy people.

5

≈

THE POSSIBILITIES ARE ENDLESS

EECP's Benefits beyond Heart Disease

S INCE EECP STIMULATES THE BLOOD FLOW that is so crucial to good health, it is natural to think it can be useful in treating a variety of other health problems that have poor blood flow as a root cause, and even offer a boost to athletes looking for an edge. As I mentioned earlier, China routinely uses EECP to treat numerous noncardiac conditions with tremendous success. Indeed, research has been and continues to be conducted throughout the world on EECP's effect on a wide variety of ailments. In my own practice, I am constantly awed by the extent to which my patients experience improvement in their noncardiac medical conditions as a side benefit of EECP. In this chapter, we will look at a sampling of EECP's many noncardiac benefits.

EECP AND THE AILING BODY

EECP can benefit people with a wide variety of ailments, from hearing and visual disorders to diabetes, and from Alzheimer's disease and Parkinson's disease to arthritis. By aiding blood flow, EECP brings unexpected healing and comfort to many people.

Stroke

A stroke is essentially a "heart attack of the brain." It is most commonly caused by a sudden blockage of an artery in the brain, just as a heart attack is the result of a sudden blockage of an artery in the heart. These types of strokes are called *ischemic*, meaning they are caused by a lack of blood and oxygen delivery.

EECP improves blood flow to the brain. Accordingly, Chinese physicians have integrated EECP into their routine rehabilitation of recent ischemic stroke survivors. These patients recover faster and more completely than stroke survivors who do not receive EECP, thanks to the improved blood flow to the brain that EECP provides. Anecdotal reports indicate the treatment may even benefit patients who suffered a stroke years earlier.

Alzheimer's Disease

Many types of dementia are thought to be the result of poor blood flow to the parts of the brain responsible for cognitive abilities. In one study, conducted at Nanfang Hospital in China, patients with dementia related to Alzheimer's disease who were treated with EECP experienced an increase in blood flow to the brain as well as an increase in biological markers related to thinking and memory.[1] These exciting findings suggest that EECP may offer hope for Alzheimer's sufferers. Indeed, many of my patients have reported that they could think more clearly and remember more accurately after completing their treatment program. One patient, a vascular surgeon, told me he found it much easier to remember details about his patients without referring to their charts after his course of EECP. There is no doubt that we are on to something here, which is why more research on the effects of EECP on moderate and severe dementia is currently underway.

CASE STUDY

Anna K., age seventy-six, had angina, heart failure, peripheral vascular disease, and diabetes. In addition, she had suffered two strokes several years earlier, leaving her unsteady on her feet and dependent on a walker. As she progressed through the EECP program, her fatigue and shortness of breath steadily improved, and she also noted that her sense of balance was returning. On the day of her twenty-eighth EECP treatment, she walked into my office using only a cane. It was the first time in years she had been able to leave home without her walker!

CASE STUDY

William R., age seventy-five, was a semiretired engineer who still conducted research. However, he had experienced progressive cognitive decline in recent years. When he first started his EECP program to treat his angina and congestive heart failure, his wife had to accompany him in the car because he had trouble remembering the way to the office. Halfway through his seven-week course of treatment, he was able to drive alone without any difficulties. By the end of the program, he noted improved clarity of thought. He was able to perform mathematical computations more quickly and accurately, and he had become significantly more productive in his research.

CASE STUDY

Norm B., age seventy-five, had long-standing coronary artery disease and heart failure, had suffered multiple heart attacks, had undergone bypass surgery, and had a pacemaker. He experienced severe shortness of breath with minimal exertion, and he had chest pain when carrying packages, climbing steps, and breathing cold air. In addition, Norm had chronic deafness in his left ear. As he progressed through the EECP program, in addition to his chest pain subsiding, shortness of breath diminishing, and energy improving, he noted that he could hear in his left ear for the first time in nearly twenty years.

Hearing Disorders and Tinnitus

Lack of blood flow to the sensory systems in the ears is thought to cause hearing disorders and tinnitus (persistent ringing in the ears). In Germany, the standard therapy for sudden deafness and tinnitus involves medications designed to improve blood flow to the inner ear. Not surprisingly, these disorders have also been shown to improve with EECP. In one study, thirty patients with acute hearing disorders and/or tinnitus that persisted despite standard drug therapy received five to ten one-hour EECP treatments. Blood flow to the brain via the internal carotid artery (feeding the front of the brain) improved by 19 percent and via the vertebral artery (feeding the back of the brain) by 11 percent. Tinnitus significantly decreased in 47 percent of the patients, and the hearing threshold markedly increased in 28 percent. Hearing tests (audiometry studies) conducted after the study demonstrated that the improvement persisted throughout a one-year follow-up period.[2]

In a Chinese study, EECP used in combination with traditional Chinese and Western medicines was found to improve deafness after only thirteen treatments in 75 percent of cases (versus 55 percent in patients treated with medications alone). Just 17 percent (versus 33 percent) of patients experienced a recurrence in deafness in the three years following the study.[3]

Visual Disorders

Severe narrowing (atherosclerosis) of the ophthalmic arteries, which bring blood to the eyes, can result in vision impairment. Any improvement in their function or in the function of retinal vessels is likely to result in better vision. EECP has been found to improve blood flow to the eyes, particularly to the retina. A study from Friedrich Alexander University in Erlangen, Germany, involving patients with severe atherosclerosis in the ophthalmic arteries showed that EECP increased diastolic blood flow velocity in these arteries by 21 percent and overall blood flow velocity in the arteries

CASE STUDY

In addition to chronic angina, Franklin S., age sixty-seven, had diabetic retinopathy. EECP not only greatly reduced the severity of his angina, restored his energy, and enabled him to exercise again (he could swim for forty-five minutes without chest pain), it also improved his vision.

CASE STUDY

Mitchell C., age fifty-seven, had diabetes, hypertension, congestive heart failure, and peripheral vascular disease. Despite undergoing bypass surgery and several angioplasties and stent procedures, he continued to experience chronic angina. After completing his EECP program, he had much less angina, significantly more energy, and was able to engage in more activities in and out of the house. But he was most excited about his improved vision as a result of EECP. For the first time in years, he no longer needed his glasses for reading or for driving.

by 11 percent. No change in blood flow to the eyes was found in patients with normal ophthalmic arteries, providing a powerful illustration of the body's inherent safety mechanisms to protect organs from too much blood flow.[4] Clearly, the future holds promise for other visual disorders where blood flow plays a role, such as macular degeneration and diabetic retinopathy. As the case studies describe, we already have abundant anecdotal evidence of EECP's ability to improve these conditions.

Parkinson's Disease

Anecdotal reports also provide encouraging news about EECP's ability to improve symptoms associated with Parkinson's disease. Lack of blood flow to the part of the brain that makes dopamine, the key chemical that is lacking in patients with Parkinson's disease, is a major contributing factor to the condition. Parkinson's patients have responded to EECP with a reduction in tremor, improvement in their balance and ability to walk, and improvement in their facial expressions. These benefits have been reported to last for as long as two years.[5]

Erectile Dysfunction

Erectile dysfunction (ED) is a condition that severely compromises quality of life for many men living with heart disease. It is most commonly a result of a lack of blood flow to the penis. While there are medications for erectile dysfunction, most men with heart disease are unable to take them because of the risk of serious side effects when they are taken in combination with cardiac medications. EECP may very well be the long-sought-after solution to this often devastating problem. In a study conducted at Technical University in Dresden, Germany, men reported significant improvement in penile rigidity and erectile function after completing only twenty EECP treatments. Their experience corresponded to measured improvement in blood flow to the penis. Perceived quality of erection improved by nearly 100 percent, and there were no negative side effects.[6] Many of my male patients remark about this unexpected and welcome benefit of EECP. One patient asked, "Doc, is this normal? I feel like a twenty-year-old again!"

Chronic Wounds

In order for the body to heal a wound, it must deliver blood to the affected skin and underlying tissue. Blood delivers the needed cells and chemicals that fight infection and supply nutrients, oxygen, and the building blocks of healthy tissue to the wound. Remember, EECP increases blood flow throughout the body, including the skin.[7] So it is not surprising that EECP, by improving circulation to wounded areas, promotes healing. I have observed this many times in my practice, and it is always a thrilling side benefit of the treatment for patients who are struggling with chronic wounds.

CASE STUDY

Charles B., age sixty-nine, had nonhealing ulcers on his left leg for thirty-one years—a complication of a trauma and orthopedic surgery. He would get angina after eating, doing household activities, and climbing steps. He had multiple stents placed after a heart attack, but he continued to have angina that forced him to limit his activities. After receiving EECP, he had no angina and was able to engage in increasingly demanding physical activities without limitation. As a side benefit of EECP, he was able to get so much blood flowing in his leg that his ulcer began to bleed, and he was finally able to undergo a skin graft. Recently he said, "I am walking without pain for the first time in more than thirty years, and I owe it all to EECP."

Peripheral Vascular Disease

In addition to heart disease, many of my patients suffer from poor circulation in their legs, a condition called *peripheral vascular disease,* or PVD. This is not surprising, since the same disease that affects the arteries of the heart affects the arteries in the legs. In fact, although they are heart patients, those who also suffer with peripheral vascular disease often primarily complain of poor leg circulation and leg pain, known as *claudication.* This leg pain is "angina in the legs," as the legs cry out for more blood, and it can be so severe that it limits patients' ability to walk, rendering them essentially inactive. While many sufferers undergo bypass surgery, angioplasties, and stent placements in their legs to treat the condition, the debilitating claudication often returns.

It is incorrect to conclude that patients with peripheral vascular disease do not have enough blood flowing in their legs to benefit from EECP. On the contrary, that is exactly why they need the treatment. The journey these patients typically take during their EECP program is fascinating. As a matter of course, the procedure improves their leg circulation, enabling them to walk more and do more before pain sets in. As their activity level climbs, their heart disease–related symptoms—which had been masked by their inactivity—reemerge. Continued EECP treatments improve blood flow to their hearts as well as to their legs, their angina begins to subside, and they finally return to the lifestyle they have been missing for years.

Based on the impressive results I, and EECP providers across the country, have seen in so many peripheral vascular disease sufferers, I predict that EECP will become an approved treatment specifically for peripheral vascular disease in the very near future.

Diabetes

Diabetes is a major risk factor for heart disease, so it is not surprising that many of my patients suffer from the condition. In addition to the obvious benefits of improved heart and leg circulation that EECP brings to these patients, I am continually struck by another positive side effect that individuals with diabetes often enjoy: improved blood sugar control. This is a logical effect, when you consider that blood flow helps determine the body's ability to utilize sugar. As increased blood flow reaches the pancreas, insulin production is enhanced, thus improving overall blood sugar control. Since the cornerstone of successful long-term diabetes management is tight blood sugar control, adding EECP to the scope of treatments used to fight the growing epidemic of diabetes in this country is urgently needed. Much research is currently underway in this area.

Peripheral Neuropathy

Peripheral neuropathy is a condition that results in pain and numbness in the feet, legs, and hands. Typically, a patient suffering from peripheral neuropathy will lose most, if not all, of their sensation in these areas, which means they cannot feel, distinguish temperature, or recognize the location of their extremities in space with their eyes closed. This devastating condition is frequently due to a lack of blood flow to the tiny nerves responsible for sensations. EECP stim-

CASE STUDY

Bernice J., age seventy-seven, had diabetes and a thirty-year history of heart disease and angina. She had suffered three heart attacks and had angioplasty. She was not able to undergo bypass surgery due to her small vessels. At age sixty-one, because of her severe circulatory problems, both of her legs were amputated below the knee. But until her most recent heart attack, she could walk independently on two prostheses. Her third heart attack had a profound effect on her condition, leaving her without enough stamina to even stand, let alone walk. After her EECP treatment, her angina disappeared, her energy and stamina returned, and she was once again able to walk independently on her prostheses.

CASE STUDY

Mariya G., age seventy-four, had angina and a history of heart attack, bypass surgery, congestive heart failure, and peripheral vascular disease. She also had suffered from diabetes for fifteen years, requiring insulin injections for the last several years to adequately control her blood sugar. After completing fifty EECP treatments, Mariya's chest pain and shortness of breath disappeared, and her stamina was greatly increased. In addition, her blood sugar control improved markedly, allowing her to completely discontinue using insulin and to control her diabetes with diet and oral medications alone.

CASE STUDY

Michael T., age sixty-seven, had diabetes and severe peripheral neuropathy in addition to coronary artery disease and angina. As he progressed through his EECP program, he said, "I started getting more feeling in my toes. Also, my hands, feet, and body are now warm. Wow! I can now work or be on my feet for hours! I have lots more pep and stamina, and I can do more and walk farther without getting out of breath."

> ## CASE STUDY
>
> Prior to starting EECP, Charles L., age eighty-four, was having angina approximately ten times per week with basic activities. After EECP, his angina was eliminated, and he was able to exercise, climb steps, and engage in all daily activities without difficulty. Nearly two years after completing his EECP treatment, this engineer and author told me, "I am having the time of my life. I am happy and feel good all the time. My memory of names has improved, and my mind is sharper than it has ever been. I'm doing original think-tank work again! I now walk two miles, every other day, in forty minutes. I have not experienced any angina or used any nitro tabs. I am having a ball!"

ulates more blood to flow to the affected nerves, improving their function, reducing related symptoms, and offering another major quality of life benefit of the treatment.

Sleep Cycle and Thought Clarity

Healthy sleep patterns are critical to overall health and well-being. Adequate sleep brings increased energy and improved mood, memory, and clarity of thought. Many heart disease sufferers experience disturbed sleep patterns for one reason or another. One of the earliest benefits that EECP patients consistently report is the ability to sleep better, and they enjoy all the positive ripple effects that brings.

Arthritis

Many chronic pain conditions, such as rheumatoid arthritis, Lyme disease, and low back pain, also respond well to EECP. I once had a patient who suffered from rheumatoid arthritis with severe hand deformities. At the completion of his EECP program, he told me his hands were pain free for the first time in twenty years! Another patient with arthritis related to Lyme disease remarked that, thanks to EECP, she could wake up and walk without hip or knee pain for the first time since her diagnosis. I have had similar conversations with patients who had chronic neck, shoulder, and back pain. Again, it makes perfect sense, and it comes down to the enhanced blood flow that EECP creates. By improving blood flow, the chemicals responsible for transmitting pain signals in your nervous system are washed away, and you are able to move your joints more freely without discomfort. The more you can move around and exercise, the more your blood flows and the better you feel.

Restless Legs Syndrome

Restless legs syndrome (RLS) is a neurological disorder that sends extremely uncomfortable sensations down the legs, causing people who live with the condition to move their legs frequently in an effort to find relief. These individuals most often suffer symptoms in the evening, as they attempt to relax or sleep. The disrupted sleep that results from constantly trying to "shake off" the intrusive condition can lead to severe fatigue, which eventually impairs daily functioning and quality of life.

The cause of restless legs syndrome is not clear, but blood flow is thought to play a key role, and that is where EECP comes in. One study followed six patients who suffered from restless legs syndrome for many years, in some cases since childhood. Immediately after completing thirty-five EECP treatments, their restless legs syndrome symptoms improved by nearly 80 percent. Three patients, including one with a nine-year history and another with a twenty-three-year

CASE STUDY

Sara D., age sixty-nine, had struggled with restless legs syndrome for many years. The condition prevented her from sleeping more than two hours per night. She received EECP treatment for her angina and congestive heart failure. At the completion of EECP, not only was her angina greatly reduced, her restless legs syndrome had substantially improved. She had fewer cramps and less discomfort, allowing her to sleep much better.

history of frequent and disruptive restless legs syndrome, maintained the improvement for three to six months after completing EECP. Two others enjoyed sustained improvement for a full year.[8] These are astounding and significant results for an ailment that has very few, if any, effective treatment options. Clearly, EECP's ability to improve blood flow in the central and peripheral nervous systems and in the legs is what lies behind its remarkable success in treating this condition.

At this moment, researchers around the globe are continuing to work to expand EECP's applications. Because it is safe, noninvasive, comfortable, and inexpensive, we should certainly use it to treat everything we can. Ten years from now (but hopefully sooner), this chapter will be much, much longer, as we discover even more uses for EECP.

EECP AND THE HEALTHY BODY

How does EECP affect a healthy body? I'm sure you have already considered this question. If EECP, by stimulating blood flow, can get even the sickest heart patients moving again and alleviate countless other circulatory conditions, what are the possibilities for healthy people? Sure enough, many researchers and athletes have already taken notice of the astounding effects the treatment has on the healthy population.

For individuals who are too ill or unable to exercise, EECP gives them the next best thing: passive exercise. They simply lie down and rest for an hour while the machine exercises their circulation for them. EECP's effect on the body is similar to that of endurance training: it enables the major arteries in the heart, limbs, and throughout the body to function better and become more efficient at delivering blood, oxygen, and nutrients.[9] For this reason, some consider EECP to be the exercise for those who cannot exercise. But, since everyone can benefit from the treatment's positive effects, I consider EECP to be the exercise for everyone. For individuals who can and do exercise, whether they are leisure walkers or Olympic athletes, EECP stimulates additional blood flow, further strengthening their cardiovascular system and enhancing their health, stamina, and physical potential in the process. Fundamentally, EECP propels people to the next fitness level, no matter what level they are on. In this section, we will explore exactly what EECP does to your body that creates such healthful effects.

Remember, with EECP, blood pressure cuffs are wrapped around your legs, squeezing and releasing in sync with your heartbeat. As you consider this, you will quickly realize that EECP does not just increase blood flow to your heart, but throughout your entire body. With greater blood flow, your blood vessels grow and strengthen, and new ones develop. Your organs, in turn, get more oxygen and nutrients, and more waste is removed from your cells. The benefits of this action are endless.

Training the Heart

EECP increases, or augments, diastolic blood pressure—a measure of the blood flow to the heart while the heart is resting, between beats. This augmentation is as great as 93 percent in the aorta (the main artery in the body) and as much as 16 percent in the coronary arteries, and it leads to an overall increase in blood flow to the heart of at least 28 percent.[10] With increased blood flow to the heart, cardiac output is increased. In other words, the heart is able to squeeze more blood out to the body with each beat. At the same time, EECP decreases systolic blood pressure—a measure of how hard the heart has to work to pump blood out to the rest of the body—by 15 percent.[11] In other words, EECP makes the heart's job of delivering blood throughout the body 15 percent easier.

What might this mean to a healthy person? As EECP improves blood flow and oxygen delivery to the heart and reduces the heart's workload, it trains the heart to work more efficiently, similar to the effect of endurance training. An individual's fitness level is measured by the amount of oxygen that can be transported from the heart, throughout the body, and to the working muscles, and the efficiency with which the muscles can use this oxygen. This measure translates into the ability to perform more physical activity with less exertion. For example, let us assume that you can run one mile in twelve minutes. Adding EECP to your exercise regimen may enable you to run the same mile in, say, eight minutes if you wish, with ease.

Maintaining Healthy Blood Vessels

In addition to its direct effects on the heart muscle, EECP actually improves overall circulation.[12] Recall what we said earlier about blood vessels, which are dynamic organs, not inanimate tubes or pipes. When blood vessels are healthy, they expand and contract, actively working to deliver blood and oxygen throughout your body and to remove waste products. The healthier your blood vessels are, the better they are able to do their job, and the healthier you are. But just as muscles may weaken and atrophy if they are not exercised, blood vessels may stop functioning properly if poor blood flow leaves them underutilized. The health of your endothelial cells, the special cells that line the blood vessel walls, determines whether your blood vessels will be alive, dynamic, and healthy. Endothelial cells must be able to dilate and constrict in order for blood vessels to do the same. Individuals with abnormal endothelial cell function will have poorly functioning blood vessels and are more likely to develop circulatory complications such as heart disease.

As you might have guessed, increasing blood flow through your blood vessels is the only way to create shear stress (friction) along the endothelial cells and keep them alive and healthy. This gets to the heart of why blood flow is critically necessary to keep you alive and healthy. Exercise is one way to increase blood flow, and, of course, EECP is another and creates the same healthful effects. EECP has been shown to improve and even normalize endothelial cell function in heart patients, proof of its ability to create physiologic changes that lead to positive, long-term results.[13] If EECP can have this effect on heart disease sufferers, whose endothelial cells are already compromised, it is exciting to consider the treatment's effect on blood vessel functioning in healthy people. Indeed, researchers have confirmed that, in addition to enhancing blood flow in and around the heart, EECP strengthens the circulatory system in healthy people. The treatment increases pulsatility, which is an important measure of blood vessels' health and responsiveness to blood flow and plays a critical role in maintaining normal endothelial function.[14] Just as there is no such thing as too much blood flow, there is no such thing as circulation that is too strong or a body that is too healthy.

Detoxifying the Body

EECP also has a profound effect on two organs responsible for ridding the body of waste products: the kidneys and the liver.

The kidneys are the body's filters. As blood passes through them, the kidneys remove waste products by creating urine, and they regulate the balance of salt and water in the body. So, the more blood that flows through the kidneys, the greater the amount of waste the body will be able to eliminate. EECP increases renal blood flow (blood flow to the kidneys) by 21 percent, increases urine production by 60 percent, and nearly doubles salt excretion. EECP decreases renin, a hormone produced in the kidneys that causes the body to retain salt and water, by 37 percent. With lower renin levels, blood pressure is decreased and more effectively controlled. In short, EECP increases blood flow to the kidneys, improves the kidneys' ability to produce urine, promotes salt excretion, and reduces renin.[15] While our focus here is on healthy people, anyone who receives the treatment will enjoy its natural detoxifying effects.

The liver has three major functions. First, it breaks down a variety of cellular waste products, medications, and other substances in the blood that might be harmful to your body if not filtered out, and it delivers them to the kidneys or the intestine to be eliminated. Second, the liver helps process food into proteins and other substances that your body needs for nourishment. For example, it makes bile, which breaks up fats and allows you to absorb vitamins such as A, D, and E from the foods you eat. Third, the liver acts as a storage place for sugars and vitamins (especially vitamin B$_{12}$) and releases them when you need them. The liver can only perform these critical jobs when it receives sufficient blood flow. The more blood flow it receives, the more thoroughly and efficiently the liver is able to help detoxify your body. EECP aids the liver by increasing its blood flow by as much as 25 percent.[16]

Boosting Antioxidants

There is a furnace called the *mitochondria* within every cell of your body. As the mitochondria utilizes oxygen to create energy during normal cellular metabolism, a charged oxygen molecule called a *free radical* is occasionally created. This molecule has at least one unpaired electron in its outer orbit, giving it a negative electrical charge and enabling it to damage cell membranes, vessel walls, proteins, fats, and even DNA. If the free radical is not quickly neutralized, it can go on to create new ones that are just as dangerous. Your body uses its stores of natural antioxidants to neutralize free radicals, but if its supply is not great enough, the free radicals will dominate, and oxidative stress will occur. When oxidative stress persists over a long period of time, your body will likely develop a chronic degenerative disease. It is this type of progressive damage that has implicated free radicals as an underlying cause of premature aging and many chronic diseases and conditions, including heart attacks, strokes, diabetes, cancer, arthritis, Alzheimer's disease and dementia, macular degeneration, lupus, fibromyalgia, chronic fatigue, and more. Oxidative stress and free radicals also damage the cholesterol molecule, making it more likely to layer out in your arteries as plaque. People with heart disease, for example, experience higher levels of free radical production and oxidative stress than healthy individuals. In other words, their antioxidant defenses are impaired.

In order for your body to use natural antioxidants to attack free radicals, neutralize them, and render them harmless before they can wreak havoc, it must have enough antioxidants to match the number of free radicals your body produces. Unfortunately, as we age, our natural stores of antioxidants diminish, which is why physicians, nutritionists, fitness experts, and antiaging specialists so often recommend that we take oral supplements or eat foods rich in antioxidants to boost our reserves.

While EECP is a physical treatment, it also has proven antioxidant effects. Malondialdehyde is a substance that is created when cell membranes are damaged by oxidative stress. Vitamin E, a potent antioxidant, decreases malondialdehyde levels by a chemical reaction. EECP also causes a steady decrease in malondialdehyde levels by improving blood flow and removing this toxic metabolic byproduct from cells, indicating an antioxidant effect similar to that of vitamin E. EECP's antioxidant effects are among the biochemical changes that help explain the long-term benefits of this treatment.[17]

Could EECP be the fountain of youth? I don't know if I would go *that* far, but there is no doubt that the blood flow it stimulates, combined with the myriad physiological responses to this blood flow, all work to maximize the body's health and well-being.

Oxygenating Muscles

In order to work harder during exercise, muscles demand extra oxygen. And of course, the only way to boost oxygen delivery is to boost blood flow. To meet this demand for more oxygen, muscles have a built-in mechanism to distribute more blood throughout their fibers during exercise. The mechanism is made up of two key components. First, exercise stimulates additional capillaries in the muscle to open, allowing for more blood flow. Second, as muscles contract, the shape of these capillaries changes in order to maximize their surface area and the number of muscle fibers they are able to reach.

Muscles also demand extra oxygen *after* exercise. They need it to recover, to minimize postexercise fatigue and soreness, and to get ready for the next workout. Muscle fatigue comes from lactic acid buildup during exercise, a byproduct of muscle metabolism, while soreness comes from small tears in muscle cells or fibers (known as *delayed onset muscle soreness,* or DOMS). Delayed onset muscle soreness typically manifests several hours after exercise, and if left untreated, will likely resolve in three to seven days, as long as you avoid rigorous activities that increase pain. Both fatigue and soreness increase the risk of injury in athletes and in those who exercise regularly.

Athletes can lessen the effects of fatigue and soreness, reduce their risk of injury, and reduce their recovery time between workouts by increasing blood flow to tired muscles after exercise. The oxygen and nutrients delivered through blood aid the healing process and help wash out the irritating chemicals that were released when the muscle tears occurred. With a faster rebound time and less soreness and fatigue, the athlete can count on a stronger performance the next time they hit the court, track, or field.

Many athletes looking for an edge incorporate a cooldown period into their training as a means of decreasing the lactic acid in their blood. This cooldown period often consists of easy, low-impact aerobic exercise because it increases blood flow to the affected muscles without creating more significant trauma. However, these athletes face a problem: although cooldown (active recovery) decreases lactic acid levels more quickly than rest (passive recovery), it further depletes the very energy stores that need to be replenished, since any active muscle movement requires energy. In other words, exercising to help muscles recover from the strain of previous exercise actually increases the risk of even more muscle fatigue, soreness, and injury.

This dilemma leads many professional athletes to receive massage therapy after a workout or competition. Massage's many benefits are well-documented. It stimulates blood flow without exertion and spurs the healing process. Specifically, massage increases circulation, improves range of motion and flexibility, stimulates the lymphatic system, strengthens the immune system, improves joint mobility, breaks up scar tissue, relaxes muscles, and rids muscles of lactic acid and toxins, allowing an individual to rebound from exercise two to three times faster than they would without massage. Massage also reduces anxiety, injury risk, and pain.

I mentioned before that patients say EECP feels like a deep muscle massage. They are right on target. As the leg cuffs squeeze and release, they create all the benefits of traditional massage. But as passive exercise, EECP offers athletes an even better aid than massage. EECP stimulates significantly more blood flow than is possible from massage, to a degree similar to vigorous exercise but without expending energy and bringing the accompanying risk. Muscles respond to the treatment by triggering the first component of their blood distribution mechanism described earlier: waking up additional capillaries to accommodate the increased blood flow. By squeezing the legs and subtly changing the shape of muscles, EECP fuels the second component of the mechanism, causing capillaries to change shape to reach more areas of the muscle. In the process, EECP helps get rid of lactic acid and facilitates muscle repair without draining the body of energy stores needed for the next workout. By doing so, EECP improves muscle function and performance and gets athletes back on the court, in the pool, or on the field faster and with less fatigue, pain, and risk of injury.

FLOW IS FUNDAMENTAL

EECP strengthens the most fundamental process in the human body: blood flow. As a result, it improves health and vitality in countless ways, from alleviating debilitating conditions to enhancing fitness in athletes. There is just one question that remains unanswered. In the next chapter, we will explore it.

6

~

Why Haven't I Heard about This Before?

When I first meet people and begin to speak about EECP, their response is almost universal. Whether it is an individual who has been living with heart disease for decades and undergone multiple procedures over the years, a newly diagnosed patient, a family member of a heart disease sufferer, a personal friend, or a casual acquaintance, the reaction is the same: "Why haven't I heard about this before?" The question is nearly always asked with a combination of surprise, suspicion, excitement, and anger. Even physicians who have not had direct experience with EECP approach it with caution and hesitation.

"Why haven't I heard about this before?" It is the question that echoes in my mind, day in and day out. EECP is virtually unknown, despite the fact that our new understanding of heart disease should inevitably lead us to seek a treatment that stimulates blood flow on a systemic level. It is virtually unknown, despite more than a hundred scientific studies that demonstrate EECP's incredible benefits. It is virtually unknown, despite its FDA and Medicare approval, its insurance coverage, and the fact that it is noninvasive, painless, effective, and entirely safe. Despite all of these compelling facts, EECP remains medicine's best-kept secret. Why? There is no easy, politically correct answer to this question. It is complex and symptomatic of a much greater issue in the American medical system. But in this chapter, I will offer my best explanation.

AMERICAN MEDICINE: THE HIGHER-TECH, THE BETTER

The United States has a long history of innovation, discovery, and technological advances. It is inextricable from the Wild West and frontier symbolism that characterized America's early days and, to a large degree, continues to define what we represent as a country. The American way is one of trailblazing and forging new ground, and the American medical establishment follows the same tradition. It is why United States physicians and researchers are responsible for so many life-changing and lifesaving discoveries. Without this drive, we would not have the polio vaccine, cesarean section, kidney transplant, MRI, vitamin C, open-heart surgery, or countless other critical tools for keeping people alive and healthy.

These discoveries and many others are tremendous points of pride, and they stem from an approach to medicine that constantly strives to achieve the impossible. This approach teaches that the impossible is within our reach, that there is no limit to discovery. But in recent decades, with the astronomical growth in high-technology capabilities (computers, laser-guided equipment, and other precise mechanical devices), a pitfall of this philosophy has emerged alongside all the advances. The focus in American medicine today, it seems, is on high-tech innovation, while low-tech options are considered less worthy, viable, or exciting. The United States medical establishment has come to adopt the philosophy that the more complicated, risky, aggressive, and expensive the treatment, the better it must be. "In the U.S.," said William Boden, MD, professor of medicine at the University of Connecticut School of Medicine, "there is the belief that 'more aggressive' is synonymous with 'better outcomes.'"[1] Such treatments typically fall into two categories: medications and invasive procedures or surgery. Treatments that fall outside these categories are not given much credence. They are not considered to be "real" medicine. In short, the American medical mind-set currently does not allow room for a noninvasive option.

This simplified, one-or-the-other approach to medicine serves as the foundation for many, if not most, United States medical school curricula. While some schools have begun to incorporate holistic or alternative medicine into their courses of study, most future physicians are taught that they have two choices: operate or medicate. They learn there is very little in between or otherwise, and it is this approach that they carry into their professional practice.

The practice of cardiology is perhaps one of the best examples of this mind-set in action. Even with numerous studies showing that invasive procedures do not adequately address heart disease and only prolong life in a very small percentage of cases, their use remains widespread and even continues to grow. The attitude of many cardiologists is that the procedures are all they have, and they have to do something. This focus on invasive procedures does not allow for the consideration of EECP as a treatment option. In the context of the current Western medical tradition, EECP is too simple—too low-tech—to be credible. It is only offered to the sickest patients—those who cannot undergo additional surgery and have maximized their medications. Having exhausted the high-tech options, their cardiologist may then suggest EECP. And guess what? In the vast majority of cases, after EECP, they finally feel better! Then most ask, "Why didn't my doctor tell me about this sooner? Why did I have to go through all those procedures before I could try this?"

As I have stated previously, this discussion is certainly not meant to imply that surgery and pharmaceuticals have no place in modern medicine. They absolutely, unequivocally do. But I believe both are vastly overprescribed, to the exclusion of other noninvasive, accessible treatments that may work as well, if not better. Unfortunately, accepting a paradigm shift to first treat heart disease patients with a noninvasive, inexpensive, outpatient procedure, and to save the more aggressive, risky, costly treatments as last resorts is a jarring thought for most Western physicians. In fact, it is one that most in the health-care industry cannot imagine. If the shift is to occur, it will do so at the demand of patients.

EECP WON'T PAY THE BILLS

In addition to being consistent with the prevailing mentality in Western medicine, the high-tech approach to managing heart disease—including all the bypasses, angioplasties, stents, hospitalizations, tests, and complex drug regimens—has one more thing going for it. It generates *hundreds of billions of dollars* every year for doctors, hospitals, pharmaceutical companies, and the health-care system at large. It is an incredibly lucrative business. The treatments provided to one heart disease patient could easily generate more than $1 million in health-care expenses over their lifetime. In 2003 (the last year for which data is available), a bypass operation cost an average of $83,919. In the same year, the average cost of an angioplasty was $39,255.[2] These figures include the significant additional costs of the hospitalization, related tests, medications, and postoperative care. On the other hand, a standard course of EECP costs approximately $6,000, and it does not involve hospitalization, tests, drugs, or any other expenses. EECP patients are also less likely to be hospitalized in the future than heart disease sufferers who have undergone invasive procedures.[3] In short, EECP is not a particularly profitable treatment, and it makes patients less likely to need other, more profitable treatments down the road.

This is a controversial notion. Accepting—or even considering—that monetary concerns could influence the way doctors and hospitals care for patients is more than most people can bear. Rather than ask you to take my word for it, I will offer a few thoughts, observations, and experiences on the subject and leave you to draw your own conclusions.

There is tremendous competition in the health-care industry. Particularly in larger cities, hospitals must fight each other for every new and returning patient. When choosing a hospital, patients typically look for the newest, most technologically advanced facilities. It is one of the many factors in deciding where to go for care, and it is consistent with our earlier discussion about the American tendency toward high technology. So in order to get and retain patients, hospitals invest in state-of-the-art equipment, renovate their campuses, and recruit prestigious physicians. Then they spend even more money advertising their top-of-the-line staff and facilities. How do they pay for all of this? One of their primary sources of income is from performing numerous expensive procedures. These operations keep hospitals in business. Additionally, state or federal regulations often require hospitals to perform a minimum number of procedures per year in order to keep certain facilities open. Catheterization labs and open-heart surgery programs, for example, are governed by such regulations in many states, including New York and New Jersey.[4] These requirements also extend to interventional cardiologists, who must often perform a minimum number of procedures to maintain their subspecialty certification.[5]

Somehow, the United States health-care system has found itself in a terrible ethical crisis. The industry and its practitioners—doctors, hospitals, pharmaceutical companies, and so on—make money when people are sick and require costly treatments. Our health-care system's need and desire to generate revenue places it at fundamental odds with the patients it serves. The ancient Greek physician and philosopher Galen recognized this dilemma, asserting that the profit motive of medicine was incompatible with a serious devotion to the art of medicine. Finding ways to bridge this chasm—or failing to do so—continues to have a profound impact on the health of our citizens and our economy. While it is our responsibility as health-care providers to reconcile these conflicting inclinations, history suggests it may require the demands of our patients to bring about real change.

THE (UN)NATURAL ORDER OF THINGS

When a new medical treatment is introduced for any condition, it is first typically offered to those who have no other treatment options—the sickest, end-stage patients. Then, as the treatment becomes more familiar, as we gain experience with it and see its value for ourselves, and as more scientific studies are published to reinforce its effectiveness, it is moved up in the sequence of disease management to be used sooner rather than later.

The introduction of EECP as a treatment for heart disease has not followed this standard pattern. When it was first made available in the United States, it was reserved for the most advanced heart patients. But more than five years have passed since Medicare began paying for the treatment, and more than a hundred studies and papers have been published in every major cardiology journal that demonstrate its overwhelming effectiveness and unquestioned safety. Some studies even go as far as to conclude that EECP should be offered as a first-line treatment for heart disease, immediately upon diagnosis, long before surgery or other invasive procedures are used.[6] It is hard to imagine a more ringing endorsement.

Despite all of this, EECP is typically only offered to the hopeless, suffering heart patient who has tried every other treatment, sometimes repeatedly, and has no remaining options. Worse yet, EECP is not being offered widely even to this desperate population. There are 2.4 million patients in the United States with coronary artery disease who are unable to undergo bypass surgery or angioplasty because their physicians consider them inoperable. Aside from medications, EECP is their only treatment option, their only hope for improved quality of life. But most are not informed that EECP exists.

Again, it appears that if a shift in this trend is to take place, it will do so at the demand of patients. We are already beginning to see many individuals, especially those who have recently been diagnosed with heart disease, who are doing their own research, discovering

EECP, and choosing to forgo surgery or invasive procedures in favor of the noninvasive option.

HEART DISEASE:
THE NOT-SO-STRAIGHT SCOOP

That EECP is unknown to so many heart disease sufferers is a serious matter, but it is indicative of an even larger problem. The fact is that the majority of heart disease patients and their families are misinformed about the true nature of the disease. I hear patients say, time and time again, that they believe blockages are the main problem in heart disease, and that "routine" procedures such as bypass surgery, angioplasty, or stent placement will clear or remove them and take care of their serious condition.

There are actually five layers to this misconception. First, of course, is that heart disease is a systemic illness. The main problem is not that blockages exist, but that poorly functioning blood vessels cause poor blood flow throughout the body and particularly to the heart, creating an environment where blockages can develop. Therefore, the second layer is that procedures and operations that focus on blockages are only targeting a manifestation of the disease, not the disease itself. This distinction explains why bypass, angioplasty, and stents do not prolong life or prevent heart attacks. The third important point is that blockages cannot be removed. They are made of calcium and fats and, once present, become a permanent part of the blood vessel wall. Fourth, there is no such thing as a "routine" stent placement, angioplasty, or bypass operation. Each procedure brings the risk of infection, cognitive impairment, stroke, or even death. Complications may arise, and efforts to open or bypass blockages are not always successful. And lastly, it is not possible to "solve the problem." There is no cure for heart disease. Instead, the goal is to help patients *live* with it in the best possible way, minimizing symptoms, delaying its progression, and preventing events such as heart attacks. The primary way to achieve this goal is to strengthen circulation and improve overall blood flow to the heart. Doing so not only reduces or eliminates symptoms such as chest pain, fatigue, shortness of breath, and a variety of others, it trains the heart and blood vessels to do their jobs more efficiently. In the process, blockages become irrelevant.

Because of the tremendous fear and anxiety a diagnosis of heart disease so often brings, many heart disease sufferers understandably want to believe there is a quick fix for their illness. This desire, supported by their misconceptions, often leads patients to undergo invasive procedures without exploring the alternatives. In fact, since the recommended procedures seem to appropriately treat the disease as they understand it, they rarely see a need to seek out other options. Unfortunately, these patients often have unreasonable expectations about what the procedures will accomplish and how simple they will be, and they are disappointed, confused, and angry when things do not go as they planned or their symptoms recur. I am frequently asked, "Why did I have to go through all of that, since I feel just as bad now as I did before?"

INFORMED CONSENT AND BIOETHICS

Why are so many heart disease sufferers misinformed about their disease? Whose responsibility is it to inform them? There are many possible answers to the first question, but only one to the last. It is a doctor's *obligation* to ensure that all of their patients fully understand their diagnosis, *all* of their treatment options, the risks and benefits of each, and what will happen if they choose to have no treatment at all.

Having an in-depth conversation like this with your doctor may be time-consuming. You may even think it sounds unlikely to happen, since your doctor's office may seem like a hectic place where one-on-one time is limited. But a physician's highest privilege and greatest responsibility is providing information to patients about their condition and treatment options and then guiding their decisions with the patient's best interests at heart. This allows the patient to give informed consent, to select a treatment based on all the relevant factors, and it is one of the central tenets of medical ethics. When we become physicians, we take the Hippocratic oath. A modern translation says, in part:

"I will apply, for the benefit of the sick, all measures which are required, avoiding those twin traps of overtreatment and therapeutic nihilism.

"I will remember that . . . warmth, sympathy, and understanding may outweigh the surgeon's knife or the chemist's drug."

In short, the physician plays a critical role as a middleman, filtering information to their patients. Patients, in turn, rely on their doctors for complete, accurate information about their choices and for treatment recommendations motivated only by what is in their best interest.

Despite this responsibility, many patients have told me that their physicians fostered a sense of urgency to undergo an invasive procedure for their heart disease. While some doctors implied that time was of the essence, others were more blatant. I have even heard of situations where patients were told, "I cannot guarantee you'll live through the weekend if you don't have a bypass immediately." But as we have seen, there are very few cases in which such procedures are true emergencies. Heart disease is a chronic, progressive condition, and it takes years for blockages to develop in arteries. In most cases, patients have time to get off the catheterization table, take a deep breath, and carefully weigh their treatment options. A physician who implies that you must make a decision immediately when that is not truly the case has violated the tenet of informed consent and deprived you of the time and opportunity to explore alternatives.

Your physician must prevent or correct the five misconceptions about heart disease we listed in the previous section. In addition, they must fully discuss all of the treatments available to you—including EECP. If they fail to do either, you will not fully understand your illness, and you will not be able to make logical, informed treatment decisions or form realistic expectations. You have a fundamental right to demand these things and to find a doctor who will provide them to you.

Unfortunately, this scenario offers one of the strongest explanations for why EECP is still relatively unknown. If more patients understood the basic truths about heart disease—that it is a systemic illness; that blockages are not the problem and cannot be eliminated; that procedures targeting blockages are misguided and potentially risky; that there is rarely a need for emergency procedures; and that a proven, noninvasive treatment exists that offers a logical, systemic solution—I would never again be asked, "Why haven't I heard about this before?" Patients would not subject themselves to invasive procedures aimed at bypassing, opening, or stenting blockages. They would demand EECP, and it would be universally recognized as the leading treatment for heart disease.

This need for information dissemination has led to a recent trend in medical practice called *information therapy.* It aims to support informed consent by providing specific, evidence-based medical information to a patient, caregiver, or consumer in writing to help that person make a particular health decision or behavior change.[7] The central premise is that information is as critical a component of one's health care as examinations, tests, and procedures. Health-care decisions should not depend upon a doctor choosing which facts to share or upon a patient accurately remembering what they were told. This approach is in keeping with the growing emphasis on patient self-management and shared decision making, and it is becoming increasingly popular, with some physicians actively pushing for its widespread use.

THE DOCTOR-PATIENT RELATIONSHIP

Patients only want to feel better, and they inherently believe their doctors have their best interests in mind when recommending treatments, procedures, and action plans. As a result, patients are often quick to follow their physicians' advice. On some level, many doctors are aware of this relationship, and they understand the high regard in which their patients hold them. Consciously or not, this power differential often plays an important role in the doctor-patient relationship: the doctor may prescribe a treatment without explaining why it is justified or discussing all of the alternatives, and the patient may follow these orders without asking questions or second-guessing them.

Ziauddin Sardar, a writer and philosopher at London's City University, offers this comment on the role of power in the doctor-patient relationship: "In non-Western traditions of medicine, the power of healing belongs to patients, not doctors. Doctors can offer remedies but they work with the power of the whole person, the patient. In the Western system, the power of the medical establishment, the consultants, and the doctors is absolute. No wonder patients arriving in a hospital perceive themselves as helpless victims whose only function is to bring diseases for the doctors to fight and defeat."[8]

Despite this imbalance of power, your doctor has an undeniable responsibility to you that goes beyond ordering tests, performing procedures, and prescribing medication. As we saw earlier, your doctor is required to educate you fully about your diagnosis, all of your treatment options, related risks and benefits, and the consequences of doing nothing. But you have a responsibility as well. You must be proactive in your health. Ask questions. Do your own research. Be armed with all the information you can gather. Doing so is the only way you can be sure to get the care you need.

Above all else, don't be afraid to upset your doctor. Many people have told me that they fear their doctor would be offended to find out they came to me to learn about EECP. The last thing they want to do, they tell me, is to offend their doctor. I appreciate this sentiment. Many people have close, trusting relationships with their physicians. It may even be that their doctor saved their life at some point and they feel indebted to them. But your doctor should not be offended or upset by your effort to learn about a treatment option. It is your right—actually, it is your *responsibility*—to educate yourself about your health. You must not be afraid of hurting your doctor's feelings in the process. You and your doctor should form a partnership for your care. It is your health that is of paramount importance, not your doctor's feelings. A physician who is truly on your side will welcome a two-way dialogue about *all* treatment options for your heart disease, including EECP. I believe most doctors fall into this category. Just try them!

INFORMATION IS POWER

In the fight against heart disease, information is your best weapon. Understanding all that you can about your systemic condition, being willing to ask questions, and forging collaborative relationships with your doctors will all but ensure that you will get the treatment you need. But your responsibility does not stop there. As we will see in the next chapter, there are many lifestyle choices you can, and must, make to maximize blood flow and stay on the path to good health.

7

~

Taking Control after EECP

W E NOW UNDERSTAND THAT BLOOD FLOW is essential to health. We have also fully explored the exciting role EECP plays in treating heart disease and numerous other illnesses and conditions related to poor circulation. By dramatically improving blood flow, EECP puts patients on an upward spiral. But the good news does not and should not end with EECP; there are many behaviors we can adopt, modify, or eliminate to do our part to ensure that EECP's positive effects last as long as possible.

Whether you are living with heart disease or are concerned that you might be someday, the time to do all you can to reduce your risk factors is *now*. While some factors are beyond your control, such as age and family history of heart disease, many others are not, and they offer important opportunities to slow the progression or even prevent the development of the disease. As you might have guessed, these risk factors have one thing in common: they all inhibit blood flow. If you have heart disease, keeping your blood flowing is the best way to fight its effects and enjoy the best possible quality of life. If you are healthy, keeping your blood flowing is the best way to stay that way. In this chapter, we will consider several critical steps you can take in your quest for strong blood flow and good health.

FIGHT THE TEMPTATION OF PHYSICAL INACTIVITY

For many Americans, life is becoming increasingly sedentary. Gone are the days when we would walk to the store, buy what we need for that day, and walk home. Instead, we drive virtually everywhere, sometimes without even getting out of the car when we arrive at our destination. (Even drugstores, banks, and dry cleaners have drive-through windows.) The Internet has brought the world to our living rooms, allowing us to shop, conduct research, and socialize without ever leaving the sofa. Many of us have come to appreciate these conveniences, but they have paved the way for an epidemic that continues to grow, claiming countless lives every day. Physical activity is a casualty of modern convenience, with many dangerous ripple effects. According to the American Heart Association, 35.8 percent of men and 41.0 percent of women lead a sedentary life with no leisure-time physical activity.[1] The United States surgeon general reports that more than 60 percent of American adults are not regularly active, and 25 percent do not exercise at all. Inactive people have higher rates of heart disease, cancer, depression, and a host of other devastating ailments than people who engage in even mild physical activity.[2] Being sedentary not only increases your risk of developing coronary artery disease, it increases your risk of *dying* from the disease by 60 percent.[3]

Prevent or Reduce Obesity

The most noticeable result of physical inactivity may be weight gain, and eventually, obesity. Nearly one-third of American adults are obese, and another 35 percent are overweight. Approximately three hundred thousand United States adults die of obesity-related causes each year.[4] Obesity inhibits blood vessel function and is recognized as a major risk factor for heart disease, stroke, insulin resistance and diabetes, high cholesterol, high blood pressure, and many other conditions. Unfortunately, Americans are showing no signs of getting this serious health risk under control. On the contrary, the percentage of obese Americans has increased by 75 percent since 1991.

The obesity epidemic is equally shocking among United States youth. Nearly 9.2 million children and adolescents aged six to nineteen—16 percent of this population—are considered overweight or obese, and an additional 31 percent are at risk of falling into this category.[5] Communities across the country are releasing even more eye-opening statistics. In my own city of Philadelphia, a recent study revealed that 51 percent of children are overweight or obese.[6] As these overweight, sedentary kids grow up, they are at extremely high risk for all the complications of obesity. Obese children have been shown to have blood vessel dysfunction similar to that seen in adult heart disease sufferers. Even obese kids as young as five years old are more likely than children of healthy weight to have high blood pressure and thickened heart muscles.[7] The thicker a person's heart muscle, the more likely they are to have reduced blood flow.

ARE YOU AT RISK?

Your body mass index (BMI), which is your weight in kilograms divided by your height in meters squared (kg/m²), determines whether you are considered obese. People with a body mass index of twenty-five or more are classified as overweight, while those with a body mass index of thirty or higher are obese.

Several recent studies shed some light on the direct link between obesity and heart disease. They found that levels of leptin, a hormone secreted by fat cells, rise in tandem with levels of C-reactive protein, an inflammatory marker in the blood that is linked to heart disease risk.[8] Leptin poses a direct risk of heart attack similar to that of high blood pressure and low HDL ("good") cholesterol.[9] These findings again reinforce the relationship among heart disease, impaired blood flow, and inflammation.

GET MOVING!

"Exercise is good for you." This is a statement we have all heard, time and again, and most of us accept it as fact. But have you ever stopped to consider *why* exercise is good for you? You may say exercise makes you stronger and raises your metabolism, allowing you to lose weight or keep your weight under control. You may also note that exercise gives you more energy, keeps you feeling young, makes you fit, and improves your looks. The list of benefits goes on and on. But on the most basic level, *exercise gets your blood flowing*. When you exercise, your heart beats faster, causing your blood to pump more forcefully throughout your body—to every organ, tissue, and cell—and allowing all the processes that define a healthy body to occur. This increased blood flow is the fundamental reason why exercise is good for you; it is what gives rise to all of the other benefits you can think of.

The Science of Exercise

Scientists have discovered a direct cause-and-effect relationship between exercise (that is, blood flow) and health that offers a compelling, tangible incentive to be physically active. The landmark research that illustrated this connection was the Harvard Alumni Study. It followed seventeen thousand middle-aged Harvard graduates over a twenty-six-year period and monitored a number of variables, including exercise habits. The researchers concluded that those who exercised vigorously (jogging, swimming, cycling, tennis, and so on) had a 25 percent lower death rate than those who were more sedentary or engaged in nonvigorous activities (such as bowling, golf, or strolling).[10] Dr. Ralph Paffenbarger, one of the principal authors of the Harvard study and one of the world's leading authorities on exercise and longevity, has offered us a simple summation: for every hour you exercise, you get back that hour plus an extra hour of life.

But why is there such a direct relationship between exercise and good health? We understand that good blood flow is crucial to good health and that exercise gets your blood pumping. But what does the blood flow do to your bodily function that is so critical? The answer is simple: by increasing your blood flow, you are increasing oxygen delivery throughout your body and particularly to your heart. In the process, you are protecting and enhancing the health of your heart by conditioning it to work more efficiently. Conversely, when you are sedentary, you are putting your heart—and therefore your life—at risk.

Exercise Prevents and Reduces the Effects of Heart Disease

An overwhelming volume of scientific evidence demonstrates that regular exercise is cardioprotective and it helps slow the progression and reduce the severity of coronary artery disease.[11] Many studies have shown that physical activity reduces several cardiovascular risk factors such as diabetes, obesity, risk of thrombosis (blood clotting), and endothelial cell (blood vessel) dysfunction.[12] Exercise also improves levels of HDL ("good") cholesterol and lowers blood pressure, both factors known to protect against heart disease.[13] By reducing cardiovascular risk factors, exercise reduces the occurrence of heart disease–related death. For example, research shows that physically active people are less likely to have a heart attack, are better able to rebound from and survive a heart attack if one should occur, and have a lower risk of death due to heart disease.[14]

But we can go one level deeper in understanding why exercise is cardioprotective. We can determine what exercise does on a biological level to help prevent and slow the development of heart disease. Recall that inflammation damages blood vessels and is a key underlying cause of countless diseases and conditions, including heart disease. Also, recall our discussion in chapter 2 regarding the mechanics of blood flow. The friction of blood flow has direct anti-inflammatory effects on blood vessels.[15] Therefore, by increasing blood flow, exercise offers a natural way to counteract inflammation and protect blood vessels. This is not just a theory based on logic; researchers have quantified the anti-inflammatory effect of exercise by measuring the drop in C-reactive protein in the blood over time.[16]

If you have heart disease, one study has shown that you would be better served by exercising regularly than by undergoing an invasive procedure. Researchers at the University of Leipzig (Germany) concluded that heart patients who do not have an invasive procedure but do exercise daily (twenty minutes on a stationary bike) were 18 percent less likely to have a heart attack or other cardiac complication over the next four years than heart patients who did not exercise regularly but did have a stent placed.[17] These results further underscore this fundamental message: improving blood flow *systemically*, throughout the body and therefore to the heart, does far more to improve health and protect the heart than focusing in on a specific blockage. Remember, heart disease is not about isolated blockages, so a localized treatment like a stent is merely a Band-Aid. It fails to address the underlying problem: lack of blood flow throughout the heart muscle. Exercise boosts health in all of the blood vessels and in the heart by stimulating blood flow everywhere.

In the case of exercise, there cannot be too much of a good thing. We have come to understand that there is a dose-response relationship between exercise and protection against cardiovascular disease, meaning the more you exercise, the healthier your heart is.[18] This is incredibly empowering news for people who are anxious to do all they can to prevent or slow the development of heart disease. It teaches us that there is something we can do every day, something that is free and does not require any special equipment or expertise, to decrease our risk of falling victim to the number-one killer in our society.

Exercise Leads to Weight Loss and Better Health

It is well understood that exercise helps you lose weight and maintain a healthy weight by increasing your energy expenditure and metabolic rate.[19] What is even more exciting, though, is the fact that as you lose weight, you open the door to the variety of other health benefits that naturally follow.

There is no better time than during childhood to reduce the damaging effects of physical inactivity and obesity. Simple lifestyle changes such as exercising regularly and adopting a low-fat diet lead to a marked improvement in blood vessel function in obese children, not only signaling a young body's ability to heal, but also again highlighting the fact that blood flow is the key underlying determinant of heart health.[20]

But while it is best to chart a healthy course when you are young and stop bad habits before they start, overweight and obese adults must never think they are too old to improve their health. Obese adults gain significant benefits from exercise, even without dieting or reducing caloric intake. One study, conducted by Duke University's Center for Health Policy and Research, followed three groups of patients aged forty to sixty-five during an eight-month period of exercise. One group jogged twenty miles per week, one jogged twelve miles per week, and one walked twelve miles per week. All three groups lost significant weight and body fat. The group that jogged twenty miles per week lost the most, and the groups that walked or jogged twelve miles per week lost about the same as each other. The researchers concluded that most obese individuals can lose substantial weight and fat mass by walking thirty minutes every day.[21]

The weight loss that results from exercise has tangible benefits in the fight against heart disease. A study from CCS Haryana Agricultural University of India recently documented that obese postmenopausal women who exercised one hour per day for three months lost weight, lowered their blood pressure and cholesterol, and enjoyed increased energy and activity levels.[22] In another study, researchers at Queen's University in Ontario, Canada, found that obese premenopausal women who exercised daily for fourteen weeks experienced substantial reductions in total fat, abdominal fat, visceral fat (which surrounds internal organs and is particularly dangerous), and insulin resistance. They obtained these benefits even without dieting or cutting back on calories.[23]

A University of Liverpool (England) study of obese individuals aged thirty-seven to forty-seven who participated in moderate aerobic exercise (walking on a treadmill or riding a stationary bicycle) for eight weeks found that the subjects reduced their body weight, body fat, and waist size. Interestingly, this study divided participants into two groups. Each group burned the same total number of calories per week (two thousand), but one group exercised five times per week and burned four hundred calories during each session, and the other exercised only twice per week, burning one thousand calories per session. Both groups achieved the same significant benefits, suggesting that total weekly energy expenditure is what is most important in using exercise as a weight-loss tool.[24]

Exercise Offers You Options

The Centers for Disease Control and Prevention, together with the American College of Sports Medicine, recommends you exercise aerobically (walking, swimming, jogging, dancing, and so on) for at least thirty minutes per day, five days per week, at your target heart rate in order to achieve cardiovascular benefit. If you cannot precisely calculate your heart rate while you exercise, here is a tip: try to achieve an intensity level that you would consider moderate to moderately hard. It should cause you to perspire a bit and to breathe more rapidly than while you are at rest. But you should not be working so intensely that you are unable to speak in full sentences.

As you know, there are countless gurus, trainers, books, videotapes, magazines, and websites that tout "the best" or "most complete" or "fastest" or "easiest" exercise regimen. But there is no one best program or technique. The point is to get moving. Certain programs and approaches may feel better to you, may be more enjoyable or convenient, or may address your particular needs more than others. But any activity that improves your blood flow will give you the

THE LIST OF EXERCISE'S BENEFITS
JUST KEEPS GROWING

As if all these facts weren't reason enough to put down this book and get moving, the list of exercise's benefits just keeps growing. Research has shown that physical activity:

- Decreases depression and anxiety and improves mood[25]
- Plays a substantial role in developing bone mass during childhood and adolescence, and in improving and maintaining skeletal mass into adulthood, decreasing the risk of hip fractures later in life[26]
- Decreases the risk of colon cancer, breast cancer, and prostate cancer[27]
- Lowers the risk of diabetes[28] and helps prevent the progression of the disease in those who have diabetes[29]
- Strengthens the body's antioxidant mechanisms, helping to slow the aging process, fight disease progression, and create a younger, healthier, and more fit appearance and attitude
- Enhances blood flow in limb muscles, thereby improving overall muscle function and performance
- Improves balance and joint flexibility
- Boosts self-image and self-esteem
- Improves sleep patterns, thereby helping individuals look and feel more relaxed and rested

CALCULATING YOUR TARGET HEART RATE

1. Determine your maximum heart rate: 220 minus your age in years. (For example, if you are 50, your maximum heart rate is 220 – 50 = 170 beats per minute.)

2. Your target heart rate is 50 to 80 percent of your maximum heart rate. (For example, 50 percent of 170 = 85; 80 percent of 170 = 136. Your target heart rate = 85 to 136 beats per minute.)

desired benefits: decreasing your risk of disease; enhancing your fitness, strength, flexibility, and body composition; and greatly improving your quality of life. On the next page is a sampling of types of physical activity and the documented benefits each has on cardiovascular health.

It is easy to find excuses not to exercise. You are too busy, the weather is not cooperating, you do not have access to an exercise facility or the proper equipment, and so on. But exercise can take many forms. It does not have to be a grand production in order to provide cardiovascular benefit and improve your health. You do not even need an uninterrupted block of time in which to do it. The National Heart, Lung, and Blood Institute at the National Institutes of Health says exercise will still be effective if it is divided into multiple ten- to twenty-minute sessions per day. It is your total amount of activity each day that counts.

The importance of being active cannot be overstated, and there are more opportunities to add physical activity to your daily life than you might realize. Take the longer route to your next meeting. Park at the far end of the parking lot. Walk around the airport while you wait for your flight. Use the steps instead of the elevator or escalator. Set aside some more time to work in the garden. Even these seemingly small lifestyle changes will increase your physical activity and be as effective as a formal exercise routine in improving your fitness level, lowering your blood pressure, and reducing your risk of heart disease.[30] So let's get moving!

MANAGE STRESS AND ANXIETY

Scientists have identified clear connections between emotional stress, persistent levels of stress hormones in your body such as adrenaline, cortisol, and norepinephrine, and various illnesses and diseases. Recently, evidence has emerged that anger, hostility, and depression raise blood levels of C-reactive protein, the inflammatory marker linked to heart disease.[31] In short, when you are emotionally

Cardiovascular Benefits of Exercise

Exercise Type — Aerobic exercise (cycling, running, etc.)
Duration/Frequency/Time — 4 months • 3x/week • 60 minutes
Benefits • Improves cardiovascular fitness, allowing greater blood flow throughout the body with less effort • Increases HDL ("good") cholesterol, protecting blood vessels from further blockage[32]

Exercise Type — Low-impact aerobics
Duration/Frequency/Time — 3 months • 3x/week • 60 minutes
Benefits • Improves cardiovascular fitness, allowing greater blood flow throughout the body with less effort[33]

Exercise Type — Tai chi
Duration/Frequency/Time — 3 months • 2x/week • 60 minutes
Benefits • Improves cardiovascular fitness, allowing greater blood flow throughout the body with less effort • Improves fluid balance and heart muscle performance[34]

Exercise Type — Strength training
Duration/Frequency/Time — 4 months • 3x/week • 60 minutes
Benefits • Decreases heart rate and blood pressure, thus relaxing the cardiovascular system and allowing for increased blood flow throughout the body with less effort[35]

Exercise Type — Walking
Duration/Frequency/Time — 6 weeks • 5x/week • 30 minutes
Benefits • Improves cardiovascular fitness, allowing greater blood flow throughout the body with less effort • Increases HDL and lowers total cholesterol and triglycerides, protecting blood vessels from further blockage[36]

Exercise Type — Swimming
Duration/Frequency/Time — 10 weeks • 3x/week • 30 minutes
Benefits • Decreases blood pressure[37]

Exercise Type — Yoga
Duration/Frequency/Time — 3 months • 7x/week • 60 minutes
Benefits • Lowers heart rate and blood pressure, relaxes the cardiovascular system allowing for increased blood flow throughout body with less effort • Decreases total cholesterol, protecting blood vessels from further blockage • Decreases the likelihood of blood clots, allowing blood to flow more freely[38]

upset, your body releases hormones that cause your blood vessels to constrict, thereby impairing blood flow. Learning to cope with stress and manage it effectively when it arises, therefore, is essential not only to your emotional and psychological health, but to your physical health as well.

Our bodies offer many signals that stress is building. You may get a headache, experience indigestion, feel muscle tension, have difficulty sleeping, or grind your teeth. You could experience a racing heart, sweaty palms, fatigue, general aches and pains, or an upset stomach. Or you may feel angry, anxious, depressed, irritable, lonely, or nervous. Any of these symptoms, alone or in combination, are signals of stress. They manifest differently in everyone, but they must not be ignored.

Once you identify the signs, you can learn to manage stress using proven techniques. By improving your coping strategies and learning to relax, your blood vessels will dilate and your blood flow will improve. Common effective stress management methods include:

- Eating and drinking sensibly

- Quitting smoking

- Improving communications with your family, friends, and coworkers

- Getting enough rest

- Exercising regularly

- Managing your time effectively

- Asking for help when you think you need it

- Learning to relax (finding the technique or techniques that work best for you, such as breathing exercises, progressive muscle relaxation, mental imagery relaxation, or biofeedback)

QUIT SMOKING

While there have been many attempts over the past several decades to raise public awareness of the dangers of cigarette smoking, it continues to be the nation's leading preventable cause of death and disease. Smoking is responsible for more than 442,000 premature deaths in the United States each year. Worldwide, there will soon be six million deaths per year due to tobacco use, putting smoking on the same level as the HIV/AIDS epidemic. Most Americans are aware that it causes emphysema, lung cancer, and other serious breathing problems, but many do not recognize that cigarette smoking has devastating effects on the cardiovascular system. In fact, tobacco use causes more deaths from heart disease and stroke than from lung cancer. Smoking is responsible for about 30 percent of all deaths from heart disease in the United States.

The World Health Organization's Multinational Monitoring of Trends and Determinants in Cardiovascular Disease (MONICA) project conducted a study of more than 131,000 men and women from twenty-one countries and found that smoking substantially raises the risk of heart attacks in adults aged thirty-five to thirty-nine. Smokers in this age group are five times more likely than their nonsmoking counterparts to have a heart attack. The MONICA project researchers concluded that half of all heart attacks in people under fifty could be prevented with smoking cessation.[39]

A British study on smoking and mortality among male doctors continues to yield new information more than fifty years after it began.[40] In 1951, the British Doctors Study, as it is known, began monitoring nearly thirty-five thousand male doctors born prior to 1930. The first data to arise from this study was published in 1954.[41] The publication was a landmark event, as it was one of the first to establish a link between smoking and lung cancer, and between smoking and heart attacks. Based on what they learned, the investigators gradually compiled a list of twenty-four diseases and conditions that are clearly caused by smoking, including high blood pressure, coronary artery disease, heart attack, heart failure, and stroke.

How Does Smoking Increase Heart Disease Risk?

It only takes three seconds for your body to begin feeling the harmful effects of smoking. Your heart beats faster, your blood pressure rises, and the carbon monoxide in smoke removes oxygen from your blood.[42] As we have discussed, blood flow is critical because it delivers the nutrients and oxygen that all the cells in your body need in order to function properly. However, it really does not matter how much blood is flowing if it has been stripped of its oxygen. Without oxygen, cells die. And when your heart senses it is not getting the oxygen it needs, it pumps faster and works harder to try to boost blood flow in hopes of boosting oxygen delivery. So when smoke removes oxygen from your blood, it is effectively killing your cells and straining your heart. Conversely, when you stop smoking, more blood and oxygen is immediately delivered throughout your body.

The chemical culprit in cigarettes, and in tobacco of any form, is nicotine. Nicotine has numerous deadly effects on the body. Primarily, it constricts your blood vessels and causes them to spasm. When blood vessels constrict, blood flow is reduced, blood pressure rises, and the heart again must strain to get its job done. (This is why smokers tend to have cold feet and hands, and they often appear pale.) In addition, it appears that smoking both accelerates the buildup of plaque in arteries and causes these plaques to rupture. At the same time, nicotine promotes blood clotting. This deadly combination can lead to the abrupt, complete blockage of an artery feeding the heart, thereby triggering a serious heart attack.[43]

There is seemingly no end to the bad news about nicotine. Endothelial cells are the critically important cells that line blood vessels and are responsible for promoting healthy blood flow throughout the body. Endothelial cells can develop from stem cells (endothelial progenitor cells), which are present in the circulation.

These progenitor cells help to repair the lining of blood vessels by settling on the blood vessel wall in a place where new, healthy endothelial cells are needed. A low progenitor cell count is a strong predictor for heart disease. Nicotine is poisonous to progenitor cells, as evidenced by the fact that smokers have lower levels of progenitor cells than nonsmokers. The more people smoke, the fewer progenitor cells they have. Tellingly, when smokers quit smoking, their levels of progenitor cells tend to rise rapidly, and when they resume smoking, their levels drop again, almost to the original low numbers.[44]

Smokers have significantly higher levels of three inflammatory and blood-clotting factors in their blood than nonsmokers. Each of the substances—C-reactive protein, homocysteine, and fibrinogen—has been linked to an increased risk of heart disease. Former smokers have only slightly elevated levels of these markers compared to nonsmokers, demonstrating again that it is never too late to quit smoking and take a positive step toward reducing your risk of heart disease.[45]

In addition to its harmful effects on blood vessel function, heart function, and blood flow, smoking aggravates a variety of other known risks for heart disease. It increases LDL ("bad") cholesterol, decreases HDL ("good") cholesterol, and increases the risk of diabetes by making the body more resistant to insulin.

Passive Smoking Kills Too

If you choose to smoke, you are not only robbing your body of oxygen, impairing your circulation and blood flow, and seriously damaging your health, you are similarly affecting those around you. Passive smoking—secondhand smoke inhaled by nonsmokers living or socializing with smokers—is thought to increase the risk of heart disease by as much as 50 percent and contributes to thirty-five thousand U.S. deaths annually.[46]

Several U.S. states—including Delaware, California, and New York—and more than 1,700 American cities and towns have instituted smoking bans in all public indoor spaces in an effort to protect nonsmokers from this health risk. Australia, Ireland, Italy, Canada,

Iran, the Netherlands, and Norway have introduced such bans nationwide. Studies suggest the positive effects of these laws on public health in the coming years will be staggering. For example, the city of Helena, Montana, passed a smoking ban in workplaces more than two years ago, and although it was overturned six months later, the number of heart attacks in that city dropped by 40 percent during the time the law was in effect.[47] Another study concluded that while only 69 percent of American indoor workers are currently protected by a smoke-free workplace policy, a nationwide ban could prevent thousands of heart attacks, strokes, and deaths each year, and it would encourage approximately 1.3 million people to quit smoking within just the first five years of the ban.[48]

The British Doctors Study arrived at an important conclusion that offers hope and incentive to current smokers: it is never too late to quit. The study found that the risks associated with smoking quickly diminish after you stop. A thirty-year-old, for example, who quits smoking will avoid almost all of the excess mortality risk associated with tobacco use. People who quit smoking by age forty will regain an extra nine years of life. Those who stop at age fifty will regain six years, and people who quit by the time they are sixty will regain three years. Whatever your age, quitting smoking—or minimizing your passive exposure to smoke—is one of the most important steps you can take toward enhancing your blood flow, lowering your heart disease risk, and improving your overall health.

DRINK ALCOHOL ONLY IN MODERATION

Much attention has been paid in recent years to the relationship between alcohol and heart disease. Many reports indicate that moderate drinking raises HDL ("good") cholesterol, lowers blood pressure, inhibits the formation of blood clots (which can be both good and bad, as it may increase the risk of bleeding but may decrease the risk of a heart attack), and helps prevent artery damage caused by elevated LDL ("bad") cholesterol. Indeed, moderate drinking does appear to offer some protection against heart disease for certain people. Moderate drinking is defined as no more than one drink for women and no more than two drinks for men per day. A drink is defined as 1.5 ounces of 80-proof or 1 ounce of 100-proof liquor, 5 ounces of wine, or 12 ounces of regular or light beer.

Of course, many of the benefits from moderate alcohol consumption listed above can be achieved through proper diet and exercise, and there is an important flipside to the encouraging reports on moderate drinking. Consuming too much alcohol can lead to many serious health problems, including high blood pressure (which inhibits blood flow), diseases of the liver and pancreas, and damage to your heart and brain. The American Heart Association cautions people *not* to start drinking if they do not currently drink alcohol. If you do drink, curtailing the amount of alcohol you consume will enable you to reduce your blood pressure and allow your blood to flow more freely.

MANAGE HIGH BLOOD PRESSURE, DIABETES, AND CHOLESTEROL

Several medical conditions, if not controlled, can increase cardiovascular risk. Chief among these are high blood pressure, diabetes, and cholesterol.

Control High Blood Pressure (Hypertension)

When you have high blood pressure, or hypertension, your blood vessels become stiff and the force of blood against your artery walls is too strong. This pressure causes damage to your blood vessels and vital organs. Hypertension is commonly called the "silent killer" because its symptoms—headache, visual disturbances, nausea, and vomiting—often do not emerge until the situation is severe and the damage has been done. An estimated sixty-five million Americans—nearly one-third of United States adults—have hypertension, defined as levels of 140/90 mmHg or higher, and an additional 30 percent of the population is considered "prehypertensive."[49]

Understanding blood pressure. A blood pressure measurement consists of two numbers. The top number is called the *systolic blood pressure*; it represents the pressure against your artery walls just after your heart has pumped to send blood out to the body. The bottom number is called the *diastolic blood pressure*; it represents the pressure against your artery walls between heartbeats, when your heart is relaxed. The numbers are measured in millimeters of mercury (mmHg) and are classified as follows, based on guidelines from the National Institutes of Health:[50]

Understand Your Blood Pressure

Classification: Systolic Blood Pressure
High blood pressure ....140 or above
Prehypertension 120-139
Normal adult blood pressure ......119 or below

Classification: Diastolic Blood Pressure
High blood pressure ....90 or above
Prehypertension 80-89
Normal adult blood pressure ......79 or below

Factors causing hypertension. We cannot usually pinpoint why high blood pressure exists in a particular person, but many factors are known to significantly contribute to the development of hypertension. These include family history of hypertension; obesity; consuming three or more alcoholic drinks per day; high salt intake; low calcium, magnesium, or potassium intake; insulin resistance; and aging. Hormones released during periods of emotional or physical stress may also raise blood pressure by causing blood vessels to narrow, thereby impairing blood flow.

Treating hypertension. Lifestyle modifications are essential to managing high blood pressure. The obvious steps include increasing your level of physical activity, losing excess weight, quitting smoking, limiting alcohol use, learning to effectively cope with stress, and cutting back on salt intake. A low-fat diet called Dietary Approaches to Stop Hypertension (DASH) is often recommended and emphasizes whole grains, vegetables, and fruit. In addition, you have to be sure your intake of calcium, magnesium, and potassium is sufficient. If you are not able to control your blood pressure by making these lifestyle changes, your doctor may prescribe medication. It is not uncommon for a patient to require more than one medication to maintain their blood pressure in the desired range.

Regardless of whether you can control your hypertension by changing your habits or you must take medication, effectively managing this condition is crucial to your overall health. It offers yet another means for promoting blood flow and reducing your risk of heart disease.

Keep Diabetes in Check

Diabetes mellitus results from problems with insulin in the body. Insulin is a hormone produced by the pancreas that transports glucose (sugar), a major form of nutrition necessary for cells to function properly, from the blood into all of the body's cells. Most individuals with diabetes do not produce enough insulin. Without adequate insulin, glucose builds up in the blood and is unavailable for use by cells. Blood sugar level, the amount of glucose in the blood, indicates whether there is enough insulin, and is therefore the gauge individuals with diabetes use to control their condition.

An important precursor to diabetes—and a syndrome that increases heart disease risk—is a phenomenon called *insulin resistance*, when the body does not efficiently use the insulin it produces. In this situation, the pancreas attempts to regulate blood sugar levels by releasing more and more insulin. Gradually, though, the pancreas's insulin-producing cells burn out and become inactive. As a result, blood sugar slowly rises and full-blown diabetes develops. Insulin resistance is part of a metabolic syndrome that includes increased LDL ("bad") cholesterol levels and triglycerides and decreased HDL ("good") cholesterol levels. More than sixty million Americans are insulin resistant, and 25 percent of them will go on to develop diabetes.

Most individuals with diabetes control their disease through proper diet, weight management, oral medications, and in some cases, insulin injections. Finding the right balance is of the utmost importance, as diabetes contributes to more than 218,000 deaths each year and leads to a host of medical complications, most of them circulatory in nature, including heart disease, stroke, peripheral vascular disease, visual impairment, neuropathy, and kidney disease. People with diabetes are two to four times more likely than those without the disorder to die from cardiovascular disease; heart disease is the leading cause of diabetes-related deaths.

Keep an Eye on Cholesterol

Contrary to popular belief, not all cholesterol is bad. In fact, it can be a very useful substance. Cholesterol helps your body build new cells, produce needed hormones, and insulate nerves. Your liver manufactures all the cholesterol your body needs, but cholesterol also enters the body through the foods you eat, primarily through animal-based foods such as meat, eggs, and milk. It is this dietary cholesterol that often poses a risk of heart disease.

Most people are aware that high cholesterol is to be avoided and that your risk of heart disease increases as your cholesterol level increases. The danger arises when excess cholesterol builds up in the walls of your arteries, causing what is commonly referred to as "hardening of the arteries." This buildup leads to atherosclerosis and compromised blood flow. But we have come to recognize that dietary cholesterol can either benefit or harm you, depending on the type. HDL (high-density lipoprotein or "good") cholesterol actually works to clear cholesterol from your blood and has some protective effects against heart disease. LDL (low-density lipoprotein or "bad") cholesterol is the main source of artery-clogging plaque that impairs circulation. High levels of triglycerides, another fat in your bloodstream, have also been linked to heart disease.

There are no outward symptoms of high cholesterol or high triglycerides. A blood test is the only way to measure your levels. It is recommended that everyone over the age of twenty have their lipid levels (that is, total cholesterol level, LDL, HDL, and triglycerides) checked every five years. Here is how to interpret your numbers:[51]

Understand Your Total Cholesterol

Total Cholesterol (in mg/dL)	Category
< 200	Desirable
200-239	Borderline
≥ 240	High

Understand Your LDL Cholesterol

LDL Cholesterol (in mg/dL)	Category
< 100	Optimal—particularly if at very high risk of heart disease
100-129	Near optimal—particularly if at moderate risk of heart disease
130-159	Borderline—particularly if at moderate to high risk of heart disease
160-189	High—particularly with one other risk factor for heart disease
≥ 190	Very high

Understand Your HDL Cholesterol

HDL Cholesterol (in mg/dL)	Category
≥ 60	Desirable
40-59	Borderline
< 40	Too Low

Understand Your Triglycerides

Triglycerides (in mg/dL)	Category
< 150	Desirable
150-199	Borderline
≥ 200	High

A variety of factors can affect your lipid levels. Eating a diet low in cholesterol and saturated fat, maintaining a healthy weight, and exercising regularly will lower cholesterol and triglyceride levels and reduce your risk for heart disease. If these lifestyle modifications do not achieve the desired results, or if you have a strong hereditary component to your high lipid level, medication might be in order.

LIVE LONG AND WELL

While some of the statistics in this chapter paint a frightening picture, we have the power to dramatically improve *all* of them. In our quest for good health, it is exciting to consider how many opportunities exist to enhance blood flow and stack the odds in our favor. It may be enormously challenging to make some of the lifestyle changes we discussed here, but consider the benefits! Eliminating these serious risk factors or bringing them under control can help you win the fight against heart disease and so many other conditions and live a longer, healthier, fuller life.

In the next chapter, we will see that the future of medicine is here now. EECP has placed us on the brink of conquering heart disease and countless other conditions—and transforming an entire industry in the process.

8

~

EECP and the Future of Medicine

ONE OF A PHYSICIAN'S GREATEST CHALLENGES is to accept the fact that the truth changes. What is medical fact today may easily be disproved tomorrow. We study and train for years, only to discover that a cornerstone of thought and practice has become a thing of the past. Embracing this reality is often a humbling experience.

It is equally challenging—and equally important—to allow the changing truth to bring progress to our routine. We must ensure that our practice of medicine keeps pace with science. I strive to expand my knowledge every day so that I may offer my patients the most up-to-the-minute medical guidance possible. But as we discovered earlier, history suggests we have not always met this challenge, and it can take many, many years for new ideas to be accepted and integrated into practice. Bloodletting, for example, was used for hundreds of years after it was shown to be baseless because physicans had no other treatments to offer but felt compelled to treat anyway. It is thought to be responsible for countless illnesses and deaths as a result. And in 1847, a physician in Vienna concluded that doctors who performed autopsies and then immediately delivered babies without washing their hands were communicating deadly infections to women and children. He ordered his staff to wash and sterilize

152

their hands before treating each patient, and he was gratified to see the death rate quickly drop. But doctors were offended by the notion that they were responsible for their patients' demise. The physician who advocated hand washing was ridiculed, and the practice was abandoned. It took nearly twenty years for doctors to revisit sterilization and make it part of their routine. It is truly horrifying to consider how many patients were lost before this knowledge turned into habit.

The story of EECP's evolution in the United States provides an excellent illustration of what can happen when medical progress lags behind scientific truth. EECP was first introduced in studies on humans in the early 1970s, and it was shown to offer tremendous clinical benefits. Several years ago, I spoke to a technician who worked in one of the labs where EECP was first studied. "We just could not believe what we were seeing," he recalled. "The amount of blood flow in the coronary arteries was astounding. We knew we were onto something big." That was thirty years ago. As we have seen, the treatment has been largely ignored, primarily because the EECP machine itself was cumbersome and not as exciting to physicians as the technologically advanced surgical and invasive techniques that were emerging at the same time.

Despite the excitement it generated among researchers in the United States, EECP was all but forgotten during the next twenty years. However, China saw EECP's remarkable value, further developed it into the user-friendly, comfortable device we use today, and quickly elevated it to the heart disease treatment of choice. It was not until the early 1990s—when U.S. doctors were faced with a growing, aging population of postsurgical cardiac survivors who were more medically complex than younger patients and were suffering from reemerging heart disease symptoms—that U.S. interest in EECP was renewed. Doctors recognized that the high-risk, end-stage heart disease patient needed another treatment option. The clinical results this group enjoyed from EECP were extraordinary, just as they were two decades earlier. Again, researchers knew they were on to something big.

Only the sickest patients were included in studies on EECP's effects, making the significant, positive outcomes that much more exciting. Proponents of the treatment began to marvel that the results would be even more extraordinary if patients were offered EECP before their disease became so advanced. Still, physicians insisted on reserving EECP as a last resort, and they offered it only to end-stage patients who could not undergo surgery or invasive procedures.

There was no scientific basis for this approach. In fact, it was just the opposite. As EECP was slowly being introduced into medical practice for selected patients, researchers were making a staggering discovery. Study after study was casting doubt on what was thought to be a central truth of heart disease. We were learning that the disease is not, as we had thought for so long, defined by specific blockages. It is a systemic illness that affects the entire circulatory system. All of a sudden, fact had become fallacy, and the basis for modern heart disease management—attacking blockages by bypassing them, pushing them out of the way, scraping them, or irradiating them—was slipping away. Inflammation was now recognized as a key underlying factor in heart disease, but the invasive operations and procedures physicians used to battle the condition actually created more inflammation. They were aggravating the problem, contributing to an environment where heart disease may continue to flourish, rather than improving the situation.

To the medical community, it was a jarring and unwelcome realization. The high-tech and costly invasive approaches had become a multibillion-dollar industry, and they had prompted an exponential rise in the number of heart surgery programs, catheterization laboratories, cardiothoracic surgeons, and invasive cardiologists. In fact, the new, accepted truths about heart disease not only failed to bring about a change in the way the condition was treated, but the news did not even reach the general public for many years. On the contrary, the number of procedures aimed at opening or bypassing blockages has continued to climb steadily for the past fifteen years, with no end in sight. Only a few renegade physicians dared to speak publicly about the systemic nature of heart disease, and they were often dismissed.

Slowly, over the years, increasing numbers of well-known and well-respected cardiologists have spoken and written openly about the shift in our understanding of heart disease, calling for a systemic treatment as the first-line approach and urging that surgery and invasive procedures should be reserved only for the most critical patients who have failed all other measures. The opinion that treating the cause of the disease makes more clinical sense than simply treating the symptoms is gaining ground. In a recent continuing education course for physicians, Steven E. Nissen, MD, vice-chairman of cardiology at the Cleveland Clinic Foundation, explained, "Unless you treat [coronary artery disease] as a systemic disease, unless you change the metabolic milieu that caused this disease to develop, you will not change the outcome."[1]

In the growing number of books and articles about our new definition of heart disease and the need for a new approach, medications and lifestyle changes such as regular exercise, proper diet, and smoking cessation are the "solutions" consistently recommended. But each and every writer on this topic has stopped short of recommending a medical treatment, which has left patients asking, "If the invasive procedures don't treat heart disease, what does?"

THE SYSTEMIC SOLUTION TO A SYSTEMIC PROBLEM

What is curiously absent in these calls to action is the exciting news that a treatment exists that unequivocally provides an appropriate, systemic remedy for what we now know is a systemic disease. It is noninvasive, already clinically proven, and covered by insurance. It improves blood flow to the heart and throughout the body, improves the health of all blood vessels, and therefore is the only treatment that logically fights heart disease at its root. It is suitable for nearly every person living with the condition, from an individual who just got word of an abnormality on their stress test to a gravely ill, end-stage patient who has tried everything. It puts their bodies in a better place to live with heart disease and to fight it. It is EECP.

The ultimate goal of scientific research and development is to lead us from complexity to simplicity, from challenging to trouble free, from large to small. EECP is such an achievement. As a simple, safe, and effective treatment, there is no place to evolve from EECP. It is both low-tech and the most advanced heart disease treatment we have. It allows physicians to fulfill two of their most important charges: *above all, do no harm* and *help the body heal itself.*

A UNIQUE OPPORTUNITY FOR DOCTOR-PATIENT RELATIONSHIPS

Of course, I am not suggesting that the lifestyle changes and medications so often suggested in books and articles about the newly defined systemic heart disease are unnecessary. They are absolutely critical to a patient's success in living with heart disease in the best possible way. But many heart disease sufferers find it difficult, even impossible, to change their eating habits, quit smoking, engage in more exercise, and take their medications on their own.

In several ways, EECP offers an exciting opportunity to help patients improve their lifestyle choices and reinforce good habits. First, by increasing their stamina, energy, and overall quality of life, EECP gives patients the ability to be active in a way many could not manage before receiving their treatment. The more they are able to do, the more they want to do, and the more physically active they become. Second, because EECP is provided over a seven-week period, it offers a unique opportunity for the doctor-patient relationship to deepen. The daily visits give patients a chance to develop a genuine sense of trust in their doctor. At the same time, they give doctors a chance to counsel and encourage patients to supplement the benefits they receive from EECP by making healthier lifestyle choices. The physician may offer guidance on quitting smoking, eating a more balanced diet, expanding an exercise regimen, or all three. Whatever the case, and whatever the patient's particular needs, EECP allows a true health partnership to develop. In short, the treatment offers the physical and emotional setting necessary for patients to get back on the path to good health.

WHY WAIT?

The numerous benefits that EECP offers, combined with the fact that it is the only systemic treatment for the systemic illness of heart disease, begs an important question: why continue to wait until a patient has no other options before giving them a treatment that can slow or even stop the progression of their disease and improve their quality of life? There is no valid answer to this question. In fact, patients around the world are increasingly choosing EECP as their first treatment for heart disease, and science is on their side. A recent United States study compared patients who chose EECP instead of undergoing bypass surgery, angioplasty, or stent placement with patients who were instructed to wait to receive EECP until all surgical and invasive options had been exhausted. It found that the EECP-first patients were less likely to have a heart attack, were less likely to be hospitalized, and enjoyed a greater reduction in angina in the six months following their treatment than patients who received EECP as a last resort.[2] This groundbreaking study offers clear evidence that using EECP sooner rather than later brings significant clinical and cost benefits. Despite these findings, medical practice has not shifted. EECP is still typically reserved for end-stage, inoperable patients only—a formula that ignores the science and clinical experience that instructs us to do the opposite.

WHAT'S NEXT?

In the United States, most people living with heart disease continue to undergo procedure after procedure, surgery after surgery, test after test, without ever learning that EECP is an option. Every day, I meet patients in exactly this situation. Until they saw a news story, stumbled upon a brochure, or conducted their own research, they were not aware of EECP, let alone that it may be a treatment to consider. There are hundreds of thousands of people across the country just like them, still living without this information.

Why is EECP still unknown? In this and previous chapters, I have discussed many possible explanations, but none of them truly matter anymore. By reading this book, you are participating in a revolution. We can celebrate this wonderful treatment and all the hope it brings to millions of heart disease sufferers and their loved ones. As more people like you learn about EECP, the treatment will change heart disease management and health care as we know it.

A GLIMPSE OF THINGS TO COME

If we were to use a crystal ball to predict all the ways in which EECP will impact us in the future, the possibilities—actually, the *probabilities*—are nothing short of astounding. With its safety, effectiveness, and a list of uses we have only begun to discover, EECP is a sleeping giant offering a deceptively simple solution to many burgeoning, devastating health problems. It is noninvasive and painless, brings *none* of the risks of surgery, and—if we apply it in even a fraction of the cases where we could—promises to save countless lives and billions of dollars.

EECP allows us to envision a time when the emotional, physical, and economic impact of circulatory diseases will be all but eliminated. With it, patients and their families will no longer be held hostage by the fear, painful symptoms, hospital stays, missed work, or compromised quality of life these conditions currently bring. In

CASE STUDY

Rocco S., age forty-six, had an extensive history of heart disease. At his young age, he had already suffered three heart attacks and undergone two bypass surgeries (at age forty-four and age forty-five), eleven angioplasties, and six stent placements. Despite all of these surgeries and procedures, he had daily angina with almost all activities, and even while he slept. He had overwhelming anxiety and depression. "I'm a young guy. I can't do anything," he told me. After EECP, his angina decreased in frequency and severity; he went from taking nitro fourteen times a day to only once or twice daily. He had no more fear of his heart disease, and he had much more energy. He was able to coach Little League and volunteer at his church again. "EECP has really changed my life," he said.

short, it will allow sufferers of a staggeringly wide variety of ailments to spend more time truly *living* and less time in the operating room undergoing painful, costly, risky procedures. In addition to the savings in health-care costs, EECP will return patients to work and other activities, translating into higher productivity and consumption by society at large. EECP is the future of medicine, with the power to transform an entire industry, perhaps even our entire culture. Following are just a few ways it will do so.

Reining in the Number-One Killer

As more people understand the true nature of heart disease and learn about EECP, we will see a profound change in the way heart disease is treated and prevented.

Without question, the future of EECP is as the first treatment for heart disease. Before the bypass, before the angioplasties, before the stents, patients will choose the only logical, noninvasive, risk-free, lower-cost option. This approach, which relegates invasive procedures and surgery to their rightful place as last resorts, is simply common sense. Indeed, many informed Americans are already choosing EECP as their first treatment, and this trend will only continue to grow as more people learn all the facts about heart disease.

EECP will be used to prevent heart disease. When people are found to have an increased risk of heart disease, EECP will be used to prevent or slow its progression. The treatment promotes the development of collateral blood vessels, strengthens the circulatory system, and trains the heart to work more efficiently. In doing so, it will give potential heart disease sufferers a head start on the illness, thereby delaying and minimizing its effects.

Becoming the Standard Treatment for All Conditions Marked by Poor Blood Flow

As a systemic treatment that maximizes oxygen- and nutrient-rich blood flow throughout the body, EECP's benefits are seemingly limitless. As we have seen, lack of blood flow is the cause or a major contributing factor in numerous diseases responsible for tremendous suffering, disability, death, and expense. EECP will create a considerable shift in current treatments for some of these diseases, and it will provide a treatment where there once was none for others. Along with many other devastating circulatory disorders, EECP can and will successfully treat:

- Heart disease
- Stroke
- Peripheral vascular disease
- Diabetes
- Hypertension
- Kidney disease
- Parkinson's disease
- Dementia and memory loss (including Alzheimer's disease)
- Neuropathy

- Erectile dysfunction
- Hearing loss and tinnitus
- Vision impairment
- Autoimmune diseases (including Raynaud's phenomenon)
- Mesenteric ischemia
- Avascular necrosis
- Vertigo
- Rheumatic disease
- Restless legs syndrome

Preventing Disease and Enhancing Athletic Performance

By boosting blood flow in a healthy body, EECP improves stamina, endurance, strength, mobility, and vitality. EECP's ability to flush toxins from the body and to serve as an antioxidant and anti-inflammatory agent make it an invaluable partner in the quest for good health. As such, healthy individuals will make EECP an integral part of their lives, using it to supplement exercise regimens, promote overall wellness, and prevent disease.

Of course, athletes form the most elite group of healthy people. We have already begun to see an interest in EECP among professional athletes. In the future, they will continue to expand their use of the treatment to complement training programs, reduce players' risk of injury, and minimize recovery time between workouts. EECP may very well become the secret weapon of athletes looking for an edge.

WHAT IS AT STAKE?

Heart disease continues to claim one American life every forty-five seconds, while we continue to apply old rules to treat it. It is the leading killer, the most costly disease, and a primary cause of disability in the United States, but we have the ability to quickly change these facts. The need for EECP has never been greater, and as our population ages, that need will continue to rise exponentially. Embracing the treatment and making it widely available—sooner rather than later in the course of treating an individual's heart disease—would change the entire face of the condition. It is the only way to knock heart disease off its perch as our most deadly and most expensive illness. It is the only humane choice. Hundreds of thousands of lives and hundreds of billions of dollars are at stake. This is a public health issue, an economic issue, and a bioethical issue.

By reading this book, you have taken a critical step in improving your health and the health of your loved ones. Listen to your body. Don't minimize your symptoms or discount the importance of your quality of life. Play an active role in managing your health. Ask questions, and be sure the treatments you receive are in your best interest.

We have the tool. Now we must use it to its fullest. The possibilities are endless.

Endnotes

Introduction

1. R. Holubkov, E. D. Kennard, J. M. Foris, et al., "Comparison of Patients Undergoing Enhanced External Counterpulsation and Percutaneous Coronary Intervention for Stable Angina Pectoris," *The American Journal of Cardiology* 89 (2002): 1182–6; F. Unger, P. W. Serruys, M. H. Yacoub, et al., "Revascularization in Multivessel Disease: Comparison between Two-Year Outcomes of Coronary Bypass Surgery and Stenting," *The Journal of Thoracic and Cardiovascular Surgery* 125 (2003): 809–20; The Bypass Angioplasty Revascularization Investigation (BARI) Investigators, "Comparison of Coronary Bypass Surgery with Angioplasty in Patients with Multivessel Disease," *The New England Journal of Medicine* 335 (1996): 217–25.

2. J. E. Brush Jr., R. O. Cannon III, W. H. Schenke, et al., "Angina Due to Coronary Microvascular Disease in Hypertensive Patients without Left Ventricular Hypertrophy," *The New England Journal of Medicine* 319 (1988): 1302–7; F. I. Sax, R. O. Cannon III, C. Hanson, et al., "Impaired Forearm Vasodilator Reserve in Patients with Microvascular Angina. Evidence of a Generalized Disorder of Vascular Function?" *The New England Journal of Medicine* 317 (1987): 1366–70.

3. P. M. Ridker, N. Rifai, L. Rose, et al., "Comparison of C-Reactive Protein and Low-Density Lipoprotein Cholesterol Levels in the Prediction of First Cardiovascular Events," *The New England Journal of Medicine* 347 (2002): 1557–65.

4. C. Heeschen, S. Dimmeler, S. Fichtlscherer, et al., "Prognostic Value of Placental Growth Factor in Patients with Acute Chest Pain," *The Journal of the American Medical Association* 291 (2004): 435–41.

5. H. K. Kuramitsu, M. Qi, I. C. Kang, et al., "Role for Periodontal Bacteria in Cardiovascular Diseases," *Annals of Periodontology/The American Academy of Periodontology* 6 (2001): 41–7; S. Abou-Raya, A. Naeem, K. H. Abou-El, et al., "Coronary Artery Disease and Periodontal Disease: Is There a Link?" *Angiology* 53 (2002): 141–8.

6. S. O. Geerts, V. Legrand, J. Charpentier, et al., "Further Evidence of the Association between Periodontal Conditions and Coronary Artery Disease," *The Journal of Periodontology* 75 (2004): 1274–80.

7. M. V. Kalayoglu, P. Libby, and G. I. Byrne, "*Chlamydia pneumoniae* as an Emerging Risk Factor in Cardiovascular Disease," *The Journal of the American Medical Association* 288 (2002): 2724–31.

8. C. Grahame-Clarke, N. N. Chan, D. Andrew, et al., "Impaired Vascular Function and Increased Risk of Coronary Artery Disease with Human Cytomegalovirus," *Circulation* 108 (2003): 678–83; M. Chmiela, M. Kowalewicz-Kulbat, A. Miszczak, et al., "A Link between *Helicobacter pylori* and/or *Chlamydia* spp. Infections and Atherosclerosis," *FEMS Immunology and Medical Microbiology* 36 (2003): 187–92.

9. N. Parchure, E. G. Zouridakis, and J. C. Kaski, "Effect of Azithromycin Treatment on Endothelial Function in Patients with Coronary Artery Disease and Evidence of *Chlamydia pneumoniae* Infection," *Circulation* 105 (2002): 1298–303; D. Sander, K. Winbeck, J. Klingelhofer, et al., "Reduced Progression of Early Carotid Atherosclerosis after Antibiotic Treatment and *Chlamydia pneumoniae* Seropositivity," *Circulation* 106 (2002): 2428–33.

10. The American Heart Association, "Heart Disease and Stroke Statistics," 2005 update, 51.

11. T. B. Graboys, B. Biegelsen, S. Lampert, et al., "Results of a Second-Opinion Trial among Patients Recommended for Coronary Angiography," *The Journal of the American Medical Association* 268 (1992): 2537–40.

12. E. V. Chomka and B. H. Brundage, "Cardiovascular Ultrafast Computed Tomographic Angiography," *American Journal of Cardiac Imaging* 7 (1993): 252–64.

13. The American Heart Association, "Heart Disease and Stroke Statistics," 2005 update, 51–52.

14. Ibid.

15. R. Hill, A. Bagust, A. Bakhaj, et al., "Coronary Artery Stents: A Rapid Systematic Review and Economic Evaluation," *Health Technology Assessment* 8 (2004): iii–iv, 1–242.

16. K. Griffin, "No More Knife Guys," *AARP Magazine*, November/December 2004, 30–33.

17. T. B. Graboys, A. Headley, B. Lown, et al., "Results of a Second-Opinion Program for Coronary Artery Bypass Graft Surgery," *The Journal of the American Medical Association* 258 (1987): 1611–4.

18. G. Kolata, "New Heart Studies Cast Doubt on Artery-Opening Operations," *The New York Times*, March 21, 2004, Front section.

19. Ibid.

20. K. Griffin, "No More Knife Guys," *AARP Magazine*, November/December 2004, 30–33.

21. G. Kolata, "New Heart Studies Cast Doubt on Artery-Opening Operations," *The New York Times*, March 21, 2004, Front section.

Chapter 1

1. W. E. Lawson, J. C. Hui, and P. F. Cohn, "Long-Term Prognosis of Patients with Angina Treated with EECP: Five-Year Follow-up Study," *Clinical Cardiology* 23 (2000): 254–8; The Bypass Angioplasty Revascularization Investigation (BARI) Investigators, "Comparison of Coronary Bypass Surgery with Angioplasty in Patients with Multivessel Disease," *The New England Journal of Medicine* 335 (1996): 217–25.

2. The American Heart Association, "*Heart Disease and Stroke Statistics*," 2005 update.

3. Ibid.

4. D. L. Braverman, B. Wechsler, and A. Farooqi, "Safety and Efficacy of Enhanced External Counterpulsation in Patients with Symptomatic Ischemic Heart Disease and Cardiac Pacemakers: A Case Series," *Archives of Physical Medicine and Rehabilitation* 85 (2004): E18.

5. A. B. Ochoa, W. W. O'Neill, and S. Almany, "Atrial Fibrillation Does Not Degrade the Clinical Benefits from Enhanced External Counterpulsation Therapy in Patients with Chronic Angina: Results from the International EECP Patient Registry," *Journal of the American College of Cardiology* 41(6 Suppl 2) (2003): 379.

Chapter 2

1. National Health and Nutrition Examination Survey III (1988–94), Centers for Disease Control and Prevention/National Center for Health Statistics.

2. J. C. McSweeney, M. Cody, P. O'Sullivan, et al., "Women's Early Warning Symptoms of Acute Myocardial Infarction," *Circulation* 108 (2003): 2619–23.

3. W. C. Little, "Angiographic Assessment of the Culprit Coronary Artery Lesion before Acute Myocardial Infarction," *The American Journal of Cardiology* 66 (1990): 44G–47G.

4. A. D. Michaels, M. Accad, T. A. Ports, et al., "Left Ventricular Systolic Unloading and Augmentation of Intracoronary Pressure and Doppler Flow during Enhanced External Counterpuslation," *Circulation* 106 (2002): 1237–42.

5. G. Wu, Z. Zheng, Z. Du, et al., "[A Comparative Study of Finger Plethysmography and Aortic Pressure for Monitoring the Effect of External Counterpulsation]" [Chinese], *Sheng Wu Yi Xue Gong Cheng Xue Za Zhi* 16 (1999): 493–6.

6. D. Werner, G. Michelson, J. Harazny, et al., "Changes in Ocular Blood Flow Velocities during External Counterpulsation in Healthy Volunteers and Patients with Atherosclerosis," *Graefe's Archive for Clinical and Experimental Ophthalmology* 239 (2001): 599–602.

7. D. Werner, H. Marthol, C. M. Brown, et al., "Changes of Cerebral Blood Flow Velocities during Enhanced External Counterpulsation," *Acta Neurologica Scandinavica* 107 (2003): 405–11; H. Marthol, D. Werner, C. M. Brown, et al., "Enhanced External Counterpulsation Does Not Compromise Cerebral Autoregulation," *Acta Neurologica Scandinavica* 111 (2005): 34–41.

8. D. Werner, C. Freidel, J. Kropp, et al., "Pneumatic External Counterpulsation—A New Treatment for Selected Patients with Symptomatic Coronary Artery Disease," *Circulation* 98 (17 Suppl) (1998): I-350(1839).

9. S. Kho, J. Liuzzo, K. Suresh, et al., "Vascular Endothelial Growth Factor and Atrial Natriuretic Peptide in Enhanced External Counterpulsation," *Program and Abstracts of the 82nd Annual Meeting of the Endocrine Society* June 21–24, 2000, Toronto, Ontario, Canada (abstract 561).

10. J. Y. Ji, H. Jing, and S. L. Diamond, "Shear Stress Causes Nuclear Localization of Endothelial Glucocorticoid Receptor and Expression from the GRE Promoter," *Circulation Research* 92 (2003): 279–85.

11. P. O. Bonetti, G. W. Barsness, P. C. Keelan, et al., "Enhanced External Counterpulsation Improves Endothelial Function in Patients with Symptomatic

Coronary Artery Disease," *Journal of the American College of Cardiology* 41 (2003): 1761–8.

12. G. F. Wu, S. Z. Qiang, Z. S. Zheng, et al., "A Neurohormonal Mechanism for the Effectiveness of Enhanced External Counterpulsation," *Circulation* 100 (1999): I-832(4390); X. X. Qian, W. K. Wu, Z. S. Zheng, et al., "Effect of Enhanced External Counterpulsation on Nitric Oxide Production in Coronary Disease," *Journal of Heart Disease* 1 (1999): 1.

13. D. Werner, F. Wonka, L. Klinghammer, et al., "Improvement of Renal Perfusion and Function by Pneumatic External Counterpulsation," *European Heart Journal* 19 (Abstract Suppl) (1999): 3660(655).

14. G. F. Wu, S. Z. Qiang, Z. S. Zheng, et al., "A Neurohormonal Mechanism for the Effectiveness of Enhanced External Counterpulsation," *Circulation* 100 (1999): I-832(4390).

15. L. Lu, Z. S. Zheng, W. K. Wu, et al., "Effect of Enhanced External Counterpulsation on Circulating and Tissue Angiotensin II in Experimental Myocardial Infarction," *Journal of Cardiac Failure* 7(3 Suppl 2) (2001): 35(123).

16. G. F. Wu, S. Z. Qiang, Z. S. Zheng, et al., "A Neurohormonal Mechanism for the Effectiveness of Enhanced External Counterpulsation," *Circulation* 100 (1999): I-832(4390).

Chapter 3

1. A. Kantrowitz, "Experimental Augmentation of Coronary Flow by Retardation of the Arterial Pressure Pulse," *Surgery* 34 (1953): 678–87.

2. W. C. Birtwell, H. S. Soroff, M. Wall, et al., "Assisted Circulation: An Improved Method for Counterpulsation," *Transactions—American Society of Artificial Internal Organs* 8 (1962): 35–42; H. S. Soroff, W. C. Birtwell, H. J. Levine, et al., "Effect of Counterpulsation upon the Myocardial Oxygen Consumption and Heart Work," *Surgical Forum* 13 (1962): 174–6.

3. L. Campeau, "Grading of Angina Pectoris" (letter to the editor), *Circulation* 54 (1976): 522–3.

4. J. S. Banas, A. Brilla, and H. J. Levine, "Evaluation of External Counterpulsation for the Treatment of Angina Pectoris," *The American Journal of Cardiology* 31 (1973): 118.

5. E. A. Amsterdam, J. Banas, J. M. Criley, et al., "Clinical Assessment of External Pressure Circulatory Assistance in Acute Myocardial Infarction. Report of a Cooperative Clinical Trial," *The American Journal of Cardiology* 45 (1980): 349–56.

6. H. S. Soroff, C. T. Cloutier, W. C. Birtwell, et al., "Management of Cardiogenic Shock," *The Journal of the American Medical Association* 229 (1974): 1441–50.

7. The American Heart Association, "Heart Disease and Stroke Statistics," 2005 update, 51.

8. Ibid.

9. Y. Y. Xu, D. Y. Hu, Z. S. Zheng, "External Counterpulsation—Review Article," *Chinese Medical Journal* 103 (1990): 762–71.

10. W. E. Lawson, J. C. K. Hui, H. S. Soroff, et al., "Efficacy of Enhanced External Counterpulsation in the Treatment of Angina Pectoris," *The American Journal of Cardiology* 70 (1992): 859–62.

11. W. E. Lawson, J. C. K. Hui, Z. S. Zheng, et al., "Three-Year Sustained Benefit from Enhanced External Counterpulsation in Chronic Angina Pectoris," *The American Journal of Cardiology* 75 (1995): 840–1.

12. I. Taguchi, K. Ogawa, A. Oida, et al., "Comparison of Hemodynamic Effects of Enhanced External Counterpulsation and Intra-aortic Balloon Pumping in Patients with Acute Myocardial Infarction," *The American Journal of Cardiology* 86 (2000): 1139–41.

13. W. E. Lawson, J. C. K. Hui, and P. F. Cohn, "Long-Term Prognosis of Patients with Angina Treated with Enhanced External Counterpulsation: Five-Year Follow-up Study," *Clinical Cardiology* 23 (2000): 254–8.

14. D. Masuda, R. Nohara, T. Hirai, et al., "The New Therapeutic Approach with Enhanced External Counterpulsation in Patients with Chronic Stable Angina: Evaluation of Myocardial Flow and Flow Reserve by N-13 Ammonia PET," *Circulation* 100 (1999): I-732(3865).

15. S. Karim, M. Kasim, R. Suwita, et al., "Enhanced External Counterpulsation Protects Coronary Artery Disease Patients from Future Cardiac Events," *Journal of Heart Disease* 1 (1999): 223(889).

16. The Bypass Angioplasty Revascularization Investigation (BARI) Investigators, "Comparison of Coronary Bypass Surgery with Angioplasty in Patients with Multivessel Disease," *The New England Journal of Medicine* 335 (1996):

217–25; W. E. Lawson, J. C. K. Hui, and P. F. Cohn, "Long-Term Prognosis of Patients with Angina Treated with Enhanced External Counterpulsation: Five-Year Follow-up Study," *Clinical Cardiology* 23 (2000): 254–8.

17. The Bypass Angioplasty Revascularization Investigation (BARI) Investigators, "Comparison of Coronary Bypass Surgery with Angioplasty in Patients with Multivessel Disease," *The New England Journal of Medicine* 335 (1996): 217–25.

18. C. W. Hamm, J. Reimers, T. Ischinger, et al., "A Randomized Study of Coronary Angioplasty Compared with Bypass Surgery in Patients with Symptomatic Multivessel Coronary Disease. German Angioplasty Bypass Surgery Investigation (GABI)," *The New England Journal of Medicine* 331 (1994): 1037–43.

19. R. A. Henderson, S. J. Pocock, S. J. Sharp, et al., "Long-Term Results of RITA-1 Trial: Clinical and Cost Comparisons of Coronary Angioplasty and Coronary-Artery Bypass Grafting. Randomised Intervention Treatment of Angina," *Lancet* 352 (1998): 1419–25.

20. R. Holubkov, E. D. Kennard, J. M. Foris, et al., "Comparison of Patients Undergoing Enhanced External Counterpulsation and Percutaneous Coronary Intervention for Stable Angina Pectoris," *The American Journal of Cardiology* 89 (2002): 1182–6; The Bypass Angioplasty Revascularization Investigation (BARI) Investigators, "Comparison of Coronary Bypass Surgery with Angioplasty in Patients with Multivessel Disease," *The New England Journal of Medicine* 335 (1996): 217–25; W. E. Lawson, J. C. K. Hui, and P. F. Cohn, "Long-Term Prognosis of Patients with Angina Treated with Enhanced External Counterpulsation: Five-Year Follow-up Study," *Clinical Cardiology* 23 (2000): 254–8.

21. R. Holubkov, E. D. Kennard, J. M. Foris, et al., "Comparison of Patients Undergoing Enhanced External Counterpulsation and Percutaneous Coronary Intervention for Stable Angina Pectoris," *The American Journal of Cardiology* 89 (2002): 1182–6.

22. W. E. Lawson, J. C. Hui, Z. S. Zheng, et al., "Can Angiographic Findings Predict Which Coronary Patients Will Benefit from Enhanced External Counterpulsation?" *The American Journal of Cardiology* 77 (1996): 1107–9.

23. J. Tartaglia, J. Stenerson Jr., R. Charney, et al., "Exercise Capability and Myocardial Perfusion in Chronic Angina Patients with Enhanced External Counterpulsation," *Clinical Cardiology* 26 (2003): 287–90.

24. T. P. Stys, W. E. Lawson, J. C. Hui, et al., "Effects of Enhanced External Counterpulsation on Stress Radionuclide Coronary Perfusion and Exercise Capacity in Chronic Stable Angina Pectoris," *The American Journal of Cardiology* 89 (2002): 822–4.

25. A. S. Brown, E. Ho, D. Heavery, et al., "The Improvements in Exercise Tolerance Post Enhanced External Counterpulsation in Patients with Chronic Refractory Angina Are Related to Diastolic Augmentation," *Heart* 85(Suppl I) (2001): 41(125).

26. G. L. Fricchione, K. Jaghab, W. Lawson, et al., "Psychosocial Effects of Enhanced External Counterpulsation in the Angina Patient," *Psychosomatics* 36 (1995): 494–7.

27. S. Springer, A. Fife, W. Lawson, et al., "Psychosocial Effects of Enhanced External Counterpulsation in the Angina Patient: A Second Study," *Psychosomatics* 42 (2001): 124–32.

28. K. A. Eagle, R. A. Guyton, R. Davidoff, et al., "ACC/AHA Guidelines for Coronary Artery Bypass Graft Surgery: Executive Summary and Recommendations: A Report of the American College of Cardiology/American Heart Association Task Force on Practice Guidelines [Committee to Revise the 1991 Guidelines for Coronary Artery Bypass Graft Surgery]," *Circulation* 100 (1999): 1464–80.

29. R. R. Arora, T. M. Chou, D. Jain, et al., "The Multicenter Study of Enhanced External Counterpulsation (MUST-EECP): Effect of EECP on Exercise-Induced Myocardial Ischemia and Anginal Episodes," *Journal of the American College of Cardiology* 33 (1999): 1833–40.

30. R. R. Arora, T. M. Chou, D. Jain, et al., "Effects of Enhanced External Counterpulsation on Health-Related Quality of Life Continue 12 Months after Treatment: A Substudy of the Multicenter Study of Enhanced External Counterpulsatikon," *Journal of Investigative Medicine* 50 (2002): 25–32.

31. W. Lawson, J. C. K. Hui, and G. Lang, "Treatment Benefit in the Enhanced External Counterpulsation Consortium," *Cardiology* 94 (2000): 31–5.

32. "IEPR-I Clinical Outcomes," *IEPR Newsletter Special Edition* (November 2002), 4.

33. K. Griffin, "No More Knife Guys," *AARP Magazine*, November/December 2004, 30–33.

34. O. Soran, A. Sengul, C. Ikizler, et al., "Enhanced External Counterpulsation (EECP) Treated Angina Patients from Turkey and the United States Have

Similar Good Outcomes Despite Different Baseline Profiles: A Report from the International EECP Patient Registry (IEPR)," *Cardiovascular Surgery* 11(Suppl II) (2003): 135.

35. R. R. Arora, M. F. Timoney, E. D. Kennard, et al., "The Safety and Efficacy of Enhanced External Counterpulsation as Therapy for Unstable Angina," *Circulation* 102(18 Suppl 2) (2000): II-615(2982).

Chapter 4

1. W. Lawson, "Current Use of Enhanced External Counterpulsation and Patient Selection," *Clinical Cardiology* 25(12 Suppl 2) (2002):II: 16–21.

2. W. E. Lawson, J. C. Hui, E. D. Kennard, et al., "Treatment Hours and Angina Improvement with Enhanced External Counterpulsation," *Journal of the American College of Cardiology* 43(5 Suppl A) (2004): 11A(1059-4).

3. W. E. Lawson, J. C. Hui, T. Guo, et al., "Prior Revascularization Increases the Effectiveness of Enhanced External Counterpulsation," *Clinical Cardiology* 21 (1998): 841–4.

4. C. P. Fitzgerald, W. E. Lawson, J. C. K. Hui, et al., "Enhanced External Counterpulsation as Initial Revascularization Treatment for Angina Refractory to Medical Therapy," *Cardiology* 100 (2003): 129–35.

5. T. P. Stys, W. E. Lawson, J. C. K. Hui, et al., "Safety and Effectiveness of Enhanced External Counterpulsation in Improving Angioplasty Restenosis," *Journal of Heart Disaease* 2 (2001): 131(524).

6. A. D. Michaels, G. W. Barsness, O. Soran, et al., "Frequency and Efficacy of Repeat Enhanced External Counterpulsation for Stable Angina Pectoris (from the International EECP Patient Registry)," *The American Journal of Cardiology* 95 (2005): 394–7.

7. R. Holubkov, E. Kennard, J. M. Foris, et al., "Comparison of Patients Undergoing Enhanced External Counterpulsation and Percutaneous Coronary Intervention for Stable Angina Pectoris," *The American Journal of Cardiology* 89 (2002): 1182–6; W. E. Lawson, G. Barsness, O. Soran, et al., "Frequency and Results of Repeat Enhanced External Counterpulsation for Refractory Angina," *Journal of the American College of Cardiology* 43(5 Suppl A) (2004): 308A(891-5).

8. W. E. Lawson, J. C. K. Hui, Z. S. Zheng, et al., "Three-Year Sustained Benefit from Enhanced External Counterpulsation in Chronic Angina Pectoris," *The American Journal of Cardiology* 75 (1995): 840–1; W. E. Lawson, J. C. K.

Hui, and P. F. Cohn, "Long-Term Prognosis of Patients with Angina Treated with Enhanced External Counterpulsation: Five-Year Follow-up Study," *Clinical Cardiology* 23 (2000): 254–8.

9. D. L. Braverman and B. Wechsler, "Enhanced External Counterpulsation and Functional Improvement in Octogenarians with Symptomatic Ischemic Heart Disease," *Archives of Physical Medicine and Rehabilitation* 84 (2003): E10(23).

10. G. Linnemeier, A. D. Michaels, O. Soran, et al., "Enhanced External Counterpulsation in the Management of Angina in the Elderly," *The American Journal of Geriatric Cardiology* 12 (2003): 90–4.

11. L. Jans and S. Stoddard, *Chartbook on Women and Disability in the United States. An InfoUse Report* (Washington, D.C.: U.S. National Institute on Disability and Rehabilitation Research, 1999).

12. N. K. Wenger, "Coronary Heart Disease: An Older Woman's Major Health Risk," *British Medical Journal* 315 (1997): 1085–90.

13. D. J. Malenka, D. O'Rourke, M. A. Miller, et al., "Cause of In-Hospital Death in 12,232 Consecutive Patients Undergoing Percutaneous Transluminal Coronary Angioplasty. The Northern New England Cardiovascular Disease Study Group," *American Heart Journal* 137 (1999): 632–8.

14. V. Vaccarino, Z. Q. Lin, S. V. Kasl, et al., "Gender Differences in Recovery after Coronary Artery Bypass Surgery," *Journal of the American College of Cardiology* 41 (2003): 307–14.

15. G. C. Linnemeier, E. D. Kennard, O. Soran, et al., "Enhanced External Counterpulsation Improves Functional Capacity and Quality of Life in Women with Chronic Angina," *Journal of the American College of Cardiology* 43(5 Suppl A) (2004): 308A(891-3).

16. O. Soran, E. Kennard, and A. Feldman, "Do Women with Left Ventricular Dysfunction and Refractory Angina Respond as Well as Men to Enhanced External Counterpulsation?" *IEPR Newsletter* 4 (2002): 7.

17. G. Linnemeier, M. K. Rutter, G. Barsness, et al., "Enhanced External Counterpulsation for the Relief of Angina in Patients with Diabetes: Safety, Efficacy and 1-Year Clinical Outcomes," *American Heart Journal* 146 (2003): 453–8.

18. K. M. V. Narayan, J. P. Boyle, T. J. Thompson, et al., "Lifetime Risk for Diabetes Mellitus in the United States," *The Journal of the American Medical Association* 290 (2003): 1884–90.

19. O. Soran, E. D. Kennard, S. F. Kelsey, et al., "Enhanced External Counterpulsation as Treatment for Chronic Angina in Patients with Left Ventricular Dysfunction: A Report from the International EECP Patient Registry (IEPR)," *Congestive Heart Failure* 8 (2002): 297–302.

20. O. Z. Soran, T. DeMarco, L. E. Crawford, et al., "Efficacy and Safety of Enhanced External Counterpulsation in Mild to Moderate Heart Failure: A Preliminary Report," *Journal of Cardiac Failure* 5(3 Suppl 1) (1999): 53(195).

21. O. Soran, B. Fleishman, T. DeMarco, et al., "Enhanced External Counterpulsation in Patients with Heart Failure: A Multicenter Feasibility Study," *Congestive Heart Failure* 8 (2002): 204–8, 227.

22. J. Gorcsan III, L. Crawford, O. Soran, et al., "Improvement in Left Ventricular Performance by Enhanced External Counterpulsation in Patients with Heart Failure," *Journal of the American College of Cardiology* 35(2 Suppl A) (2000): 230A(901-5).

23. D. Masuda, R. Nohara, T. Hirai, et al., "Enhanced External Counterpulsation Improved Myocardial Perfusion and Coronary Flow Reserve in Patients with Chronic Stable Angina: Evaluation by (13)N-Ammonia Positron Emission Tomography," *European Heart Journal* 22 (2001): 1451–8; H. Urano, "Enhanced External Counterpulsation Improves Exercise Tolerance, Reduces Exercise-Induced Myocardial Ischemia and Improves Left Ventricular Diastolic Filling in Patients with Coronary Artery Disease," *Journal of the American College of Cardiology* 37 (2001): 93–9.

24. U. Kansra and S. Sircar, "Microvascular angina," *Journal of the Indian Academy of Clinical Medicine* 2 (2001): 67–72.

25. R. Bugiardini and C. N. Bairey Merz, "Angina with 'Normal' Coronary Arteries: A Changing Philosophy," *The Journal of the American Medical Association* 293 (2005): 477–84.

26. K. D. Kronhaus and W. E. Lawson, "Long-Term Improvement in Microvascular Angina Patients Treated with Enhanced External Counterpulsation," *Journal of the American College of Cardiology* 43(5 Suppl A) (2004): 308A(891-6).

27. M. Mary-Krause, L. Cotte, A. Simon, et al., "Increased Risk of Myocardial Infarction with Duration of Protease Inhibitor Therapy in HIV-Infected Men," *AIDS* 17 (2003): 2479–86, 2529–31.

28. Y. Asanuma, A. Oeser, A. K. Shintani, et al., "Premature Coronary-Artery Atherosclerosis in Systemic Lupus Erythematosus," *The New England Journal of Medicine* 349 (2003): 2407–15.

29. S. Manzi, E. N. Meilahn, J. E. Rairie, et al., "Age-Specific Incidence Rates of Myocardial Infarction and Angina in Women with Systemic Lupus Erythematosus: Comparison with the Framingham Study," *American Journal of Epidemiology* 145 (1997): 408–15.

30. H. Maradit-Kremers, C. S. Crowson, P. J. Nicola, et al., "Increased Unrecognized Coronary Heart Disease and Sudden Deaths in Rheumatoid Arthritis. A Population-Based Cohort Study," *Arthritis and Rheumatism* 52 (2005): 402–11.

31. P. J. Nicola, H. Maradit-Kremers, V. L. Roger, et al. "The Risk of Congestive Heart Failure in Rheumatoid Arthritis: A Population-Based Study over 46 Years," *Arthritis and Rheumatism* 52 (2005): 412–20.

Chapter 5

1. W. P. Li, Z. B. Yao, W. J. Yang, et al., "Study of the External Counterpulsation (ECP) Therapy for Senile Dementia of the Alzheimer's Type (SDAT)," *Chinese Medical Journal* 107 (1994): 755–60.

2. C. Offergeld, D. Werner, M. Schneider, et al., "[Pneumatic External Counterpulsation (PECP): A New Treatment Option in Therapy for Refractory Inner Ear Disorders?]" [German], *Laryngorhinootologie* 79 (2000): 503–9.

3. Z. F. Yu, "[Thirty-two Cases of Sudden Deafness Treated with Sequential External Counterpulsation in Addition to Combined Traditional Chinese Medicine and Western Medicine Therapy]" [Chinese], *Chung-Kuo Chung Hsi i Chieh Ho Tsa Chih* 13 (1993): 603–5, 581.

4. D. Werner, G. Michelson, J. Harazny, et al., "Changes in Ocular Blood Flow Velocities during External Counterpulsation in Healthy Volunteers and Patients with Atherosclerosis," *Graefe's Archives of Clinical and Experimental Ophthalmology* 239 (2001): 599–602.

5. C. Rousseau, "Doctor Embarks on Parkinson's Research," Associated Press, May 17, 2004.

6. S. E. Froschermaier, D. Werner, S. Leike, et al., "Enhanced External Counterpulsation as a New Treatment Modality for Patients with Erectile Dysfunction," *Urologia Internationalis* 61 (1998): 168–71.

7. M. J. Hilz, D. Werner, H. Marthol, et al., "Enhanced External Counterpulsation Improves Skin Oxygenation and Perfusion," *European Journal of Clinical Investigation* 34 (2004): 385–91.

8. S. Rajaram, A. S. Walters, J. Shanahan, et al., "External Counterpulsation (ECP) as a Novel Treatment Modality for Restless Legs Syndrome (RLS)," 56th Annual Meeting of the American Academy of Neurology, April 24–May 1, 2004.

9. M. Huonker, M. Halle, and J. Keul, "Structural and Functional Adaptations of the Cardiovascular System by Training," *International Journal of Sports Medicine* 17(Suppl 3) (1996): S164–72.

10. A. D. Michaels, M. Accad, T. A. Ports, et al., "Left Ventricular Systolic Unloading and Augmentation of Intracoronary Pressure and Doppler Flow during Enhanced External Counterpuslation," *Circulation* 106 (2002): 1237–42.

11. Ibid.

12. D. Werner, M. Schneider, M. Weise, et al., "Pneumatic External Counterpulsation: A New Noninvasive Method to Improve Organ Perfusion," *The American Journal of Cardiology* 84 (1999): 950–2, A7–8; R. M. Applebaum, R. Kasliwal, and P. A. Tunick, "Sequential External Counterpulsation Increases Cerebral and Renal Blood Flow," *American Heart Journal* 133 (1997): 611–5.

13. H. Urano, S. Lida, K. Fukami, et al., "Intermittent Shear Stimuli by Enhanced External Counterpulsation (EECP) Restores Endothelial Function in Patients with Coronary Artery Diseases," *Circulation* 102(18 Suppl 2) (2000): II-57(266).

14. L. Liu, S. Zhou, Z. Zheng, et al., "[Effects of External Counterpulsation on the Pulsatility of Blood Pressure in Human Subjects]" [Chinese], *Sheng Wu Yi Xue Gong Cheng Xue Za Zhi* 19 (2002): 467–70.

15. D. Werner, A. John, T. Tragner, et al., "Improvement of Renal Perfusion and Function by Pneumatic External Counterpulsation," *European Heart Journal* 19(Abstr Suppl) (1998): 655(P3660).

16. D. Werner, M. Schneider, M. Weise, et al., "Pneumatic External Counterpulsation: A New Noninvasive Method to Improve Organ Perfusion," *The American Journal of Cardiology* 84 (1999): 950–2, A7–8.

17. X. Qian, W. Wu, Z. S. Zheng, et al., "Effect of Enhanced External Counter-pulsation on Lipid Peroxidation in Coronary Disease," *The Journal of Heart Disease* 1 (1999): 116(462).

Chapter 6

1. K. Griffin, "No More Knife Guys," *AARP Magazine*, November/December 2004, 30–33.

2. Healthcare Cost and Utilization Project 2003.

3. A. S. Brown, E. Ho, D. Heavery, et al., "The Improvements in Exercise Toler-ance Post Enhanced External Counterpulsation in Patients with Chronic Refractory Angina Are Related to Diastolic Augmentation," *Heart* 85(Suppl I) (2001): P41(125).

4. New Jersey A.C. Title 8, Chapter 33E: Cardiac Diagnostic Facilities and Car-diac Surgery Centers. New York State R.R. Title 10, Section 405.22: Critical Care and Special Care Services.

5. T. Graboys, "Coronary Angiography. A Long Look at a Short Queue," *The Journal of the American Medical Association* 282 (1999): 184–6.

6. C. P. Fitzgerald, W. E. Lawson, J. C. K. Hui, et al., "EECP as Initial Revascu-larization Treatment for Angina Refractory to Medical Therapy," *Cardiology* 100 (2003): 129–135.

7. M. Mettler and D. W. Kemper, "Information Therapy: Prescribed Informa-tion as a Reimbursable Medical Service," *Healthwise*, 2002.

8. Ziauddin Sardar, "Medicine and Multiculturalism," *New Renaissance*, 11:2 (Summer 2002): 6–8.

Chapter 7

1. National Health Interview Study (1999–2001), Centers for Disease Control and Prevention/National Center for Health Statistics.

2. S. Weyerer, "Physical Activity and Depression in the Community. Evidence from the Upper Bavarian Field Study," *International Journal of Sports Medi-cine* 13 (1992): 492–6; R. E. Frisch, G. Wyshak, N. L. Albright, et al., "Lower Prevalence of Breast Cancer and Cancers of the Reproductive System among Former College Athletes Compared to Non-Athletes," *British Journal of Cancer* 52 (1985): 885–91; I. Bairati, R. Larouche, F. Meyer, et al., "Life-

time Occupational Physical Activity and Incidental Prostate Cancer," *Cancer Causes and Control* 11 (2000): 759–64.

3. K. E. Powell, P. D. Thompson, C. J. Caspersen, et al., "Physical Activity and the Incidence of Coronary Heart Disease," *Annual Review of Public Health* 8 (1987): 253–87; J. A. Berlin and G. A. Colditz, "A Meta-analysis of Physical Activity in the Prevention of Coronary Heart Disease," *American Journal of Epidemiology* 132 (1990): 612–28.

4. D. B. Allison, K. R. Fontaine, J. E. Manson, et al., "Annual Deaths Attributable to Obesity in the United States," *The Journal of the American Medical Association* 282 (1999): 1530–8.

5. The American Heart Association, "Heart Disease and Stroke Statistics," 2005 update, 39.

6. 2004 Southeastern Pennsylvania Household Health Survey, Philadelphia Health Management Corporation, Community Health Database, 2004.

7. C. Hanevold, J. Waller, S. Daniels, et al., "The Effects of Obesity, Gender, and Ethnic Group on Left Ventricular Hypertrophy and Geometry in Hypertensive Children: A Collaborative Study of the International Pediatric Hypertension Association," *Pediatrics* 113 (2004): 328–33.

8. A. S. Shamsuzzaman, M. Winnicki, R. Wolk, et al., "Independent Association between Plasma Leptin and C-Reactive Protein in Healthy Humans," *Circulation* 109 (2004): 2181–5.

9. S. Soderberg, B. Ahren, J. H. Jansson, et al., "Leptin Is Associated with Increased Risk of Myocardial Infarction," *Journal of Internal Medicine* 246 (1999): 409–18; A. M. Wallace, A. D. McMahon, C. J. Packard, et al., "Plasma Leptin and the Risk of Cardiovascular Disease in the West of Scotland Coronary Prevention Study (WOSCOPS)," *Circulation* 104 (2001): 3052–6.

10. I. M. Lee, C. C. Hsieh, and R. S. Paffenbarger Jr., "Exercise Intensity and Longevity in Men. The Harvard Alumni Study," *The Journal of the American Medical Association* 273 (1995): 1179–84.

11. D. Ornish, S. E. Brown, L. W. Scherwitz, et al., "Can Lifestyle Changes Reverse Coronary Heart Disease? The Lifestyle Heart Trial," *Lancet* 336 (1990): 129–33; W. L. Haskell, E. L. Alderman, J. M. Fair, et al., "Effects of Intensive Multiple Risk Factor Reduction on Coronary Atherosclerosis and Clinical Cardiac Events in Men and Women with Coronary Artery Disease. The Stanford Coronary Risk Intervention Project (SCRIP)," *Circulation* 89 (1994): 975–90.

12. R. J. Shephard and G. J. Balady, "Exercise as Cardiovascular Therapy," *Circulation* 99 (1999): 963–72.

13. W. E. Kraus, J. A. Houmard, B. D. Duscha, et al., "Effects of the Amount and Intensity of Exercise on Plasma Lipoproteins," *The New England Journal of Medicine* 347 (2002): 1483–92; P. F. Kokkinos and V. Papademetriou, "Exercise and Hypertension," *Coronary Artery Disease* 11 (2000): 99–102.

14. I. M. Lee, C. C. Hsieh, and R. S. Paffenbarger Jr., "Exercise Intensity and Longevity in Men. The Harvard Alumni Study," *The Journal of the American Medical Association* 273 (1995): 1179–84; J. A. Berlin and G. A. Colditz, "A Meta-analysis of Physical Activity in the Prevention of Coronary Heart Disease," *American Journal of Epidemiology* 132 (1990): 612–28; A. S. Leon, J. Connett, D. R. Jacobs Jr., et al., "Leisure-Time Physical Activity Levels and Risk of Coronary Heart Disease and Death. The Multiple Risk Factor Intervention Trial," *The Journal of the American Medical Association* 258 (1987): 2388–95; H. A. Demirel, S. K. Powers, M. A. Zergeroglu, et al., "Short-Term Exercise Improves Myocardial Tolerance to In Vivo Ischemia-Reperfusion in the Rat," *Journal of Applied Physiology* 91 (2001): 2205–12.

15. J. Y. Ji, H. Jing, and S. L. Diamond, "Shear Stress Causes Nuclear Localization of Endothelial Glucocorticoid Receptor and Expression from the GRE Promoter," *Circulation Research* 92 (2003): 279–85.

16. T. S. Church, C. E. Barlow, C. P. Earnest, et al., "Associations between Cardiorespiratory Fitness and C-Reactive Protein in Men," *Arteriosclerosis, Thrombosis, and Vascular Biology* 22 (2002): 1869–76; K. Okita, H. Nishijima, T. Murakami, et al., "Can Exercise Training with Weight Loss Lower Serum C-Reactive Protein Levels?" *Arteriosclerosis, Thrombosis, and Vascular Biology* 24 (2004): 1868–73.

17. R. Hambrecht, C. Walther, S. Möbius-Winkler, et al., "Percutaneous Coronary Angioplasty Compared with Exercise Training in Patients with Stable Coronary Artery Disease," *Circulation* 109 (2004): 1371–8.

18. H. D. Sesso, R. S. Paffenbarger Jr., and I. M. Lee, "Physical Activity and Coronary Heart Disease in Men: The Harvard Alumni Health Study," *Circulation* 102 (2000): 975–80.

19. M. L. Stefanick, "Exercise and Weight Control," *Exercise and Sport Sciences Review* 21 (1993): 363–96.

20. K. S. Woo, P. Chook, C. W. Yu, et al., "Effects of Diet and Exercise on Obesity-Related Vascular Dysfunction in Children," *Circulation* 109 (2004): 1981–6.

21. C. A. Slentz, B. D. Duscha, J. L. Johnson, et al., "Effects of the Amount of Exercise on Body Weight, Body Composition, and Measures of Central Obesity: STRRIDE—A Randomized Controlled Study," *Archives of Internal Medicine* 164 (2004): 31–9.

22. S. Dahiya and C. Arora, "Impact of Exercise on Nutritional Status and Health Profile of Urban Obese Women in Hisar City," *Asia Pacific Journal of Clinical Nutrition* 13(Suppl) (2004): S138.

23. R. Ross, I. Janssen, J. Dawson, et al., "Exercise-Induced Reduction in Obesity and Insulin Resistance in Women: A Randomized Controlled Trial," *Obesity Research* 12 (2004): 789–98.

24. K. Sykes, L. L. Choo, and M. Cotterrell, "Accumulating Aerobic Exercise for Effective Weight Control," *Journal of the Royal Society of Health* 124 (2004): 24–8.

25. F. Dimeo, M. Bauer, I. Varahram, et al., "Benefits from Aerobic Exercise in Patients with Major Depression: A Pilot Study," *British Journal of Sports Medicine* 35 (2001): 114–7.

26. R. Chow, J. E. Harrison, and C. Notarius, "Effect of Two Randomized Exercise Programs on Bone Mass of Healthy Postmenopausal Women," *British Medical Journal* 285 (1987): 1441–4.

27. I. M. Lee, R. S. Paffenbarger Jr., and C. Hsieh, "Physical Activity and Risk of Developing Colorectal Cancer among College Alumni," *Journal of the National Cancer Institute* 83 (1991): 1324–9; A. McTiernan, C. Kooperberg, E. White, et al., "Recreational Physical Activity and the Risk of Breast Cancer in Postmenopausal Women: The Women's Health Initiative Cohort Study," *The Journal of the American Medical Association* 29 (2003): 1377–9; I. Bairati, R. Larouche, F. Meyer, et al., "Lifetime Occupational Physical Activity and Incidental Prostate Cancer," *Cancer Causes and Control* 11 (2000): 759–64.

28. S. P. Helmrich, D. R. Ragland, R. W. Leung, et al., "Physical Activity and Reduced Occurrence of Non-Insulin-Dependent Diabetes Mellitus," *The New England Journal of Medicine* 325 (1991): 147–52.

29. T. Ronnemaa, K. Mattila, A. Lehtonen, et al., "A Controlled Randomized Study on the Effect of Long-Term Physical Exercise on the Metabolic Control in Type 2 Diabetic Patients," *Acta Medica Scandinavica* 220 (1986): 219–24.

30. A. L. Dunn, B. H. Marcus, J. B. Kampert, et al., "Comparison of Lifestyle and Structured Interventions to Increase Physical Activity and Cardiorespiratory Fitness: A Randomized Trial," *The Journal of the American Medical Association* 281 (1999): 327–34.

31. E. C. Suarez, "C-Reactive Protein Is Associated with Psychological Risk Factors of Cardiovascular Disease in Apparently Healthy Adults," *Psychosomatic Medicine* 66 (2004): 684–91.

32. J. A. Blumenthal, C. F. Emery, D. J. Madden, et al., "Effects of Exercise Training on Cardiorespiratory Function in Men and Women Older Than 60 Years of Age," *The American Journal of Cardiology* 67 (1991): 633–9; J. A. Blumenthal, A. Sherwood, M. A. Babyak, et al., "Effects of Exercise and Stress Management Training on Markers of Cardiovascular Risk in Patients with Ischemic Heart Disease: A Randomized Controlled Trial," *The Journal of the American Medical Association* 293 (2005): 1626–34; J. Toman, L. Spinarova, T. Kara, et al., "[Physical Training in Patients with Chronic Heart Failure: Functional Fitness and the Role of the Periphery]" [Czech], *Vnitrni Lekarstvi* 47 (2001): 74–80.

33. D. R. Hopkins, B. Murrah, W. W. Hoeger, et al., "Effect of Low-Impact Aerobic Dance on the Functional Fitness of Elderly Women," *The Gerontologist* 30 (1990): 189–92; H. Shimamoto, Y. Adachi, M. Takahashi, et al., "Low Impact Aerobic Dance As a Useful Exercise Mode for Reducing Body Mass in Mildly Obese Middle-Aged Women," *Applied Human Science: Journal of Physiological Anthropology* 17 (1998): 109–14.

34. G. Y. Yeh, M. J. Wood, B. H. Lorell, et al., "Effects of Tai Chi Mind-Body Movement Therapy on Functional Status and Exercise Capacity in Patients with Chronic Heart Failure: A Randomized Controlled Trial," *American Journal of Medicine* 117 (2004): 541–8.

35. N. D. Parker, G. R. Hunter, M. S. Treuth, et al., "Effects of Strength Training on Cardiovascular Responses during a Submaximal Walk and a Weight-Loaded Walking Test in Older Females," *Journal of Cardiopulmonary Rehabilitation* 16 (1996): 56–62.

36. M. Murphy, A. Nevill, C. Neville, et al., "Accumulating Brisk Walking for Fitness, Cardiovascular Risk, and Psychological Health," *Medicine and Science in Sports and Exercise* 34 (2002): 1468–74.

37. H. Tanaka, D. R. Bassett Jr., E. T. Howley, et al., "Swimming Training Lowers the Resting Blood Pressure in Individuals with Hypertension," *Journal of Hypertension* 15 (1997): 651–7.

38. A. Damodaran, A. Malathi, N. Patil, et al., "Therapeutic Potential of Yoga Practices in Modifying Cardiovascular Risk Profile in Middle Aged Men and Women," *The Journal of the Association of Physicians of India* 50 (2002): 633–40; I. S. Chohan, H. S. Nayar, P. Thomas, et al., "Influence of Yoga on Blood Coagulation," *Thrombosis and Haemostasis* 30 (1984): 196–7.

39. M. S. Mahonen, P. McElduff, A. J. Dobson, et al., "Current Smoking and the Risk of Non-fatal Myocardial Infarction in the WHO MONICA Project Populations," *Tobacco Control* 13 (2004): 244–50.

40. R. Doll, R. Peto, J. Boreham, et al., "Mortality in Relation to Smoking: 50 Years' Observations on Male British Doctors," *British Journal of Cancer* 92 (2005): 426–9.

41. R. Doll and A. B. Hill, "The Mortality of Doctors in Relation to Their Smoking Habits: A Preliminary Report. 1954," *British Medical Journal* 328 (2004): 1529–33.

42. W. W. Worick and W. E. Shaller, *Alcohol, Tobacco, and Drugs, Their Use and Abuse* (Englewood Cliffs, N.J.: Prentice-Hall, 1977), 78.

43. L. A. Bazzano, J. He, P. Muntner, et al., "Relationship between Cigarette Smoking and Novel Risk Factors for Cardiovascular Disease in the United States," *Annals of Internal Medicine* 138 (2003): 891–7.

44. T. Kondo, M. Hayashi, K. Takeshita, et al., "Smoking Cessation Rapidly Increases Circulating Progenitor Cells in Peripheral Blood in Chronic Smokers," *Arteriosclerosis, Thrombosis, and Vascular Biology* 24 (2004): 1442–7.

45. L. A. Bazzano, J. He, P. Muntner, et al., "Relationship between Cigarette Smoking and Novel Risk Factors for Cardiovascular Disease in the United States," *Annals of Internal Medicine* 138 (2003): 891–7.

46. P. H. Whincup, J. A. Gilg, J. R. Emberson, et al., "Passive Smoking and Risk of Coronary Heart Disease and Stroke: Prospective Study with Cotinine Measurement," *British Medical Journal* 329 (2004): 200–5; Centers for Disease Control and Prevention/National Center for Health Statistics, *Morbidity and Mortality Weekly Report* 51 (April 12, 2002): 297–320.

47. R. P. Sargent, R. M. Shepard, and S. A. Glantz, "Reduced Incidence of Admissions for Myocardial Infarction Associated with Public Smoking Ban: Before and After Study," *British Medical Journal* 328 (2004): 977–80.

48. M. K. Ong and S. A. Glantz, "Cardiovascular Health and Economic Effects of Smoke-Free Workplaces," *The American Journal of Medicine* 117 (2004): 32–8.

49. National Health and Nutrition Examination Survey (1999–2002), Centers for Disease Control and Prevention/National Center for Health Statistics.

50. Joint National Committee on Prevention, Detection, Evaluation, and Treatment of High Blood Pressure, *The Seventh Report of the Joint National Committee on Prevention, Detection, Evaluation, and Treatment of High Blood Pressure*, NIH Publication No. 03-5233 (Bethesda, Md.: U.S. Department of Health and Human Services, 2003).

51. S. M. Grundy, J. I. Cleeman, C. N. Merz, et al., "Implications of Recent Clinical Trials for the National Cholesterol Education Program Adult Treatment Panel III Guidelines," *Circulation* 110 (2004): 227–39.

Chapter 8

1. P. Libby, A. M. Gotto, P. H. Jones, et al., CME activity based on transcripts and slides of presentations as delivered by the faculty at the "Examining the Dyslipidemia Constellation: An Interactive Forum on New Treatment Advances" symposium, Chicago, IL, March 29, 2003. Release date: August 29, 2003. www.medscape.com/viewprogram/2590_index.

2. C. P. Fitzgerald, W. E. Lawson, and J. C. Hui, "Enhanced External Counterpulsation as Initial Revascularization Treatment for Angina Refractory to Medical Therapy," *Cardiology* 100 (2003): 129–35.

Test Your Heart Disease Knowledge: Answer Key

1. True (see the introduction)
2. False (see chapter 7)
3. False (see chapter 7)
4. False (see chapter 7)
5. True (see chapter 7)
6. True (see chapter 7)
7. False (see the introduction)
8. True (see chapter 7)
9. True (see chapter 2)
10. False (see chapter 7)
11. False (see the introduction)
12. True (see chapter 2)
13. False (see the introduction)
14. True (see the introduction)
15. True (see chapter 7)
16. True (see chapter 2)
17. True (see chapter 7)
18. True (see chapter 7)
19. True (see chapter 7)
20. False (see chapter 7)

Frequently Asked Questions

What is angina?

Angina is the variety of symptoms associated with a lack of blood flow to the heart. It occurs when vessels that carry blood to the heart muscle become dysfunctional, and are often narrowed or blocked. Angina may feel like chest pain or pressure; shortness of breath; pain in the jaw, neck, arms, or back; nausea; or generalized fatigue.

What does the acronym EECP stand for?

The acronym EECP stands for enhanced external counterpulsation.

What is EECP?

EECP is a noninvasive, outpatient treatment for heart disease that is used to relieve or eliminate angina. During EECP, blood pressure cuffs are wrapped around your legs, and they squeeze and release in sync with your heartbeat, promoting blood flow throughout your body and particularly to your heart. In the process, EECP develops new pathways around blocked arteries in the heart by expanding networks of tiny blood vessels ("collaterals") that help increase and normalize blood flow to the heart muscle. For this reason, EECP is often called the "natural bypass."

What are the advantages of EECP?

Unlike bypass surgery, balloon angioplasty, and stenting procedures, EECP is noninvasive, carries no risk, is comfortable, and is administered in outpatient sessions.

Does EECP have any risks or side effects?

EECP is safe. Occasionally, some patients experience mild skin irritation underneath the blood pressure cuffs. Experienced EECP therapists address this irritation by using extra padding where needed to make the patient comfortable. Some patients experience a bit more fatigue at the beginning of their course of treatment, but it usually subsides after the first few sessions. In fact, patients typically feel energized by EECP.

How long does EECP take?

The standard course of treatment is one hour per day, five days per week, for seven weeks (a total of thirty-five one-hour sessions). Some patients have two treatments in one day to complete the program more quickly. Some patients extend the program beyond thirty-five treatments, depending on their particular medical situation and goals.

How quickly will EECP help me to feel better?

Most patients begin to experience beneficial results from EECP between their fifteenth and twenty-fifth treatments. These benefits include increased stamina, improved sleeping patterns, decreased angina, and less reliance on nitroglycerin and other medications. There is variation, certainly, and some patients start to feel better as soon as their first week of treatment.

What happens if I miss a treatment?

You are encouraged to have your EECP treatment every day. However, missing a day will not have a negative effect on your overall results. When you come back, you will simply pick up where you left off, and the missed treatment will be added to the end of your program until you have a total of thirty-five sessions. Just like exercise, the more consistent you are with your EECP schedule, the better your results will be.

What does EECP feel like?

EECP feels like a deep muscle massage to your legs. During the treatment, you do not feel anything in your chest or heart. You only feel the cuffs that are wrapped around your legs squeezing in time to your own heartbeat. Our patients have affectionately described this sensation as "gentle hugs." Most of our patients relax, listen to music, or read during their treatments. Some even sleep.

Do the benefits of EECP last?

Yes. In patients followed for three to five years after treatment, the benefits of EECP—including less angina, less nitroglycerin usage, and improved blood flow patterns documented on stress tests—had lasted.

How does EECP compare to angioplasty or bypass surgery?

The five-year outcomes for EECP patients are virtually the same as for angioplasty and bypass surgery patients.

Is EECP approved by the FDA? What kind of research has been done on it?

The FDA approved EECP in 1995 as a treatment for coronary artery disease and angina, for cardiogenic shock, and for use during a heart attack. In 2002, the FDA approved EECP as a treatment for congestive heart failure. EECP has undergone rigorous clinical trials at leading universities around the country and has been the subject of more than a hundred scientific studies published in leading medical journals throughout the world.

Does insurance pay for EECP?

Yes. Medicare and private insurance carriers pay for EECP.

I have a pacemaker. Is that a problem with EECP?

No. Pacemakers and defibrillators do not interfere in any way with EECP.

I am on Coumadin. Is that a problem with EECP?

No. Patients on Coumadin are able to undergo EECP treatments safely.

I have congestive heart failure. Is that a problem with EECP?

No. In fact, in July 2002 the FDA approved EECP as a treatment for congestive heart failure (CHF). After completing a course of EECP treatment, patients with congestive heart failure typically have less swelling in their legs, less shortness of breath, and less fatigue, and they often require less diuretic medication.

Is there an age limit for EECP?

No. We have successfully treated patients as young as thirty-six and as old as ninety-seven without any difficulties. Many of our patients are in their eighties and nineties, and they complete the entire EECP program with excellent results.

I have already had bypass surgery/angioplasty/stents. Can I still have EECP?

Yes. Most of our patients have already had one (or many) of these procedures. They come for EECP treatment because they still have angina.

Can EECP dislodge plaque and cause a stroke or heart attack?

No. Our bodies obey the laws of physics, and one principle law is that fluid will follow the path of least resistance. Atherosclerotic plaques are calcified and hard, and they create an obstruction that detours the blood through alternate routes. During EECP, when your blood is flowing to your heart, it will naturally bypass arteries with plaque and enter healthy, nondiseased blood vessels to go around the blockages. Going around the blockages is a longer trip, but it is a much easier one. In time, these new pathways are reinforced and become lasting routes for blood to reach your heart beyond the blockages. Every EECP patient has had multiple, serious blockages. No one has ever had a heart attack or a stroke as a result of the treatment.

Are there any patients who *cannot* have EECP?

There are very few patients who are unable to have EECP. Those who should not be treated include pregnant women, individuals with a severe leakage in their aortic valve requiring surgical repair, and patients who have an active blood clot in their leg.

I had a blood clot in my leg three years ago. Can I have EECP?

Yes. Having a history of a blood clot (deep vein thrombosis, or DVT) in your leg does not preclude you from having EECP. It is recommended that you have a Doppler ultrasound of your leg to confirm that the blood clot has resolved before beginning the EECP program.

Does EECP aggravate high blood pressure (hypertension)?

No. If you have hypertension that is properly managed, you may undergo EECP without difficulty. Oftentimes, patients with hypertension find that their blood pressure improves as they proceed with EECP. If your hypertension is uncontrolled, you must seek medical care to get your blood pressure under control with proper medications before proceeding with EECP.

I have poor circulation in my legs (peripheral vascular disease, or PVD). May I still have EECP?

Yes, and you should! EECP improves blood flow throughout the entire body, including your legs. If you have poor leg circulation, you might need more than thirty-five treatments. My patients with poor leg circulation typically require at least fifty treatments to get the full benefit of the program. In addition to improved stamina, less angina, and less nitroglycerin use, patients with peripheral vascular disease have a marked improvement in their leg circulation in response to EECP.

I have atrial fibrillation and an irregular heartbeat. May I still have EECP?

Yes. An irregular heartbeat, including one caused by atrial fibrillation, will not interfere with EECP if the heart rate is controlled and no faster than one hundred beats per minute.

I have varicose veins. May I still have EECP?

Yes. Varicose veins are typically a cosmetic issue, not a medical one. As such, they do not preclude individuals from receiving EECP. We often use extra padding with patients who have varicose veins to ensure maximum comfort.

What happens if my angina returns months or years after I finish my EECP treatment course? Can I come back for more?

Yes. EECP is not a once-in-a-lifetime treatment. Heart disease is a chronic illness, and symptoms may return at some point in the future. The door is always open for you to return for additional courses of EECP as needed.

Is EECP similar to chelation therapy?

No. There is no relationship between EECP and chelation therapy. Chelation is an invasive procedure whereby a substance called EDTA is given intravenously in an attempt to bind to calcium and remove it from atherosclerotic plaques. The fundamental problem with the concept of chelation is that atherosclerotic plaques are not only made of calcium; they include fat, cholesterol, and cellular deposits as well. Scientific research has not shown chelation to have any therapeutic value for heart disease. Since it has never been proven to work, Medicare and insurance carriers do not pay for chelation, and therefore it is not accessible to most heart disease patients. Patients who choose to try it must pay out of pocket. Each treatment costs approximately eighty to one hundred dollars, and patients often go for numerous treatments over a period of several months and then continue indefinitely on a maintenance regimen. Chelation can actually be harmful—even fatal—when administered to the wrong person or under the wrong circumstances. It poses particular danger to individuals with congestive heart failure. The amount of fluid administered with each treatment may overtax their weakened heart, leading to severe fluid overload and problems including pulmonary edema (a life-threatening condition that is characterized by an excess of fluid in the lungs).

In contrast, EECP is entirely noninvasive, proven by more than a hundred published scientific studies, and safe. It is an accepted, mainstream medical treatment and, as such, is approved by

Medicare and covered by insurance. Chelation does not interfere with EECP, so you may undergo both therapies simultaneously if you choose.

Is there a difference between EECP and ECP?

Yes. EECP and ECP are uniquely different. EECP is a registered trademark of Vasomedical, Inc., the leading manufacturer of EECP equipment in the United States. Vasomedical has a patent on the EECP machine's timing mechanism, which determines when the cuffs squeeze and release in time to the patient's EKG—the most critical part of the treatment. This timing mechanism makes the EECP machine by far the most clinically effective device on the market, distinguishing it from other external counterpulsation (ECP) equipment. Every published U.S. study (more than one hundred of them) and most studies originating in countries around the world and published in the leading English-language medical journals have used EECP equipment exclusively. Accordingly, EECP—not ECP— machines are the ones found in every university hospital, major community hospital, and well-known practice that offers the treatment.

Resource Directory

Braverman EECP Heart Centers

Braverman EECP Heart Centers (formerly VitalHeart EECP Clinics) is the largest EECP practice in the United States and the only one solely dedicated to the treatment. In its offices throughout the Philadelphia area, the practice has treated more than two thousand patients with EECP. Its website is a comprehensive source of information on EECP, including thorough descriptions of the treatment, news updates, clinical studies, patient testimonials, and more. The website also features an "Ask the Doctor" section, where you may email Dr. Braverman directly with your questions.

> Braverman EECP Heart Centers (Corporate Office)
> 1740 South Street, Suite 305 • Philadelphia, PA 19146
> Phone: (215) 772-9800
> Toll-Free: (800) 5-HEART-5 (800-543-2785)
> Fax: (215) 772-0329
> www.bravermancenters.com

Vasomedical, Inc.

Vasomedical, Inc. is the leading manufacturer of EECP equipment in the United States. EECP is currently available in more than 650 locations throughout the United States, as well as in twenty-four countries around the world. To find a location near you, call Vasomedical's toll-free number: (800) 455-EECP. Vasomedical's website is also a good source of information for both patients and physicians about all aspects of EECP.

> Vasomedical, Inc.
> 180 Linden Avenue • Westbury, NY 11590
> Phone: (516) 997-4600
> Toll-Free: (800) 455-EECP (800-455-3327)
> Fax: (516) 997-2299
> www.naturalbypass.com

International EECP Therapists Association

The International EECP Therapists Association (IETA) is a multidisciplinary organization of EECP therapists dedicated to setting standards of excellence in the delivery of enhanced external counterpulsation. Its website offers information for patients and their families, as well as professional development guidance for EECP therapists. IETA is an excellent resource for EECP therapists with clinical questions or concerns about providing the most effective treatment to particular patients with individual needs.

International EECP Therapists Association
P.O. Box 650005
Vero Beach, FL 32965-0005
Phone: (800) 376-3321, ext. 140
www.ietaonline.com

International EECP Patient Registry

The International EECP Patient Registry (IEPR) is a volunteer patient registry at the University of Pittsburgh's Epidemiology Data Center. The study enrolls patients receiving EECP treatment and follows them for several years to measure their outcomes. The IEPR has published many groundbreaking studies documenting EECP's long-term benefits, including reduced angina, improved quality of life, and reduced nitroglycerin use. Its studies also focus on subpopulations of heart disease patients, including the elderly, women, those with congestive heart failure, and those with diabetes. The IEPR's website offers access to numerous research publications on EECP.

International EECP Patient Registry
University of Pittsburgh
Graduate School of Public Health
Epidemiology Data Center
127 Parran Hall
130 DeSoto Street • Pittsburgh, PA 15261
Phone: (412) 624-5157
Fax: (412) 624-3775
www.edc.gsph.pitt.edu/iepr

Mended Hearts

Mended Hearts is a national nonprofit organization dedicated to facilitating patient-centered care for heart disease sufferers. Its services—which include educational forums, support groups, and visiting programs—are offered to patients, their families and caregivers, and others impacted by heart disease. Mended Hearts' mission is to "inspire hope in heart disease patients and their families." It is affiliated with the American Heart Association and offers its programs in partnership with 460 hospitals and rehabilitation clinics across the country.

> The Mended Hearts, Inc.
> 7272 Greenville Avenue
> Dallas, TX 75231-4596
> Phone: (214) 706-1442
> Toll-Free Information Line: (888) HEART-99 (888-432-7899)
> Fax: (214) 706-5245
> www.mendedhearts.org

American Heart Association

The American Heart Association is a national voluntary health agency whose mission is to reduce disability and death from cardiovascular diseases and stroke. It is a comprehensive educational resource, providing information on warning signs, management tools, treatments, healthy lifestyle choices, children's health, and much more. Through its website, the American Heart Association offers a wealth of information about cardiovascular disease, as well as extensive data on its social and economic impact on various populations and racial and ethnic groups.

> American Heart Association
> 7272 Greenville Avenue
> Dallas, TX 75231-4596
> Toll-Free: (800) AHA-USA-1 (800-242-8721)
> www.americanheart.org

Glossary

Abdominal aortic aneurysm (AAA). A localized, saclike widening of the abdominal aorta due to a weakness in the blood vessel wall.

Angina/angina pectoris. The symptom that indicates the heart is not receiving enough blood and oxygen. Commonly, angina is experienced as chest pain, chest pressure, and/or chest tightness. See also "Anginal equivalents."

Anginal equivalents. Symptoms other than chest pain that indicate the heart is not getting enough blood and oxygen. These symptoms include shortness of breath; fatigue; decreased exercise tolerance; nausea; vomiting; burning or discomfort in the chest or throat; pain in the jaw, neck, arms, upper back, or shoulder blades; or palpitations.

Angiogenesis. The growth of new blood vessels. These vessels help to alleviate coronary artery disease by rerouting blood flow around clogged arteries so it can reach the heart.

Angiogram. The clinical report that results from an angiography or cardiac catheterization.

Angiography. See "Catheterization, cardiac."

Angioplasty. Also called *percutaneous transluminal coronary angioplasty* (PTCA). A procedure in which a balloon is inserted into the center of a blockage in an artery and inflated in order to crack the plaque and push the blockage out to the perimeter of the artery.

Anticoagulant. A blood-thinning medication that prevents blood from clotting.

Aorta. The largest artery in the body. All blood pumped out of the heart's left ventricle travels through the aorta on its way to other parts of the body.

Aortic insufficiency (AI). Also called *aortic regurgitation* (AR). An aortic valve leakage that does not allow for complete valve closure.

As a result, blood flows back into the left ventricle (regurgitation) rather than through the aorta and into the coronary arteries.

Aortic regurgitation (AR). See "Aortic insufficiency."

Aortic valve. The valve between the left ventricle and the aorta. Closure of the aortic valve signals the end of systole and the beginning of diastole.

Arrhythmia. An irregular heartbeat.

Arteries. Blood vessels that carry oxygenated blood away from the heart and throughout the body.

Atherosclerosis. Also known as "hardening of the arteries." The process whereby deposits of fat, cholesterol, and plaque build up in arteries, leading to the blockages in coronary artery disease and other cardiovascular problems.

Atrial fibrillation ("A-fib"). A condition in which chaotic activity in the upper chambers of the heart results in a disorganized, rapid, and irregular heart rhythm.

Atrium. An upper chamber of the heart. (Plural: atria.)

Augmentation. The increase in diastolic blood pressure that occurs as a result of the inflating EECP cuffs and the subsequent creation of a retrograde (from the legs up to the heart) arterial pressure wave.

Autoimmune. A condition in which the body's immune system fights against the body's own tissues.

Blood pressure. The force of pressure exerted by the heart when pumping blood. Also, the pressure of blood against the artery walls.

B-type natriuretic peptide (BNP). Also known as *plasma brain natriuretic peptide.* A substance secreted by the ventricles of the heart in response to changes in blood pressure that occur during heart failure.

Bypass surgery. See "Coronary artery bypass graft."

CABG. See "Coronary artery bypass graft."

CAD. See "Coronary artery disease."

Cardiac. Relating to the heart.

Cardiac cycle. The sequence of events between one heartbeat and the next, normally occupying less than one second. See also "Diastole" and "Systole."

Cardiac output. The amount of blood ejected by the heart in one minute. (The average amount in a healthy adult is four to six liters per minute.)

Cardiomyopathy. A condition in which the heart may have poor pumping power ("dilated"), have an impaired ability to fill with blood ("restricted"), or be thickened ("hypertrophic").

Cardiovascular disease. A family of diseases of the heart and circulatory system, including hypertension, coronary artery disease, stroke, and congestive heart failure.

CAT scan. See "Computed tomography."

Catheterization, cardiac. Also called *angiography*. A procedure in which a catheter is inserted into an artery in the arm or leg and is guided to the heart, contrast dye is injected, and X-rays of the coronary arteries, heart chambers, and valves are taken so that blood circulation can be studied and blockages in arteries can be identified.

Cerebral vascular accident (CVA). Also known as *stroke*. A complete blockage in a cerebral artery (a blood vessel in the brain), commonly due to a ruptured plaque and the resulting blood clot or an embolus. May also be caused by a hemorrhage (or bleeding) in the brain.

CHD. See "Coronary heart disease."

CHF. See "Congestive heart failure."

Chronic stable angina. See "Stable angina."

Claudication. A symptom of peripheral vascular disease (poor leg circulation), most commonly leg pain or fatigue due to a poor supply of blood and oxygen in the muscles.

Collateral blood vessels. Small vessels that develop over time in response to increased blood flowing through them; often a result of narrowed coronary arteries. Collaterals naturally bypass the narrowed area and restore blood flow to the heart, beyond the blockage.

Computed tomography (CT, CAT scan). A diagnostic imaging procedure that uses a combination of X-rays and computer technology to produce detailed, cross-sectional images of any part of the body.

Congestive heart failure (CHF). The condition in which the heart muscle is weak and fails to pump sufficient blood throughout the body. It leads to fluid buildup and associated symptoms such as shortness of breath and swelling in the legs.

Coronary. Relating to the heart.

Coronary artery bypass graft (CABG). Also known as "open-heart surgery" or "bypass surgery." A surgical procedure utilizing an artery or vein graft to bypass a blockage in a coronary artery.

Coronary artery disease (CAD). The narrowing or "hardening" of the arteries that supply blood to the heart muscle, usually caused by a buildup of fats, cholesterol, and calcium (atherosclerosis).

Coronary heart disease (CHD). A disease of the heart caused by a lack of blood flow due to coronary artery disease.

Coumadin. The brand name for warfarin. An anticoagulant, or blood-thinning, medication.

C-Reactive protein (CRP). A protein the liver produces that is present in the blood during episodes of acute inflammation. Elevated levels have been linked to many conditions associated with inflammation, including coronary artery disease.

CT scan. See "Computed tomography."

Deep vein thrombosis (DVT). A blood clot (thrombus) in a deep vein. It most commonly occurs in the legs, and may also rarely occur in the pelvis or arms.

Diabetes. A condition in which the body does not produce or respond appropriately to insulin, the hormone produced by the pancreas that enables blood sugar to enter the cells and be used for energy.

Diastole. The resting phase of the cardiac cycle, during which the heart receives 70 to 80 percent of its blood supply. It begins with the closure of the aortic valve.

Diastolic augmentation. A measure of blood flow in the arteries of the heart.

Diastolic blood pressure. The lowest blood pressure measured in the arteries, occurring between heartbeats.

Diuresis. The process by which the body rids itself of excess fluid. It may be assisted by the use of diuretic medications.

Diuretic. A medication that lowers blood pressure by stimulating the kidneys to rid the body of excess fluid. Commonly known as a "water pill."

Doppler ultrasound. A noninvasive diagnostic test that uses sound waves to evaluate the heart and blood vessels.

DVT. See "Deep vein thrombosis."

ECG. See "Electrocardiogram."

Echocardiogram ("Echo"). A noninvasive imaging procedure that creates a moving picture outline of the heart's valves and chambers using high-frequency sound waves (ultrasound).

Edema. A swelling. An excess accumulation of fluids, usually in the feet and legs. It may also occur in the hands or abdomen.

EECP. See "Enhanced external counterpulsation."

Ejection fraction. The ratio of blood that is pumped with each beat of the heart to the volume of blood that fills the heart between beats. It is expressed as a percentage.

EKG. See "Electrocardiogram."

Electrocardiogram (EKG or ECG). A recording of the heart's electrical activity.

Embolus. A blood clot that moves through the bloodstream.

Endothelial cells. The cells that line blood vessels and are actively involved in regulating blood flow.

Endothelin (ET-1). A substance released by endothelial cells that causes blood vessels to constrict.

Enhanced external counterpulsation (EECP). A noninvasive treatment for heart disease that increases blood flow to the heart, improves heart muscle function, decreases the heart's workload, and decreases resistance to the heart's pumping action. During EECP, blood pressure cuffs wrapped around the patient's legs inflate and deflate in sync with their heartbeat, enhancing blood flow throughout the body.

Heart attack. See "Myocardial infarction."

Heart disease. A generic term comprising all of the various diseases of the heart. Commonly refers to coronary artery disease and/or coronary heart disease.

Heart failure. The condition in which the heart muscle is weak and unable to pump sufficient blood to meet the body's needs.

Hypertension (HTN). High blood pressure.

Implantable cardioverter defibrillator (ICD). A surgically inserted electronic device that constantly monitors heart rate and rhythm. When it detects a potentially dangerous arrhythmia, it delivers an electrical shock to the heart muscle (cardioversion), causing the heart to beat in a normal rhythm again.

International normalized ratio (INR). The standard measurement of coagulation in the blood, commonly used to regulate Coumadin dosage.

Ischemia. The deficiency of blood supply and oxygen delivery, signaling that oxygen demand is greater than supply.

Myocardial infarction (MI). Commonly referred to as a *heart attack*. It occurs when one or more of the coronary arteries are suddenly and completely blocked, causing an area of the heart muscle to die.

Myocardial perfusion. The blood flow patterns in the heart muscle.

Myocardium. The heart muscle.

Nitric oxide (NO). A substance released by endothelial cells that causes blood vessels to relax and dilate.

Nitroglycerin (NTG). A medication that dilates blood vessels (vasodilator), improving blood flow.

Occlusion. A blockage.

Open-heart surgery. See "Coronary artery bypass graft."

Pacemaker. A surgically implanted electronic device that sends electrical impulses to the heart muscle to maintain a stable heart rate and rhythm.

Palpitation. A fluttering sensation in the chest that is often related to a missed heartbeat or a rapid heartbeat.

PCI. See "Percutaneous coronary intervention."

Percutaneous coronary intervention (PCI). An invasive procedure in which a catheter and a guide wire are inserted into a peripheral artery (usually in the groin) and threaded to a blockage in a coronary artery. Once there, an angioplasty, stent implantation, or other procedure is performed.

Percutaneous transluminal coronary angioplasty (PTCA). See "Angioplasty."

Peripheral vascular disease (PVD). Diseases of blood vessels outside the heart and brain, most commonly involving atherosclerotic narrowing of arteries that bring blood to the legs.

PET scan. See "Positron emission tomography."

Plaque. Deposits of fats, cholesterol, inflammatory cells, proteins, and calcium in the lining of arteries, which cause narrowing and slow blood flow.

Plasma brain natriuretic peptide (BNP). See "B-type natriuretic peptide."

Positron emission tomography (PET). Nuclear scanning that creates a three-dimensional picture of blood flow through the coronary arteries to the heart muscle.

Premature ventricular contraction (PVC). An irregular heartbeat in which the ventricles beat before they are supposed to.

PTCA. Percutaneous transluminal coronary angioplasty. See "Angioplasty."

PVD. See "Peripheral vascular disease."

Refractory angina. Persistent, severe angina in patients who are considered inoperable and on maximum medications.

Restenosis. The closing or narrowing of an artery that was previously opened by a PCI, such as an angioplasty or a stent.

Risk factor, cardiac. A condition, element, or activity that may adversely affect the heart.

Silent ischemia. Ischemia without symptoms.

Stable angina. Also called *chronic stable angina*. Angina that occurs at predictable times, at predictable levels of exertion or activity, and usually lasts twenty to thirty minutes or less. May continue without significant change for years. Rest and/or nitroglycerin provide short-term relief.

Stenosis. The narrowing or restriction of a blood vessel, which reduces blood flow.

Stent. A scaffoldlike metal device inserted into a blockage in an artery and expanded in order to allow blood to flow through the vessel.

Stress test. An exercise test that examines how well the heart works, during which patients walk on a treadmill to increase their heart rate while their EKG is monitored for any abnormalities.

Stroke. See "Cerebral vascular accident."

Stroke volume. The volume of blood pumped by the heart in one heartbeat.

Systemic vascular resistance (SVR). The resistance blood encounters as it flows out of the left ventricle of the heart and throughout the body.

Systole. The contraction, or "pumping," phase of the cardiac cycle.

Systolic blood pressure. The highest pressure measured in the arteries; it occurs during a heart muscle contraction.

Thallium stress test. A stress test in which a radioactive substance is injected into and carried by the blood, and its progress through the circulation of the heart is followed by X-ray.

Thrombophlebitis. The inflammation of a vein, often in conjunction with a blood clot. It commonly occurs in the superficial veins of the legs.

Thrombus. A blood clot.

Ultrasound. A noninvasive diagnostic tool used to provide a moving picture of an area of the body by measuring high-frequency sound vibrations.

Unstable angina. Angina that is different than usual in terms of severity, duration, and/or type of symptoms. It occurs without exertion or with decreasing levels of exertion.

Vascular endothelial growth factor (VEGF). A hormone that promotes the growth of new blood vessels.

Vasoconstrict. To narrow a blood vessel, causing a decrease in blood flow to a particular area of the body.

Vasoconstrictor. A medication or substance that causes vasoconstriction.

204 | Heal Your Heart *with* EECP

Vasodilate. To relax and dilate a blood vessel, causing an increase in blood flow to a particular area of the body.

Vasodilator. A medication or substance that causes vasodilation.

Vasospasm. The sudden constriction of a blood vessel due to a muscular spasm of the vessel wall.

Veins. Blood vessels that carry deoxygenated blood toward the heart.

Ventricles. The two bottom chambers of the heart that pump blood into the arteries.

Warfarin. The generic name for Coumadin.

Index

About the Author

Debra Braverman, MD, is a nationally recognized expert in EECP treatment who has been featured on the *Early Show*, in *Time*, and in other national publications. Dr. Braverman is a graduate of Cornell University Medical College (now known as the Weill Medical College of Cornell University) and is board-certified by the American Board of Physical Medicine and Rehabilitation. She is a clinical assistant professor at the University of Pennsylvania School of Medicine and the founder of Braverman EECP Heart Centers (formerly VitalHeart EECP Clinics), the largest EECP practice in the United States. Dr. Braverman has treated more patients with EECP than any other physician in the country. She lives in Philadelphia.